Outlines of Theoretical Chemistry

You are holding a reproduction of an original work that is in the public domain in the United States of America, and possibly other countries.You may freely copy and distribute this work as no entity (individual or corporate) has a copyright on the body of the work.This book may contain prior copyright references, and library stamps (as most of these works were scanned from library copies).These have been scanned and retained as part of the historical artifact.

This book may have occasional imperfections such as missing or blurred pages, poor pictures, errant marks, etc. that were either part of the original artifact, or were introduced by the scanning process. We believe this work is culturally important, and despite the imperfections, have elected to bring it back into print as part of our continuing commitment to the preservation of printed works worldwide. We appreciate your understanding of the imperfections in the preservation process, and hope you enjoy this valuable book.

OUTLINES

OF

THEORETICAL CHEMISTRY

PRINTED BY
SPOTTISWOODE AND CO., NEW STREET SQUARE
LONDON

OUTLINES

OF

THEORETICAL CHEMISTRY

BY

LOTHAR MEYER

PROFESSOR OF CHEMISTRY IN THE UNIVERSITY OF TÜBINGEN

TRANSLATED BY

P. PHILLIPS BEDSON, D.Sc. (LOND.), B.Sc. (VIC.), F.C.S.

PROFESSOR OF CHEMISTRY IN THE DURHAM COLLEGE OF SCIENCE
NEWCASTLE-ON-TYNE

AND

W. CARLETON WILLIAMS, B.Sc., F.C.S.

PROFESSOR OF CHEMISTRY IN THE FIRTH COLLEGE
SHEFFIELD

WITH A PREFACE BY THE AUTHOR

LONDON
LONGMANS, GREEN, AND CO.
AND NEW YORK: 15 EAST 16th STREET
1892

AUTHOR'S PREFACE

TO

ENGLISH TRANSLATION

As Messrs. BEDSON and WILLIAMS some years ago made a careful and accurate translation into English of my 'Modern Theories of Chemistry,' I very gladly accepted their friendly proposal to undertake the translation of this smaller book.

It may appear somewhat doubtful whether the long-felt want of a small text-book on Theoretical Chemistry has not been satisfied by the books recently published by Polis, Remsen, and Ostwald. These books are themselves so different from one another and from mine in method and intention and in their conclusions, that they all may be able to exist side by side. This conclusion is satisfactorily confirmed by the ready reception which the German edition of my book has received.

In writing this work I have not considered the requirements of students alone, but have been desirous of offering something to those friends of scientific investigation who have neither the intention nor the time to concern themselves with the details of chemical investigation, but wish to become acquainted with the general conclusions arrived at.

With this object in view I have abstained from too large a

use of the numerical results of observations and measurements, and have avoided giving detailed descriptions of experimental methods.

The book has, therefore, in the main been written from memory, and numerical examples have been taken from the existing literature only where it appeared absolutely necessary for the clearer understanding of the subject. The general—I may say the philosophical—review of the subject has been my chief aim, to which the details should be subordinated. I may, perhaps, be permitted to express the hope that this mode of treatment will especially meet with approval in England, where so wide a circle of readers interest themselves in the general results and conclusions of scientific investigations.

LOTHAR MEYER.

TÜBINGEN. *December* 30, 1891.

TRANSLATORS' PREFACE.

THE reception which our translation of Lothar Meyer's 'Modern Theories' met with, has encouraged us to present to the public an English version of the author's smaller and less technical work on Chemical Philosophy.

The revised sheets have been submitted to the author, and we have gladly availed ourselves of the valuable suggestions he has made. As the nature of the book is set forth in the author's preface specially written for this translation, there remains only to add that we trust this book may not only be found valuable to the student of chemistry, but also to those who are interested in science generally.

THE TRANSLATORS.

January, 1892.

CONTENTS

SECTION		PAGE
1	DEFINITION AND PROVINCE	1
2.	CHARACTERISTICS OF CHEMICAL CHANGE	2
3.	METHOD OF INVESTIGATION	3
4.	DEVELOPMENT OF CHEMICAL THEORIES	5
5	STŒCHIOMETRIC LAWS	6
6.	ATOMIC HYPOTHESIS	8
7	SYMBOLS	10
8	UNIT OF ATOMIC WEIGHTS	11
9	DETERMINATION OF ATOMIC WEIGHTS FROM STŒCHIOMETRIC VALUES	11
10	FIRST ATTEMPTS TO DETERMINE THE ATOMIC WEIGHTS	12
11.	CHEMICAL EQUIVALENTS	13
12.	ELECTROLYTIC EQUIVALENTS	16
13	CRYSTALLOGRAPHIC EQUIVALENCE. ISOMORPHISM	17
14.	THERMIC EQUIVALENTS	21
15.	EXCEPTIONS	24
16	SPECIFIC HEAT OF ATOMS IN COMPOUNDS	25
17.	RELATION BETWEEN ATOMIC WEIGHT AND VAPOUR DENSITY	28
18.	WANT OF AGREEMENT BETWEEN THE DIFFERENT EQUIVALENTS	30
19.	AVOGADRO'S HYPOTHESIS	30
20.	PHYSICAL BASIS OF AVOGADRO'S HYPOTHESIS. KINETIC THEORY OF GASES	31
21.	MOLECULAR WEIGHTS OF GASES	33
22.	UNIT OF MOLECULAR WEIGHTS	35
23	CALCULATION OF MOLECULAR WEIGHTS	36
24.	CORRECTION FOR ERRORS OF EXPERIMENT	37
25.	DETERMINATION OF ATOMIC WEIGHTS FROM MOLECULAR WEIGHTS	39
26.	POSSIBLE ERRORS	41
27.	MOLECULAR WEIGHTS OF THE ELEMENTS	42
28.	NASCENT STATE	44

SECTION		PAGE
29.	Determination of Stœchiometric Values	44
30.	Relation of Stœchiometric Determinations to each other	46
31.	Selection from different Determinations	49
32.	Accuracy of Atomic Weights	50
33.	Prout's Hypothesis	51
34.	Doebereiner's Triads	52
35.	Arrangement of the Elements in the Order of their Atomic Weights	54
36.	Periodicity of the Physical Properties of the Elements	57
37.	Periodicity of the Electro-chemical Properties	60
38.	Theoretical Prediction of Properties	63
39.	Periodicity of Valency	64
40.	Determination of Chemical Valency	64
41.	Possible Errors in the Determination of Chemical Valency	68
42.	Irregularities of the Chemical Valency	71
43.	Theoretical Significance of the Chemical Valency Nature of Affinity	71
44.	Investigation of the Constitution of Chemical Compounds	75
45.	Theoretical Determination of the possible Forms of Combination	77
46.	Determination of the Linking by Synthesis and Analysis	80
47.	Determination of Atomic Linking from Physical Properties	83
48.	Determination of Atomic Linking from Chemical Behaviour	84
49.	History of the Development of the Theory of Atomic Linking	85
50.	Examples of the Determination of Atomic Linking	85
51.	Aromatic Compounds	91
52.	Physical Isomerism Allotropy	95
53.	Polymorphism	96
54.	Physical Isomerism of the Molecules	97
55.	Optical Isomerism	98
56.	Asymmetrically-linked Carbon Atoms	99
57.	Active and Inactive Forms	101
58.	Physical Isomerism, with Double Linking	102
59.	Absolute Dimensions of Molecules and Atoms	103
60.	Aggregation of the Molecules	104
61.	The Effect of Heat	105
62.	Homogeneous Solid Bodies	106
63.	Heterogeneous Solid Molecular Aggregates	107
64.	Density of Solid Bodies	108

CONTENTS

SECTION		PAGE
65.	Fusion and Solidification	112
66	Melting Points of the Elements . . .	113
67.	,, ,, Compounds . . .	115
68.	,, ,, Mixtures . . .	118
69	Homogeneous Liquids, Cohesion, Capillarity, Friction .	119
70.	Density of Liquids	120
71.	Expansion by Heat	123
72.	Refraction of Light by Liquids . .	123
73.	Influence of Atom-Linkage on Refraction .	126
74.	Interaction of Liquids with other Substances. Wetting and Imbibition	128
75.	Heterogeneous Mixtures of Liquids. Solutions .	129
76	Effect of Heat on Solubility . . .	130
77	Crystallisation. Supersaturation . .	132
78.	Relations between the Freezing Points of Solutions and the Molecular Weight of their Constituents	133
79.	Exceptions to Raoult's Law . . .	138
80.	Diffusion	138
81	Osmosis and Dialysis	140
82	Evaporation and Ebullition . . .	143
83.	Boiling Points	146
84	Vapour Pressure of Mixed Liquids .	148
85.	Relation of Density and Pressure of Vapours to Molecular Weights	149
86.	Critical Temperature . .	152
87.	Nature of the Gaseous State . . .	154
88	Constitution of Gases . . .	156
89	Boyle's Law	158
90.	Mixture of Gases Diffusion Effusion Transpiration	159
91.	Mixing of Gases and Liquids. Absorption of Gases	160
92	Chemical Change . . .	162
93.	Causes of Chemical Change . .	165
94.	Heat as Cause and Effect of Chemical Change .	165
95.	Propagation of Chemical Change. Temperature of Ignition. Explosion . . .	167
96	Dissociation of Gases . . .	169
97.	,, Liquids and Solids . . .	172
98	,, in Solution . . .	174
99	Electrolysis	174
100.	Faraday's Law . . .	177
101	Relationship between Conductivity and Dissociation .	178
102.	Migration of the Ions . .	179
103	Velocities ,, . . .	181

OUTLINES OF THEORETICAL CHEMISTRY

SECTION		PAGE
104.	Relation between Electrolytic Conduction and Diffusion	183
105.	The Function of the Ions in the Production of Electric Currents	184
106.	Dissociation a Condition preparatory to Chemical Change	186
107.	Rates of Chemical Change	189
108.	Simple Decomposition	190
109.	Double ,,	192
110.	Reversible Reactions	194
111.	Guldberg and Waage's Theory of the Action of Mass	196
112.	Experimental Proof of Guldberg and Waage's Law by Etherification	197
113.	Avidity of Acids	199
114.	Avidity Calculated for Molecular Weights	202
115.	Relation between the Avidity and the Composition of Acids	203
116.	Connection between Avidity and other Properties of Acids	205
117.	Influence of Insolubility and Volatility on Chemical Change	205
118.	One Insoluble Substance	207
119.	Action of Mass in Gases	208
120.	Exceptions to Guldberg and Waage's Law	210
121.	Non-reversible Reactions	210
122.	Contact Action	212
123.	Kinetic Nature of Affinity	215

PLATES

Atomic Weights	To face p. 58
Natural System of the Elements	At end

Erratum

P. 32, seven lines from bottom, *instead of* 'theory of molecular impacts' *read* 'theory of starting molecules'; and in the same line, *instead of* 'molecular theory' *read* 'kinetic theory.'

OUTLINES

OF

THEORETICAL CHEMISTRY

§ 1. **Definition and Province.**—Chemistry is a most important branch of natural science. As the human mind is incapable of embracing knowledge in its entirety, it is necessary to divide science into several branches. The sciences may be classified either according to the methods of investigation employed or according to the objects investigated. In the first system we distinguish between descriptive science, sometimes inaptly termed natural history, and natural philosophy, which should in reality be styled natural history.

The investigation and description of the various objects as they occur in nature is the problem the descriptive sciences have to deal with, whilst it is the aim of natural philosophy to investigate their genesis and transformations, and to endeavour to discover the cause of these changes. Chemistry[1] belongs to both branches of science

If we examine any natural object, such as a rock, an animal, or a plant, we find, as a rule, that it is composed of many dissimilar parts. The rock is composed of different minerals, the animals and plants are composed of different organs; these, again, are built up from more elementary forms, such as cells This subdivision cannot be carried on indefinitely: we finally arrive at forms of matter which cannot be split up by mechanical means into dissimilar particles. Chemistry is the science which investigates and describes these ultimate constituents, of which

[1] The origin of the word 'Chemistry' is not known with certainty

all natural objects are composed. Chemistry is, therefore, a fundamental portion of all descriptive science.

But, on the other hand, chemistry is also one of the explanatory sciences. Almost all the natural phenomena with which we are acquainted are of a complex nature; the eruption of a volcano, an earthquake, a thunderstorm, a fire, the life and growth of animals and plants, and numerous other occurrences, are composed of several distinct phenomena, such as light, heat, sound, electricity, evaporation, and other changes of condition. Natural philosophy treats of these elementary changes into which natural phenomena resolve themselves. Natural philosophy embraces physics and chemistry. It is the aim of physics to investigate and explain those elementary changes which affect the properties of bodies without altering their material composition. Chemistry deals with the changes which affect the material nature of the substance. Chemistry, then, is the science which treats of matter and its changes.

§ 2. **Characteristics of Chemical Change.**—Numerous material changes in natural objects are continually taking place, such as the formation of organic compounds in plants, the various changes which animal and vegetable bodies undergo either in nature or by the agency of man; for example, fermentation, putrefaction, combustion, the extraction of metals from their ores, the preparation of food, drugs, dyes, and innumerable other materials. These changes in the composition of bodies have been taking place from time immemorial before the eyes of men, generally, indeed, at man's desire; but in spite of this, for thousands of years they have been involved in obscurity, and even at the present time they remain incomprehensible to the majority even of educated people. Although chemical changes are continually taking place everywhere, the cause of these changes is difficult to recognise. This peculiarity of chemical phenomena is an inherent result of their nature. By exposing one or more substances to certain conditions, an entire change in their nature is effected. This may be brought about by exposing the substance to the action of heat, light, or percussion; indeed, in some cases a chemical change takes place when the substance does not appear to have been subjected to any kind of external influence. Sulphur burns, and leaves in its place a pungent-smelling gas. Coal is heated, and produces coal gas. Ores heated with charcoal yield metals. Iron rusts in the air. Molten lead changes into litharge, a dull powder, which is reduced to lead when heated with charcoal. These changes, and thousands of similar transformations, appear to be of a mysterious and marvellous character.

Compare them with such phenomena as the movement of a falling body, the reflection or refraction of a ray of light, the heating and cooling of a body, the action of one magnet on another, &c., and we see that it is not very difficult to study the whole course of most physical phenomena; whereas in the case of chemical changes the beginning of a reaction is, as a rule, immediately followed by its conclusion, so that it is impossible to perceive the intermediate stages. This is the reason why chemistry remained for thousands of years a mere collection of recipes and mystic formulæ, in spite of the labour which had been devoted to its advancement. This explains, also, how it was possible for chemistry to exist for centuries in a condition hardly worthy of the name of a science, side by side with a highly developed state of physics.

§ 3. **Method of Investigation.**—The high state of development which science has attained at the present day has been gained by a logical application of the method of induction. The numerous isolated facts presented to our observation are so classified that allied and analogous facts are arranged together for the purpose of comparison The laws and rules resulting from this comparison are gradually expanded and generalised, or, if necessary, more sharply defined, and their application limited. The knowledge of such laws does not satisfy the human mind—it desires to learn the reason, the cause of the existence of these laws.

Now, this knowledge cannot be gained from observation. It is only attained by an effort of our intellect, which solves the connection between the phenomena under observation and the causes which produce and modify them.

The knowledge of the causal connection of phenomena is consequently subjective, and it always remains an open question to what extent it is co-ordinated to the objective world. The investigation of this point is a second problem for science to solve. We proceed by assuming more or less arbitrarily a certain cause for each group of phenomena. Then, without reference to facts, we proceed to draw or 'deduce' all the conclusions that can be logically developed from the 'hypothesis.' We call this development the theory of the events in question. A comparison of the theoretical deductions with the observed facts is the sole means of judging the correctness of the theory and of the hypothesis on which it is based. So long as facts and theory agree, we are justified in regarding the theory as accurate, but not as absolutely and infallibly true.

If the theoretical conclusions and the facts do not agree, then the hypothesis is false, or the extension of the theory has been incorrectly carried out, and the errors must be sought out and corrected. Hypotheses and theories contradicted by observation must be rejected; doubtful theories may often be usefully retained so long as they facilitate the survey of a large number of observations. The best supported theory must never be regarded as absolutely true: a high degree of probability is the utmost to which it can attain.

As examples of a few of the hypotheses which have attained this highest degree of probability, we may mention Newton's hypothesis that the heavenly bodies exert a mutual attraction on each other which is inversely proportional to the square of their distances; Huygen's hypothesis that light is an undulatory movement of the ether; and the hypothesis of Daniel Bernoulli and R. Clausius that in the gaseous state the particles are in rapid rectilinear motion; and many others might be cited.

If we ask how far a happily chosen hypothesis and a correct theory can carry us on the path of knowledge, we find we must be content if, by their aid, we can follow and discern the causal connection and the necessary results of phenomena until we arrive at certain values which remain unaltered in the various changes taking place. These unchangeable values are termed 'constants.' They may be real values or only express proportions or ratios of such things as number, weight, length, space or time. A 'constant' is not of necessity absolutely invariable. It is sufficient for our purposes if it does not undergo any appreciable change in the phenomena under investigation. Consequently the constants we arrive at, in a certain group of phenomena, need not of necessity form the limits of our knowledge, but may in turn form the subject of research, if we investigate the conditions under which they vary, and in this way arrive at constants of a higher order. But in spite of all the progress we have made the determination of the constants still remains the problem for investigation. We are content when we succeed in predicting the phenomena which result as a natural consequence from certain constants, and the varying relations which these constants bear to each other.

§ 4. Development of Chemical Theories.—The inductive method was first applied in chemistry at a comparatively late stage in its history. It was only at the end of the seventeenth, and more particularly during the eighteenth century that all the then known facts were systematically arranged and a logical classification of bodies into combustible and incombustible, burnt and unburnt, was made. The hypothesis which was employed to account for the difference between the two large classes of bodies proved incorrect. This hypothesis assumed the existence of a peculiar combustible principle, the so-called 'phlogiston,' in all combustible substances. Combustion consisted in the evolution of phlogiston. In recent times it has been shown that the phlogiston theory is not altogether devoid of truth. For what was formerly termed phlogiston is almost identical with our present notion of potential energy It was during the two hundred years when the phlogiston theory prevailed that the application of inductive methods revealed the general truth that matter can neither be created nor destroyed. This discovery led to conclusions rendering the doctrine of phlogiston untenable, and resulting in its replacement by Lavoisier's theory of combustion. According to this theory the process of combustion is not due to an evolution of phlogiston, but to 'oxidation'—that is, to the combination of the combustible body with oxygen, one of the constituents of atmospheric air.

During the period of quantitative analysis, which begins with this theory, great stress was laid on the investigation of the proportions by weight in which different substances unite together, and thus a new field of research was opened up, which rapidly acquired unexpected dimensions.

The most important result of this new development was to strengthen our knowledge of the fact that nothing is lost and nothing is gained when substances undergo chemical change. When substances unite together, the weight of the compound is exactly equal to the sum of the weights of the constituents. When several bodies act on each other, it was formerly a difficult matter to decide which were compounds and which were constituents; but by the light of this new law the question can easily be answered. When red-hot iron is hammered it yields forge-scales, and on exposure to damp air it rusts. In either case it gains in weight; consequently it has combined with something, and not lost anything as was formerly supposed. It has combined with oxygen, and the increase in weight is equal to the weight of oxygen the metal has united with in its conversion into oxide (rust or forge scales). Consequently the oxide is the compound and the metal is a constituent; but in the last century the reverse was held to be the case. In this way 'quantitative chemistry' effected an accurate distinction between elementary bodies and their compounds, and imparted a degree of exactness to the methods of investigation, of which in previous centuries there had been no conception.

We are acquainted with about seventy bodies which have up to the present time resisted all attempts to decompose them. We therefore consider these substances as invariable in composition until the contrary is proved, and consequently regard them as the fundamental constants of chemistry. The aim of the science of chemistry is to investigate the laws which govern the combination of these elements, and to determine in what way the character and properties of the compounds are affected by the nature of the constituent elements.

§ 5. **Stœchiometric Laws.**—The further investigation of the quantitative composition of chemical compounds led to the foundation of the science of stœchiometry[1] by Jeremias Benjamin Richter. The most important facts of stœchiometry were discovered almost simultaneously by Proust. The fact pointed out by Proust, that definite chemical compounds always contain their constituents in fixed and invariable proportions, was strongly disputed by no less an authority than C. L. Berthollet.

[1] τὰ στοιχεῖα, the constituents. μέτρον, the measure.

Richter's views on the laws which govern the combination of acids with bases to form salts remained for a long time neglected and almost unnoticed. The credit of establishing the value of these laws (so far as they were correct) belongs to J. J. Berzelius, who obtained important aid from an hypothesis propounded by John Dalton.

The fundamental law of stœchiometry, discovered by Richter and confirmed and developed by Berzelius, states that all true chemical changes (*i. e.* changes of composition) take place between definite volumes or weights of the substances. This is equally true whether a substance decomposes into its constituents or is formed from its constituents, or when different compounds exchange one of their constituents.

When water is formed from its constituents 7 98 parts by weight of oxygen unite with one part by weight of hydrogen, never more or less, and the two constituents are produced in exactly these proportions when water is decomposed.

All other substances, whether elements or compounds, behave in the same way; that is to say, they only enter into combination or undergo decomposition in definite and fixed proportions by weight.

It often happens that the bodies unite together in several distinct proportions, but these different proportions always bear a simple relation to each other.

This empirical law is known as the law of multiple proportions. For example, there is another compound of hydrogen and oxygen, hydrogen peroxide, which contains 15·96 parts by weight of oxygen to 1 part by weight of hydrogen—that is, twice as much oxygen as unites with 1 part by weight of hydrogen in water. By mixing these two oxides of hydrogen a liquid is obtained in which the quantity of oxygen lies between that contained in water and in hydrogen peroxide. The resulting liquid is not a chemical compound, but merely a mechanical mixture, for its properties are those of its constituents, and the act of admixture is not followed by those changes in the material nature of the substances, which are characteristic of chemical combination.

Nitrogen forms a larger number of oxides, in which one part by weight of nitrogen is combined respectively with 0·5696, 1·1392, 1·7088, 2·2784, and 2 8480 parts by weight of oxygen.

The relation between these quantities is expressed by the whole numbers 1, 2, 3, 4, 5.

The numbers indicating the proportions in which substances unite together are called 'combining weights,' or stœchiometric quantities. It is remarkable that they apply not merely to two given elements but to all elements without exception. For example, one part by weight of copper is combined with 0·1263 part by weight of oxygen in cuprous oxide, and with 0·2526 part by weight of oxygen (*i.e.* exactly double) in cupric oxide. The quantities of sulphur combined with one part by weight of copper in the sulphides are also in the proportion of 1 to 2, cupric sulphide containing 0·5062 and cuprous sulphide 0·2531 part by weight of sulphur', 0·2531 part by weight of sulphur on combustion unites with 0·2526 part by weight of oxygen. This is exactly the quantity of oxygen which unites with one part by weight of copper to form cupric oxide.

The combining weights for copper and sulphur and for copper and oxygen are also valid for the compounds of sulphur and oxygen. This rule is true of all elements. It may be generally expressed in the following words:—

If we know the proportions by weight in which a series of elements unite with a certain given element, then these elements either unite with each other in the quantities represented by these proportions or in some simple multiple of them. If A, B, C, D represent the proportions by weight in which the different elements unite with a definite quantity of another element, then any compound of these elements can be represented by the formula

$$n \cdot A + n_1 \cdot B + n_2 \cdot C + n_3 \cdot D + \ldots$$

when n, n_1, n_2, n_3 represent whole (generally small) numbers.

The values A, B, C, &c. are the fundamental constants of stœchiometry.

§ 6 **Atomic Hypothesis**—The stœchiometric laws are purely empirical, and were discovered by induction. They have been confirmed by thousands of experiments, and their validity is independent of any hypothesis. But the human mind suspects a cause for every law, and is disinclined to acknowledge the existence of a law unless it can account for the cause of it.

Consequently the stœchiometric laws, which are now regarded as the most important ever discovered in natural science, were at first treated with neglect, until John Dalton investigated these laws and discovered a simple explanation of them.

Dalton investigated two gaseous compounds of carbon and hydrogen, and found that the so-called heavy carburetted hydrogen now called ethylene contained exactly half as much hydrogen combined with one part by weight of carbon as is the case in light carburetted hydrogen or marsh-gas. To explain this and similar observations concerning the oxides of nitrogen Dalton made use of an old and much-disputed hypothesis. He assumed that all elements consist of very minute indivisible particles, having a definite weight, termed atoms,[1] and that chemical compounds are produced by the union of these atoms.

This hypothesis was by no means new. More than two thousand years ago the Greek philosophers energetically debated the continuity of matter—whether matter completely fills the space it occupies, or whether it is composed of very minute individual particles separated from each other by spaces. These particles were termed atoms on account of their indivisibility

Democritus and many others based their system of natural philosophy on these hypothetical atoms, and attempted to explain the transformations of the universe as a result of their properties and rapid movements. Aristotle and his followers could not tolerate the idea of the existence of an empty space between the atoms, but maintained that the whole space is completely filled with matter. This difference of opinion survived till recent times, but at the present day the truth of the atomic theory is no longer a matter of dispute. Dalton does not appear to have troubled himself about this discussion. He made use of the atomic theory because it enabled him to explain without difficulty the fact that the elements combine only in definite proportions by weight, and that if certain elements unite together in several different proportions these proportions bear a simple relation to each other. We assume that all the atoms of one and the same element have the same weight, but that this weight varies for different elements in the proportion of their stœchiometric quantities. Let A be the weight of the

[1] ἡ ἄτομος, the indivisible.

atom of a certain element, and B that of another; then it is obvious that a compound of one atom of the first with one atom of the second, e.g. A + B, must contain half as much of the second as another compound A + 2B.

As all particles of such a compound have the same composition, then any number of particles or any given quantity of this substance will contain the constituents in the same proportion as the individual particles, viz. in the proportion of the atomic weights or in a simple multiple of them.

The atomic theory offers an exceedingly lucid explanation of the purely empirical law of combining proportions

It is clear we can only deduce from the stœchiometric values the relative, not the absolute, weight of the atoms, as we only know the relative number of atoms contained in a compound. Black oxide of copper contains one part by weight of oxygen to 3·959 parts of copper. If we can by any means prove that this oxide contains an equal number of copper and of oxygen atoms, then it must follow that the weights of the atoms of these two elements are in the same proportion to each other that the constituents are in the oxide—namely, as 1 : 3·959. The copper atom is 3·959 times heavier than the atom of oxygen. This proportion by weight always remains the same, and is independent of the number of atoms of the elements entering into combination.

§ 7. **Symbols.**—Dalton imagined the atoms to be small spheres, and represented the atoms of different elements by various symbols enclosed in a ring or circle, thus:—

1 Atom	Oxygen	Hydrogen	Nitrogen	Carbon	Sulphur	Phosphorus
	○	⊙	⊕	●	⊕	⊗

Atoms of the metallic elements were represented by circles containing the initial letters of their names. Berzelius omitted the circle as inconvenient, and used the initial of the Latin name to represent the atom of any element. This system of notation is now universally adopted. Both Dalton and Berzelius placed two or more symbols close together to indicate that the atoms had entered into combination.

The number of atoms is indicated by prefixing a numeral or by the use of indices. The device of Berzelius for representing a double atom by drawing a bar through the symbol is no longer used. Two atoms of hydrogen may be represented by the following symbols, 2H, H_2, H^2, HH. The second of these symbols is most frequently employed

§ 8. **Unit of Atomic Weights.**—We have already seen (§ 6) that the weight of the atoms cannot be deduced directly from the combining proportions, and that it is only possible to decide how many times heavier or lighter one atom is than another. This, however, is all that is requisite for the development of chemical theory. It is not necessary to know the weight of individual atoms. The composition of any mixture of different substances can be equally well expressed in grams, ounces, or pounds, and in the same way the composition of any chemical compound can be expressed in terms of any unit of weight that may be selected. If we choose the weight of an atom of a given element as unity, we can by means of the stœchiometric values express the atomic weights of the others in terms of this standard, so that a number is obtained for each element, which shows how many times heavier it is than the unit.

Dalton's proposal to take the atom of hydrogen, the lightest of all the atoms, as unity is at the present time universally adopted. But for many years it was the custom to follow the example of Wollaston and Berzelius, who, for certain practical reasons, took the atom of oxygen as their standard. It is obvious that there will be a great difference in the atomic weights according to the standard selected. If hydrogen is taken as unity, it is clear that the atomic weights will be proportionally larger than is the case when the heavier atom of oxygen is taken as the standard. Just as in measuring distances, the numbers are larger if we reckon by feet instead of metres or by kilometres instead of miles. Now some atomic weights are smaller than that of oxygen, so in order to avoid fractions Wollaston took as his standard the tenth part, and Berzelius chose the hundredth part of an atom of oxygen, so that an atom of oxygen=10 or 100. This standard yielded atomic weights which were in some cases larger than 1000, and are now no longer used.

§ 9. **Determination of Atomic Weights from Stœchiometric Values.**—We have already seen (§ 6) that the relative values of the atomic weights can only be calculated from the composition of a chemical compound as determined by synthesis or analysis, when the number of atoms contained in the compound is known. But the number of atoms cannot be directly determined, and can only be deduced by the help of hypotheses varying in degree of probability. Water is composed of oxygen and hydrogen in the proportion by weight of 7·98 : 1. It does not follow that the atomic weights of these elements are in this ratio, but only that the weight of all the hydrogen atoms in a given quantity of water bears this proportion to the total weight of the oxygen atoms combined with them, so that

$$n \cdot H : m \cdot O = 1 : 7 \cdot 98$$

when n and m represent whole (unknown) numbers. The atomic theory only teaches us that a certain number of whole atoms of one substance has combined with a definite number of whole atoms of a second element, e.g., n H with m O. The values of m and n are not known. It is one of the most important problems in theoretical chemistry to determine the number of atoms which are united together in different compounds.

§ 10. **First Attempt to determine the Atomic Weights.**—At first sight it would appear to be the simplest plan to regard the proportion by weight in which two elements unite together as identical with their atomic weights. But this is not possible, because many elements unite together in different proportions. In black oxide of copper one part by weight of oxygen is united to 3·959 parts by weight of copper; but in the red oxide, twice as much copper, viz 7·918, is contained. Is the atomic weight of copper 3·959 or 7·918 times heavier than that of oxygen? There does not appear to be any reason why one number should be selected in preference to the other. If we choose the first, then we have the formulæ

$$Cu\ O = 3 \cdot 958 + 1, \text{ for the black oxide}$$

and

$$Cu_2\ O = 7 \cdot 918 + 1, \text{ for the red oxide}$$

If we take the second value, then we have

$$Cu\ O_2 = 7 \cdot 918 + 2, \text{ for the black oxide}$$

and

$$Cu\ O = 7 \cdot 918 + 1, \text{ for the red oxide.}$$

Berzelius selected the second value, but it has been replaced by the first, which is now universally regarded as correct.

Dalton advocated the greatest simplicity. He assumed the existence of only one atom of each constituent in many compounds, in which, according to our present views, several atoms of one of the constituents are contained, e g.

	Proportion by Weight.	FORMULÆ. Dalton.	Berzelius
Water	1 : 7·98	HO	H_2O
Ammonia	1 : 4·67	HN	H_3N
Ethylene	1 : 5 985	HC	H_4C_2

According to Dalton's views, the atomic weights of oxygen, nitrogen, and carbon are to the atomic weight of hydrogen in the ratio of

$$O : N : C : H = 7·98 : 4·67 : 5·985 : 1;$$

but according to Berzelius they stand to each other in the proportion of

$$O : N : C : H = 15·96 : 14·01 : 11·97 : 1.$$

The weights which Dalton regarded as the atomic weights of oxygen and carbon are only half, and in the case of nitrogen only one-third, of the atomic weights accepted by Berzelius.

§ 11. **Chemical Equivalents.**—At the beginning of the present century Wollaston proposed that the chemical symbols should represent the equivalents as determined by experiment. In this way he hoped to avoid the want of uniformity resulting from the use of the hypothetical atomic weights. Those quantities of different substances which produce the same, or nearly the same, effect were regarded as equivalent. The expression was originally applied to those quantities of different acids which are required to neutralise a fixed quantity of a given base, and also to those quantities of different bases which are required to neutralise a certain weight of a given acid The expression was afterwards used in a wider sense, and was applied to all kinds of substances, including the elements. It is obvious that no element can be strictly equivalent to another. It is only equivalent in certain respects—namely, in its capacity for uniting with a third substance, or displacing it in a compound.

We regard as equivalent weights of the elements those quantities which have in this respect the same value, and we compare them as we do the atomic weights with one part by weight of hydrogen as unity. The equivalent weights of the elements are, therefore, those quantities of the elements which can enter into the same combinations as one part by weight or one atom of hydrogen, or can unite with one part by weight or one atom of hydrogen. The first definition holds good for the metals and semi-metals; the second is true of the non-metals, because all the latter can combine with hydrogen; but only a few of the metals are able to form hydrides

By means of this definition the equivalent weights can easily be determined by experiment. One part by weight of hydrogen unites with—

19 06	parts by weight of	fluorine
35·37	,,	chlorine
79 76	,,	bromine
126·54	,,	iodine
7·98	parts by weight of	oxygen
15 99	,,	sulphur
39 48	,,	selenium
62·50	,,	tellurium
4·67	parts by weight of	nitrogen
10 32	,,	phosphorus
24·97	,,	arsenic
39·87	,,	antimony
2 99	parts by weight of	carbon
7·08	,,	silicon

One part by weight of hydrogen is replaced in its compounds by the following quantities of different metals. These quantities of the metals will consequently be able to unite with the non-metals in the proportions stated in the preceding table, e.g.

35·37 parts by weight of chlorine, 7·98 of oxygen, &c. Of the lighter metals—

7·01 parts by weight of		lithium
23·00	,,	sodium
39·03	,,	potassium
85·2	,,	rubidium
132·7	,,	cæsium
4·54 parts by weight of		beryllium
12·15	,,	magnesium
19·95	,,	calcium
43·65	,,	strontium
68·45	,,	barium
9·01	,,	aluminium

The following quantities of the heavier metals expel one part by weight of hydrogen from water or hydrochloric acid, and replace it directly or indirectly:—

27·4 parts by weight of		manganese
27·94	,,	iron
29·3	,,	cobalt
29·3	,,	nickel
32·55	,,	zinc
37·8	,,	indium
55·85	,,	cadmium
59·4	,,	tin
103·2	,,	lead
107·66	,,	silver
203·7	,,	thallium

Totally different results are obtained in the case of many metals if we determine directly the quantity of metal which will unite with one equivalent weight of oxygen (7·98 parts) or of chlorine (35·37 parts).

The oxides, sulphides, chlorides, and bromides contain the following quantities of metals united to 1 equivalent weight of oxygen (7·98), sulphur (15·99), chlorine (35·37), or bromine (79·76).

These different proportions stand in a simple relation to each other:—

7·83, or 9·13, or 13 7, or 18·27, or 20 55, or 27·4 parts by weight of manganese; the ratio is $\frac{2}{7} : \frac{1}{3} : \frac{1}{2} : \frac{2}{3} : \frac{3}{4} : 1$.

8 74, or 17·48, or 26·22 parts of chromium; ratio, $\frac{1}{3} : \frac{2}{3} : 1$.

18·63, or 20 95, or 27·94 parts of iron; ratio, $\frac{2}{3} : \frac{3}{4} : 1$.

65·6, or 98·4, or 196 8 parts of gold; ratio, $\frac{1}{3} : \frac{1}{2} : 1$.

31·59 or 63·18 parts of copper, and 99 9 or 199·8 parts of mercury; ratio, $\frac{1}{2} : 1$—and so on, for all the other elements.

It was soon found to be very difficult to decide which of these different values should be regarded as the true equivalent weight, and be represented by the chemical symbol of the element For a long time the quantities of the non-metals contained in the first table were regarded as the true equivalent weights; but the values in the second table have never come into actual use. On the other hand, the equivalent weights for the metals contained in the table were, with the exception of those of beryllium and aluminium, in use for a considerable period.

§ 12 **Electrolytic Equivalents.**—The electrolytic law of Michael Faraday has been used to insure the uniform determination of equivalent weights. Faraday found that when an electric current is passed through a so-called conductor of the second class, an electrolyte (*i.e.* a substance which can only conduct electricity when it is decomposed by the current), the quantity of the substance decomposed is proportional to the intensity of the current.

If one and the same current passes through two electrolytes, then the several constituents deposited are electrically and chemically equivalent to each other.

To determine the equivalent weights of the elements by means of this law, it is only necessary to decompose some of their compounds by a current which simultaneously decomposes a hydrogen compound, and determine experimentally what weight of the given element has been liberated in the same time as one part by weight of hydrogen. On the whole, this method yielded more uniform results than those obtained by chemical analysis; but still different values were obtained for certain metals, according to the nature and composition of the compound investigated.

For example :—

Copper	.	. 31·59	and	63·18
Mercury		. 99·9	,,	199·8
Iron	.	. 18·27	,,	27·4

Another difficulty presented itself. The compounds of many elements would not conduct electricity and were found not to be decomposed by it, and consequently the determination of the equivalents by electrolysis could not be systematically carried out.

§ 13. **Crystallographic Equivalence. Isomorphism.**—In 1819 Eilhard Mitscherlich discovered the important law of isomorphism, which has been used by Berzelius and other investigators for the determination of equivalence. Mitscherlich found that certain elements can replace others in their compounds without producing any essential alteration in the crystalline form of the substance.

These compounds and the elements which mutually replace each other are said to be isomorphous even when the elements in the isolated state do not exhibit any similarity of crystalline form. The replacement always takes place in stœchiometric quantities, so that a certain quantity of one element replaces or is replaced by a definite quantity of another, its crystallographic equivalent, while the other constituents of the compound remain unchanged. Isomorphous compounds have the power of crystallising together in such a way that they form homogeneous crystals independently of the proportions in which they are mixed. The alums, the vitriols and their double salts, the phosphates and arsenates are well-known examples of groups of isomorphous compounds.

Unfortunately no element has yet been discovered which is isomorphous with hydrogen, so that the crystallographic equivalents of the other elements cannot be directly compared with hydrogen, the usual standard. But by starting with the equivalent weight of an element which has been determined by one of the other methods, we can ascertain the crystallographic equivalents of any other elements of the same isomorphic group. If any members of this group exhibit isomorphism with other elements we can go on step by step until the equivalents of a large number of elements have thus been determined. Potassium is isomorphous with rubidium, cæsium, and thallium.

The equivalent weight of potassium 39·03 (§ 11) is isomorphously replaced by 85·2 parts by weight of rubidium, 132·7 of cæsium, and in many compounds by 203·7 parts of thallium. This last quantity is isomorphous with 113·4 parts of indium.

Whether sodium is, strictly speaking, isomorphous with potassium is a disputed point; many analogous compounds of these two elements certainly exhibit identical crystalline forms, but as a rule they do not crystallise together. If we are justified in regarding the instances of identity of crystalline form as cases of isomorphism, then 39·03 parts by weight of potassium are equivalent to 23 parts of sodium, and these are equivalent to 7·01 parts of lithium and 107·66 of silver.

But the equivalent of silver can be replaced isomorphously by 63·18 parts by weight of copper, and the latter metal is a member of the group of metals forming vitriols and can be isomorphously replaced by—

58·6 parts by weight of nickel
58·6   ,,   cobalt
55 88   ,,   iron
54·8   ,,   manganese
65·1   ,,   zinc
24·3   ,,   magnesium

The four last elements are isomorphous with 39 91 parts of calcium, and iron is isomorphous with 27·04 parts of aluminium and 52·45 parts by weight of chromium.

Calcium is also isomorphous with 87·3 parts of strontium, 136·9 parts of barium, and 206 4 of lead.

In some compounds zinc can be replaced by 111 7 parts of cadmium. The highest oxides of chromium and manganese enable us to pass on to the non-metals and semi-metals For the chromates and manganates have the same crystalline form as the sulphates, selenates, tellurates, molybdates, and tungstates, and the permanganates have the same crystalline form as the perchlorates. The isomorphism of these salts provides us with the following crystallographic equivalent weights :—

31·98 parts of sulphur
78·87 ,,   selenium

125·0 parts of tellurium
95·9 ,, molybdenum
183·6 ,, tungsten
35·37 ,, chlorine

Further 79·76 parts of bromine, 126·53 parts of iodine, and probably 19·06 of fluorine are isomorphous with 35·37 parts by weight of chlorine.

There are several other large groups of isomorphous elements. The phosphates, vanadates, and arsenates are isomorphous. In the free state arsenic is isomorphous with antimony, bismuth, and tellurium. But it is obvious that the crystallographic equivalent can only be deduced from the isomorphism of the compounds, and not from the isomorphism of the free elements, for in the latter case there are no means of ascertaining what weight of the one element can replace a given weight of the other.

It is assumed in certain minerals that sulphur is isomorphously replaced by arsenic and antimony; if this is really the case then we have the following crystallographic equivalents:—

30·96 parts by weight of phosphorus
74·9 ,, arsenic
207·3 ,, bismuth
51·1 ,, vanadium
119·6 ,, antimony

Silicon, titanium, zirconium, thorium, and tin form another isomorphous group, and tin is related to the isomorphous group of the platinum metals containing platinum, iridium, osmium, palladium, rhodium, and ruthenium; these two groups are thus brought into relation with each other, and the following equivalents are obtained:—

28·33 parts by weight of silicon
48·01 ,, titanium
90·4 ,, zirconium
232·0 ,, thorium
118·8 , tin

194·3 ,, platinum
192·5 ,, iridium

191·0 parts by weight of osmium
106·2 ,, palladium
102·7 ,, rhodium
101 4 ,, ruthenium

If the somewhat doubtful isomorphism of titanium and iron be admitted, this group may thus be brought into relationship with the iron group. Some of the crystallographic equivalent weights arrived at in this way may not be correct, for doubtless some of the cases of isomorphism may prove not to be genuine. But the great advantage of this method is that it can only give one equivalent weight for each element, whereas the other methods would yield two or more equivalent weights

After the discovery of the law of isomorphism Berzelius regarded the crystallographic equivalent weights as identical with the atomic weights, except in the case of K, Na, Li, Ag, of which he determined the atomic weights by the use of their electrolytic equivalents. The identification of the crystallographic equivalents with the atomic weights offered a lucid explanation of the phenomena of isomorphism. Imagine that a crystal is a regular structure composed of small particles of matter, called molecules, the molecules being themselves systematically built up of a definite number of atoms. If in each of these particles one atom is replaced by another of similar shape and size it is clear that the whole structure will remain unaltered in shape and arrangement. This is obvious, for experience shows us that, although the crystallographic equivalents vary considerably in weight, they all occupy approximately the same space.

We are, however, acquainted with a series of cases in which it is apparently not permissible to assume that replacement takes place atom for atom. In innumerable compounds the equivalent of potassium (39 03) is isomorphously replaced by 14·01 parts of nitrogen and 4 parts of hydrogen, and scarcely the slightest difference between the two classes of compounds is to be found. Consequently since Mitscherlich's first discoveries it has been assumed that an atom of potassium can be isomorphously replaced by the 'compound radical' ammonium (NH_4 = 18 01), composed of one atom of nitrogen (N = 14·01) and four atoms of hydrogen But if this is possible in one case, it may frequently happen that several atoms replace one single atom. If we admit this, then the whole foundation of these considerations is weakened: 107·66 parts by weight of silver are isomorphously replaced by 63 18 parts by weight of copper: this may mean that one atom of silver is replaced by one of copper. But if we assume that each atom of silver is replaced by two atoms of copper, then the atomic weight of copper will be 31·59, which is identical with the chemical equivalent weight given in § 11.

Another weak point in determining atomic weights by isomorphism is that many elements must be omitted, and hydrogen amongst the number. As a natural consequence the atomic weights can only be referred to the unit by making certain arbitrary assumptions. In fact we have already started with the arbitrary assumption that the equivalent weight of potassium as compared with hydrogen is 39·03. If we had taken it as half, or, like Berzelius, as double this value, we should have obtained for all the other elements values half or double their present atomic weights, and it would not have been possible to prove that these values were incorrect.

§ 14. **Thermic Equivalents.**—In 1819, at the time when Mitscherlich discovered the law of isomorphism, two French chemists, Dulong and Petit. observed the existence of another simple relation between the chemical combining weights of the elements and a physical property, viz. their specific heat or capacity for heat in the solid state. The atomic weights are approximately inversely proportional to the specific heats, and consequently the product of these two values is nearly the same for all elements. In order to make this law valid Dulong and Petit found it necessary to alter the combining weights of some of the elements. Although these changes were not at the time generally welcomed, they are now universally adopted (except in the case of a few small errors), and all the more recent specific heat determinations have confirmed the accuracy of the law of Dulong and Petit. This important law is of general application It gives the same values as the law of isomorphism and meets with the same difficulty, for here again the results cannot be directly referred to hydrogen as the standard, for solid hydrogen has not yet been investigated. If we take any of the crystallographic equivalents mentioned in the preceding paragraph, and multiply each by the specific heat of the element, we obtain approximately the same product.

The explanation of this fact is very simple. As the specific heat is the amount of heat required to raise the unit weight of a substance from 0° to 1° C. this product represents the amount of heat required to raise the equivalent weight by 1° C. The weight of the given element, which is heated 1° C., is termed the thermic equivalent weight. If we regard this as the atomic weight, then the product of the atomic weight into the specific heat is the atomic heat, i.e. the amount of heat taken up by one atom. It is clear that the atoms of the different elements have the same capacity for heat. The law may be simply expressed by saying that the atomic heats of all the elements are approximately equal.

This law applies without exception to all the malleable metals, to almost all the brittle metals, and to the majority of the non-metals. The following table contains in the first column the names of the elements, in the second column under c the specific heats, in the third the thermic equivalent or thermic atomic weight A, and in the fourth the product $A \cdot c$, the atomic heat. The specific heat of most of the elements has been determined between the boiling point of water and the mean temperature of the atmosphere, but in the case of easily fusible elements the determinations are made at temperatures below their melting points, as most bodies exhibit abnormal specific heats at a temperature near their melting point.

Element	Specific Heat c	Atomic Weight A	Atomic Heat $A \cdot c$
Lithium	0·941	7·01	6·6
Sodium	0·293	23·00	6·7
Magnesium	0·250	24·3	6·1
Aluminium	0·214	27·0	5·8
Phosphorus	0·174	30·96	5·4
Sulphur	0·178	31·98	5·7
Potassium	0·166	39·03	6·5
Calcium	0·170	39·91	6·8
Titanium	0·129	48·0	6·2
Chromium	0·121	52·4	6·3
Manganese	0·122	54·8	6·7

ATOMIC HEAT

Element	Specific Heat c	Atomic Weight A	Atomic Heat A . c
Iron	0·114	55·88	6·4
Cobalt	0·107	58·6	6·3
Nickel	0·108	58·6	6·4
Copper	0·095	63·18	6·0
Zinc	0·094	65·1	6·1
Gallium	0·079	69·9	5·5
Germanium	0·077	72·3	5·6
Arsenic	0·081	74·9	6·1
Selenium	0·076	78·87	6·0
Bromine	0·084	79·76	6·7
Zirconium	0·066	90·4	6·0
Molybdenum	0·072	95·9	6·9
Ruthenium	0·061	101·4	6·2
Rhodium	0·058	102·7	6·0
Palladium	0·059	106·35	6·3
Silver	0·057	107·66	6·1
Cadmium	0·054	111·7	6·0
Indium	0·057	113·6	6·5
Tin	0·055	118·8	6·5
Antimony	0·051	119·6	6·1
Tellurium	0·048	125·0	6·0
Iodine	0·054	126·54	6·8
Lanthanum	0·045	138·0	6·2
Cerium	0·045	139·9	6·3
Tungsten	0·033	183·6	6·1
Osmium	0·031	191·0	6·1
Iridium	0·032	192·5	6·3
Platinum	0·032	194·3	6·3
Gold	0·032	196·7	6·4
Mercury	0·032	199·8	6·4
Thallium	0·033	203·7	6·8
Lead	0·031	206·4	6·4
Bismuth	0·030	207·3	6·4
Thorium	0·028	232·0	6·4
Uranium	0·028	239·0	6·6

The atomic heats in this table do not exhibit absolute uniformity—the values vary between 5·4 and 6·8. The thermic equivalent or atom may now be defined as that stœchiometric quantity which on multiplication by the specific heat yields a constant which is approximately 6. If the specific heat of ice is taken as the unit, or the equivalent weight of some other element instead of hydrogen is taken as the standard, then different values would be obtained. If the atomic weight of oxygen is taken as 100, then the atomic heats would vary between 38 and 40.

As the atomic heat is almost constant, and as

$A \cdot c = \text{const.} = 6\cdot 3$ approximately,

it is clear that the value of A or c can be calculated approximately if one of these values is known.

§ 15. Exceptions.—In attempting to calculate the thermic equivalents of the elements by this method, we occasionally obtain values which cannot represent the true atomic weights. Regnault found for pure carbon in the form of diamond the specific heat $c = 0.147$, and for graphite, another modification of the same element, $c = 0.198$. The chemical equivalent of carbon is in § 11 stated to be 2.9925. The atomic weight must either be 2.9925 or a simple multiple of this number.

If $a = 2.9925$, then $A = n.a$, where n is a whole number, and $c.A = c.n.a = 6.3$ approximately.

Let $n = 1.2.3$, &c.; then we have for

Diamond		Graphite	
n	$n.a.c$	n	$n.a.c$
1	0.44	1	0.59
2	0.88	2	1.18
.	.	.	.
10	4.40	10	5.92
11	4.84	11	6.52
12	5.28	12	7.11
13	5.72	13	—
14	6.12	14	—

The atomic weight of carbon, calculated from the specific heat of the diamond, would be

$$13.a = 38.90, \text{ or } 14.a = 41.89.$$

But if it is deduced from the specific heat of graphite, then

$$10.a = 29.92; \text{ or } 11.a = 32.92.$$

Even if we disregard the want of agreement between these results, such atomic weights would lead to monstrous formulæ for the numerous compounds of carbon, and on this ground alone they could not be accepted.

Carbon forms the most pronounced exception to the law. Boron, silicon, and beryllium also form exceptions, and the values for phosphorus and sulphur do not agree closely with the atomic heats of the other elements.

It is a well-known fact that the specific heat, and therefore the atomic heat, is different at different temperatures. A careful comparison of all the determinations of specific heat led H. F. Weber to the conclusion that the influence of temperature on the specific heats of those elements which form exceptions to the law is so great that they would follow the law at temperatures above 100°. Weber proved by experiment this hypothesis to be correct in the case of carbon, silicon, and boron. Nilson, Pettersson, and Humpidge have recently proved the same for beryllium. The specific heats of these elements increase with the temperature, at first rapidly, afterwards more slowly, until they become almost constant at high temperatures. The values obtained at high temperatures agree fairly well with the law of Dulong and Petit. The smallest stœchiometric quantities (equivalent to one part by weight of hydrogen) of these four elements are—carbon 2·99, boron 3·63, silicon 7·08, and beryllium, 4·55. The atomic weights must be simple multiples of these numbers.

In the following table c gives the specific heats at high temperatures, A the atomic weights, which on multiplication by the specific heats yield the atomic heats $A \cdot c$.

	c	A	$A \cdot c$
Beryllium	0·621 at 500° C.	9·1	5·64
Boron	0·5 [1] ,, 600°	10·9	5·5
Carbon	0·459 ,, 980°	11·97	5·51
Silicon	0·203 ,, 230°	28·3	5·74

These values of A obey the law of Dulong and Petit fairly well; but it is clear that this law would not have led to their adoption if they had not already been discovered by other methods.

All the elements which exhibit deviations from the law, their atomic heats being too low, have small atomic weights, and are, as a rule, non-metals. The law always applies to elements with atomic weights thirty-six or forty times that of hydrogen.

§ 16. **Specific Heat of Atoms in Compounds.**—The law of Dulong and Petit also holds good for elements in the state of combination. The specific heat of a compound in the solid

---

[1] Calculated by interpolation from the observations. At 233° $c = 0·366$.

state is approximately equal to the sum of the specific heats of its constituents. In the case of silver iodide, for example, we have—

Silver . . A.c = 107 66 × 0·056 = 6·1
Iodine . . A.c = 126·54 × 0·054 = 6·8
Total 12·9

The specific heat of silver iodide (AgI) is $c = 0\ 061$. If this value is multiplied by the sum of the atomic weights, then we obtain the capacity for heat of that quantity of the compound represented by the formula, AgI.

$$c\ (Ag + I) = 0·061 \times (107·66 + 126\ 54) = 14·3.$$

This is only a little larger than the sum of the specific heats of the constituents. In the same way, in the case of silver bromide—

Ag.c = 107·66 × 0·056 = 6·1
Br.c = 79·76 × 0·084 = 6·7
Ag + Br = 187·42   12·8
and (AgBr)c = 187·42 × 0·074 = 13·9.

The stœchiometric quantities of these substances composed of two thermic equivalents or atoms, AgI and AgBr, require about thirteen units of heat to raise their temperature by 1° C., i.e. double as much as a single atom. Compounds containing three thermic atoms have a capacity for heat three times as great, namely, 3 × 6·4, i.e. 19 or 20. In the case of lead bromide and iodide—

$c.(Pb + 2Br) = 0·0533 \times (206·4 + 2 \times 79·76) = 19·5$
$c.(Pb + 2I) = 0·0427 \times (206\ 4 + 2 \times 126·54) = 19·6$

and the sum of the atomic heats of the elements are

$$6·4 + (2 \times 6\ 7) = 19\ 8$$
$$6·4 + (2 \times 6·8) = 20·0.$$

This fact is made use of to determine the thermic equivalents of those elements of which the specific heat cannot be directly determined. If the specific heats of iodine and bromine were unknown they could be approximately calculated from the preceding data.

35·37 parts by weight of chlorine unite with the thermic atomic weight of silver, Ag=107 66, and form 143 03 parts by weight of silver chloride, 70 74 parts by weight of chlorine unite with one atom of lead, Pb = 206·4, to form 277·14 parts by weight of lead chloride. On multiplying these quantities by the corresponding values for the specific heats, the product is the capacity for heat of the stœchiometric quantity of the compounds; deduct from this the atomic heat of the metals, and the remainder is the capacity for heat of chlorine.

$$c \,.\, 143\cdot 03 = 0\cdot 091 \times 143\cdot 03 = 13\cdot 0$$
$$c \,.\, \text{Ag} = 0\cdot 056 \times 107\cdot 66 = \underline{6\cdot 1}$$

Capacity for heat of 35·37 parts by weight of chlorine 6·9

$$c \,.\, 277\cdot 1 = 0\cdot 066 \times 277\cdot 1 = 18\cdot 3$$
$$c \,.\, \text{Pb} = 0\cdot 031 \times 206\cdot 4 = \underline{6\cdot 4}$$

Capacity for heat of 70·74 parts by weight of chlorine 11·9

Consequently the thermic equivalent of chlorine = 35·37, and the quantity which is attached to one atom of lead is twice this amount and represents two atoms, as the capacity for heat is nearly equal to twice 6 units. The thermic equivalent or atomic weight of an element can be deduced by means of the specific heat of its compounds, even when the atomic heats of the elements united with it are unknown, provided these elements form an analogous compound with an element of known atomic heat. For example:—

           11·97 parts by weight of carbon
and   47 88   ,,   oxygen

unite with the thermic equivalent of lead = 206·4 to form 266·25 parts by weight of cerussite. This mineral has the specific heat $c = 0\ 080$ and the capacity

$$0\cdot 080 \times 266\ 25 = 21\cdot 3.$$

The following metals unite with the same quantities of carbon and oxygen:—

- 136·9 parts of barium forming 196 75 parts by weight of witherite $c = 0\cdot 109$;
- 87·3 parts of strontium forming 147 05 parts by weight of strontianite $c = 0\cdot 145$;
- 39·9 parts of calcium forming 99·75 parts by weight of arragonite $c = 0\cdot 206$.

These quantities have, according to F. Neumann's discovery, the same capacity for heat as cerussite.

Witherite	. . .	$196·75 \times 0·109 = 21·4$
Strontianite	. .	$147·05 \times 0·145 = 21·3$
Arragonite	. . .	$99·75 \times 0·206 = 20·6$

From this we conclude that the amount of each metal contained in these compounds represents the thermic equivalents. Bunsen has proved by experiment that this is the case with regard to calcium.

In this way the thermic equivalents of several elements have been arrived at, which could not be determined directly, and do not on this account appear in the table on pages 22 and 23, viz.

Chlorine	. . . . .	$Cl = 35·37$
Rubidium	. . . .	$Ru = 85·2$
Strontium	. . . .	$Sr = 87·3$
Barium	. . . .	$Ba = 136·9$

But still the elements mentioned in § 15 remain exceptions, as the capacity for heat of their compounds is smaller than the value calculated from the number of their constituent atoms. This is also true of nitrogen, fluorine, oxygen, and hydrogen.

§. 17. **Relation between Atomic Weight and Vapour Density.—** As by chemical methods alone it was found impossible to fix the value of the atomic weights, other physical methods than the crystalline form and specific heat were soon employed. The most important of these is the law of combining volumes discovered by Gay Lussac and Alexander von Humboldt at the beginning of the present century. According to this law a simple relation exists between the volumes of the different gases (measured under similar conditions of temperature and pressure) entering into combination or mutually decomposing each other.

The densities of the gaseous elements at the ordinary temperature compared with air or hydrogen are as follows :—

	Air = 1	Hydrogen = 1
Hydrogen . . .	0·06926	1·00
Oxygen . .	1·10563	15·96
Nitrogen . . .	0·9713	14·02
Chlorine . .	2·450	35·37

These elements unite together in the following proportions:—

			By Volume	By Weight
Hydrogen and chlorine			1 : 1	1 : 35·37
,,	,,	oxygen	2 : 1	1 : 7·98 = 2 : 15·96
,,	,,	nitrogen	3 : 1	1 : 4·67 = 3 : 14·01
Oxygen	,,	,,	1 : 1	1 : 0·878 = 15·96 : 14·01
,,	,,	,,	1 : 2	1 : 1·756 = 15·96 : 28·02
,,	,,	,,	2 : 1	1 : 0·439 = 31·92 : 14·01

The combining weights of the gaseous elements are either directly proportional to their densities or to a simple multiple of their densities. The simplest hypothesis is that the atomic weights are proportional to the densities, *i.e.* to the weight of equal volumes of the gases. That is to say, that under similar conditions of temperature and pressure equal volumes of the different gaseous elements contain the same number of atoms. Berzelius made this assumption in opposition to Dalton's views. When this law was applied to elements which only assume the gaseous state at high temperatures the following results were obtained:—

	Air = 1	Hydrogen = 1
Sulphur	6·62	95·94
Phosphorus	4·35	62·8
Arsenic	10·4	150·2
Mercury	6·93	100

In these cases the densities compared with hydrogen cannot be regarded as the atomic weights; for the many analogies between oxygen and sulphur show that the atomic weight of the latter is almost exactly double that of the former, i.e. 31·98, not 95·94. The close analogy between the compounds of nitrogen and those of phosphorus and arsenic indicate that if N = 14, then P = 31 and As = 75; that is, the atomic weights are, in the case of phosphorus and arsenic, only half the densities; for only in the latter case will the corresponding hydrides have the analogous formulæ, NH_3, PH_3 and AsH_3; if the atomic weights are doubled the two latter must be represented by the formulæ PH_6 and AsH_6. There are also good grounds for doubting that the atom of mercury is only 100 times heavier than the atom of hydrogen; consequently

Berzelius was obliged to regard it as 200 times the weight of a hydrogen atom. The same is true of other atomic weights deduced from the density in the gaseous state; but some atomic weights arrived at by this method, e.g those of iodine and bromine, agree with the results obtained for chlorine and others in the first group of elements.

§ 18. **Want of Agreement between the different Equivalents.** The different methods used in determining the equivalent weights of the elements led to different results. The atomic weights deduced by the chemical, electrolytic, crystallographic or thermic methods occasionally agreed and occasionally disagreed It is not surprising, therefore, that there was a great want of unanimity in the views which chemists held concerning these fundamental values

In spite of great difficulties, Berzelius understood how to make use of first one and then another of these physical auxiliaries and with such success that, with a few exceptions, the atomic weights he proposed are in use at the present day, although they were for a time replaced by the values proposed by Leopold Gmelin, which were based on Dalton's results. It is true the victory of the atomic weights of Berzelius was not won by himself, but to a certain extent by his most active opponents, whose views he strongly disputed.

The result of this long and complex discussion was to clear and strengthen our views. In the present day a difference of opinion may exist for a time regarding an element which has not been thoroughly investigated, but no dispute can arise on the fundamental principles involved in the determination of atomic weights These principles were first clearly explained by S. Cannizzaro in 1858, when the apparent contradictions between certain results were satisfactorily cleared away.

§ 19. **Avogadro's Hypothesis.**—Cannizzaro was the first to point out that an entirely false construction had been placed on the relation which exists between the density of a gas or vapour and the combining weight, in spite of the fact that in 1811 Amadeus Avogadro had given perfectly correct instructions as to the manner in which this relationship was to be employed. Starting from Gay Lussac's recently discovered law of combining volumes, Avogadro enunciated the hypothesis that under similar conditions of temperature and pressure, equal volumes of gases contain the same number of particles, which need not of necessity be atoms. He called these particles 'molecules,' from *molecula*, a small mass (*moles*).

Although Avogadro's hypothesis was not the only one possible, it was by far the most probable. Nevertheless for a long time it failed to meet with approval, and the views held by chemists were in many ways directly opposed to it. For example, for half a century no one opposed the views held by Dalton and Gmelin, that water contains one atom of oxygen and one atom of hydrogen, although as a necessary consequence it follows that a volume of oxygen must contain twice as many atoms as a volume of hydrogen.

If each particle of water contains the same number of atoms of each constituent, then one volume of oxygen must contain the same number of atoms as are contained in two volumes of hydrogen. For two volumes of hydrogen unite with one volume of oxygen to form water.

The chief reason why Avogadro's hypothesis failed to meet with recognition was that at this time there was no real necessity for applying it (as Avogadro had done) not only to the elements but to their compounds. At this period only a few gaseous compounds were known, and little importance was attached to the manner in which their chemical formulæ were written. About the middle of the present century the necessity of a systematic classification of the numerous newly discovered carbon compounds, the so-called organic compounds, made itself felt. Avogadro's hypothesis, which had so long lain dormant, was admirably adapted for this purpose. At first its application was partial and limited, until C. Gerhardt made a logical use of it, although mainly with the object of classifying chemical compounds.

§ 20. **Physical Basis of Avogadro's Hypothesis. The Kinetic Theory of Gases** —Avogadro had pointed out the extraordinary similarity in the physical properties of different gases, more particularly the uniformity exhibited by the influence of temperature and pressure on their volume and density, as stated in Boyle's or Mariotte's law and in Gay Lussac's law. He was of opinion that the only possible explanation lay in the hypothesis that all gases contain the same number of particles in equal volumes, measured under similar conditions of temperature and pressure. For if one gas contained double or treble the number of particles contained in another, it would be almost impossible to understand how the relations between density, temperature, and pressure could agree under these conditions; but it is obvious that if the same number of particles of different gases are contained in equal volumes, then the same change in pressure will be effected if the volume is increased or diminished to a certain extent or the temperature altered by a certain number of degrees.

This idea of Avogadro has received decisive confirmation as a result of the new development of the mechanical theory of heat. This theory starts from an old hypothesis which was developed by Daniel Bernouilli in 1738. According to this theory, the individual particles of matter in the solid state occupy definite positions with regard to each other. In the liquid state, although the particles have the power of moving about freely they are attracted to each other; but in the gaseous state the particles are entirely detached from each other: each particle moves about with great rapidity and rushes forward in a straight line until it comes in contact with another particle or some other impediment, from which it rebounds like an elastic ball and continues its movement in a new direction. The pressure of a gas results from the sum of the impacts which the particles exert on the body they come in contact with—the sides of a vessel, for example. Consequently the pressure increases, as the number of particles in a given space and as the velocity of the particles increases.

This old hypothesis was rediscovered in 1850 by Kronig, Joule, and Clausius, and received a more systematic development at the hands of Clausius. It forms the basis of the theory known as the theory of molecular impacts or the molecular theory of gases. According to this theory the pressure exerted by a given volume of gas is proportional to the sum of the kinetic energy of the rectilinear motion of all the particles contained in the unit of volume. By kinetic energy we understand half the product of the mass into the square of the velocity. The pressure of the gas is proportional to the sum of the products obtained by multiplying the mass of each individual particle by half the square of its velocity. And as, according to Gay Lussac's law, the pressure varies in proportion to the temperature, it follows that the sum of these products is also proportional to the temperature, and consequently for constant mass the temperature is proportional to the square of the velocity.

If we have equal volumes of two different gases at the same temperature and under the same pressure, then the total kinetic energy is the same in each volume. But according to Avogadro's hypothesis the number of particles in both gases is identical; consequently the average kinetic energy of each individual particle will be the same. If the two gases are brought into communication with each other, they mix together without any change of temperature or pressure taking place, providing of course that the gases do not exert any chemical action on each other. In this mixture, again, every particle will have the same kinetic energy.

Without the aid of Avogadro's hypothesis, we are at once surrounded by difficulties. Let us assume that one gas contains twice as many particles in a certain volume as another gas, then each particle of the first gas has only half the kinetic energy of the particles of the second, for the total kinetic energy is shared by double the number of particles. By the laws of mechanics, it is impossible that this condition should continue when the gases are mixed together; and as the particles are frequently coming into collision with each other, those doubly endowed with kinetic energy must give up a portion of their energy to the other particles. But if this transference of energy takes place, then the two gases will cease to be under the same temperature and pressure, because temperature and pressure are proportional to the kinetic energy of the gases. Avogadro's hypothesis is the only means of arriving at results conforming to the laws of mechanics.

This is one of the most powerful arguments in support of Avogadro's hypothesis. Its truth is now no longer disputed.

§ 21. **Molecular Weights of Gases.**—The relative values for the molecular weights of all gases can be easily determined by means of Avogadro's hypothesis. The absolute weight of the molecules cannot be ascertained. The method depends on the

fact that the weight W of a given volume of a gas is equal to the sum of the weights of all the separate particles contained in it; so that
$$W = n \cdot m,$$
where n represents the number of particles and m the weight of a single particle, i.e. the 'molecular weight.'

For a second gas
$$W' = n' \cdot m'.$$

In these equations, n, n' and m, m' are unknown values, but the weights W and W' can be determined by experiment.

By comparing quantities of two gases which occupy equal volumes under similar conditions of temperature and pressure we have according to the hypothesis $n = n'$, and
$$W : m = W' : m';$$
$$m' : m = W' : W.$$

The relative values of the molecular weights can be easily calculated from the weights of equal volumes of the two gases as ascertained by experiment. If the unit of volume is 1 litre = 1 cubic decimetre, or even a cubic centimetre, then the weights W and W' indicate the weight of the unit volume, or the densities d and d'.

The equation
$$m' : m = d' : d$$
signifies that the molecular weights of different gases bear the same ratio to each other as do their densities, if the latter are determined at the same temperature and pressure.

The particular standard used in measuring densities is immaterial, although it is customary as well as convenient to use as the standard of comparison dry hydrogen or dry atmospheric air free from carbonic acid. It is always understood that the comparison between a given gas and the standard is made under similar conditions of temperature and pressure. With this assumption the above law may be briefly formulated thus: the molecular weights of gases are proportional to their densities.

The kinetic theory of gases has also provided a possible means for the determination of the number n eliminated from the preceding equations, but at present merely a rough estimate of the value of n has been attempted. At 0° and under a pressure of one atmosphere a single cubic centimetre of any given gas contains about 20 trillion particles or molecules. Divide the weight of a cubic centimetre of the gas by this number and we obtain the weight of a single particle. In the case of hydrogen, the lightest of all gases, a particle weighs

$$0{\cdot}000,000,000,000,000,000,000,004 \text{ grammes,}$$

or one quadrillion particles of hydrogen weigh about 4 grammes.

The particles of other gases weigh more in proportion as they are heavier than hydrogen. The minuteness of the molecular weights calculated in this way, but more especially their doubtful accuracy, has prevented the use of these absolute values, and the relative molecular weights suffice for the present.

§ 22. **Unit of Molecular Weights.**—The same reasons which led to the adoption of the atom of hydrogen as the unit of atomic weights caused hydrogen to be chosen as the standard of molecular weights. At first sight it would seem best to take the molecule of hydrogen $= 1$ and compare the molecular weights of all other gases with this unit, i.e. represent their molecular weights by numbers indicating how many times heavier they are than hydrogen. This is certainly permissible, but it is much more convenient to compare the weights of the molecules, which are composed of atoms with the same standard by which the atomic weights were measured, so that the molecular weights may be directly represented as the sum of the atomic weights. In order to do this it is necessary to know what relation the molecular weight of hydrogen bears to its atomic weight. The molecular weight cannot be smaller, but it may be larger than the atomic weight, as the molecule may contain several atoms We are compelled to assume that, it contains more than one atom, as gaseous hydrogen compounds are known which only contain half as much hydrogen as is contained in the same volume of free hydrogen.

As one volume of hydrogen combines with one volume of chlorine to form two volumes of hydrochloric acid, it follows, from Avogadro's law, that each particle of hydrogen and chlorine produces two particles or molecules of hydrochloric acid, as the two volumes of the latter gas contain, according to this hypothesis, twice as many particles as are contained in one volume of one of its constituents. And as a particle of hydrogen and a particle of chlorine can divide into two parts, it must consist of at least two atoms It cannot contain less than two, but it may contain more; but there is no reason for assuming the existence of more than two atoms in the molecule until a compound is discovered which contains less than half its volume of hydrogen.

The molecular weight of hydrogen is represented by

$$\mathfrak{H} = 2H = H_2 = 2.$$

§ 23. **Calculation of Molecular Weights.**—When the unit is chosen the calculation of the molecular weight of any other gaseous substance is extremely simple; for, according to § 21,

$$m : m' = d : d',$$
$$m = \frac{m' \cdot d}{d'};$$

and $\quad m' = \mathfrak{H} = 2,\ d' = 0\cdot 06926;$

$$m = \frac{2 \cdot d}{0\cdot 06926} = 28\cdot 876 \cdot d.$$

The molecular weight of any gas is calculated by multiplying its density compared with air at the same temperature and pressure by 28 876.

The relation is even more simple when the density is expressed in terms of hydrogen instead of air:—

$$m' = H_2 = 2 \text{ and } \delta' = 1;$$

and $\quad m = 2 \cdot \delta$

This calculation yields the same results as the previous one, for the densities compared with air d are to the densities compared with hydrogen δ, as

$$d : d' = \delta : \delta';$$
$$d : 0\ 06926 = \delta : 1;$$
$$d = 0\ 06926 \times \delta;$$
$$\delta = 14\ 438 \times d$$

The densities of gases would no doubt be directly compared with that of hydrogen if it were not for the great experimental difficulties involved. This is the reason why the comparison with air is, as a rule, preferred.

The factors 14·438 and 28·876 in the preceding formulæ have a very simple meaning. The first number represents the specific gravity or density of dry atmospheric air in terms of hydrogen; the second number, which is double the first, represents the mean value of the molecular weights of its constituents In the case of

Oxygen . $d=1·10563$, $\delta=15·963$, $m=31·93$.
Nitrogen $d=0·97137$, $\delta=14·025$, $m=28·05$.

But according to Bunsen, 100 volumes of air contain

Oxygen . . . . . 20·96 volumes
Nitrogen . . . . 79·04 „

Now, according to Avogadro's hypothesis, equal volumes of the two gases contain the same number of particles; therefore 10,000 particles of air contain

2096 particles of oxygen;
7904   „   nitrogen.

But as oxygen is heavier than nitrogen, the average weight of a particle of air is

$$m = \frac{2096 \times 31·93 + 7904 \times 28·05}{10000} = 28·86.$$

This result closely agrees with the value 28·876. This number has no real meaning, because no existing particle of air has this weight; but it may be conveniently used in molecular weight calculations, as the molecular weight of any given gas bears the same relation to this value as the density expressed in terms of air does to 1.

§ 24. **Correction for Errors of Experiment.**—The molecular weights calculated by either of these methods generally require correction. The determination of the densities of gases and vapours, like all other observations, are liable to errors of experiment, which in some cases are considerable. Another point to be noticed is, that the expansion of different gases by heat, and the relation of their volume to pressure, is almost but not absolutely identical.

Hence it follows that if two gases exactly conform to Avogadro's law at a certain temperature and pressure they will no longer do so at any other temperature and pressure, as both gases will not change their volume to absolutely the same extent. Since the deviations are but small, we may use the method mentioned in the preceding paragraphs, in order to make a fairly accurate determination of the molecular weights, and then correct the values so obtained. The correction is effected by making use of the fact that each molecule is composed of atoms; its weight must consequently be equal to the sum of the weight of the atoms contained in it.

The density of hydrochloric acid gas is found by experiment, to be 1·247. Analysis proves that this gas contains 35·37 parts by weight of chlorine to 1 part by weight of hydrogen; therefore the molecular weight of this compound must either be $m = 1 + 35·37 = 36·37$, or a simple multiple of this number, as less than a whole atom of hydrogen ($=1$) cannot be present in the compound. The product of the density by 28·87 is $d \times 28·87 = 1·247 \times 28·87 = 36·0$, which agrees with the value calculated from the atomic weights; the difference is due to errors of experiment, and 36·37 must be held to be the correct molecular weight.

Marsh gas contains 2·9925 parts by weight of carbon to 1 part by weight of hydrogen. The molecular weight must be represented as

$$m = n(1 + 2·9925) = n \times 3·9925,$$

in which n stands for a whole number (possibly $n=1$). The density compared with air $= 0·555$, and the molecular weight will be approximately

$$m' = 28·87 \times 0·555 = 16·02.$$

This is roughly four times the smallest value possible; consequently the true value is

$$m = 4 \times 3·9925 = 15·97 = (4 + 11·97).$$

The molecular weight consists of 4 parts by weight of hydrogen and 11·97 parts by weight of carbon. In this way the molecular weights of numerous substances which can be volatilised without decomposition have been determined.

§ 25. **Determination of Atomic Weights from Molecular Weights.**—As the atoms are indivisible particles ($ἄτομοι$) a molecule cannot contain less than a whole atom. Hence the molecular weights of compounds offer special facilities for the determination of the atomic weights of the elements.

The smallest quantity of an element which is found to exist in the molecular weight of any of its compounds is the maximum value of the atomic weight. This smallest quantity must contain at least one atom; it may contain two, three, or more atoms. We are justified in regarding this smallest quantity as the atomic weight, if no good reasons exist for believing that this smallest quantity consists of more than one atom. It will be seen later on that methods are not wanting which prevent the possibility of errors of this kind.

The following table comprises a list of those substances which contain the smallest quantity of the given elements in the molecular weights of their compounds. The first column contains the names of the compounds; the second, under d, the density compared with air; the third, the corrected molecular weights calculated from the densities; the fourth the amount of the element contained in the molecular weight; the fifth, the chemical equivalent; and finally the sixth contains the thermic equivalent of the element, if the element be known in the solid state.

VAPOUR DENSITIES, MOLECULAR AND ATOMIC WEIGHTS

	Density d	Molecular Weight m	Amount	Chemical Equivalent	Thermic Equivalent
Hydrofluoric acid	0·713	20·06	F : 19·06	19·06	19·06
Hydrochloric acid	1·247	36·37	Cl : 35·37	35·37	35·37
Hydrobromic acid	2·71	80·76	Br : 79·76	79·76	79·76
Hydriodic acid	4·443	127·54	I : 126·54	126·54	126·54
Water	0·623	17·96	O : 15·96	7·98	
Sulphuretted hydrogen	1·191	33·98	S : 31·98	15·99	31·98
Selenium dioxide	4·03	110·8	Se : 78·77	39·43	78·87
Tellurium dichloride	6·9	195·7	Te : 125	62·5	125
Tellurium tetrachloride	9·22	266·5	Te : 125	62·5	125
Ammonia	0·597	17·01	N : 14·01	4·67	14·01
Nitric oxide	1·039	29·97	N : 14·01	4·67	14·01
Phosphine	1·15	33·96	P : 30·96	10·32	30·96
Phosphorous chloride	4·88	137·07	P : 30·96	10·32	30·96
Arsine	2·695	77·9	As : 74·9	24·97	74·9
Arsenic chloride	6·30	181·0	As : 74·9	24·97	74·9
Antimony trichloride	7·8	225·7	Sb : 119·6	39·87	119·6

VAPOUR DENSITIES, MOLECULAR AND ATOMIC WEIGHTS—*continued*

—	Density d	Molecular Weight m	Amount	Chemical Equivalent	Thermic Equivalent
Bismuth trichloride	11·35	313·4	Bi : 207·3	69·1	207·3
Stannic chloride	9·20	260·3	Sn : 118·8	29·7	118·8
Germanium chloride	7·44	213·8	Ge : 72·3	18·07	72·3
Thorium chloride	12·42	373·5	Th . 232·0	58·00	232·0
Zirconium chloride	8·15	231·9	Zr : 90·4	22·6	90·4
Titanium chloride	6·84	189·5	Ti : 48	12·0	48
Silicon chloride	5·94	169·8	Si : 28·3	7·07	28·3
Marsh gas	0·555	15·97	C : 11·97	2·99	11·97
Carbon monoxide	0·968	27·93	C : 11·97	2·99	11·97
Boron chloride	4·02	117·0	B : 10·9	3·63	10·9
Aluminium chloride	4·56	133·15	Al : 27·04	9·01	27·04
Indium chloride	7·39	219·7	In : 113·6	3·79	113·6
Gallium chloride	4·82	176·0	Ga : 69·9	2·33	69·9
Beryllium chloride	2·77	79·82	Be : 9·08	4·54	9·08
Thallium chloride	8·2	239·07	Tl : 203·7	203·7	203·7
Lead chloride	9·5	277·1	Pb : 206·4	103·2	206·4
Zinc chloride	4·57	135·84	Zn : 65·1	32·55	65·1
Cadmium bromide	9·25	271·2	Cd : 111·7	55·85	111·7
Mercuric chloride	9·8	270·5	Hg : 199·8	99·9	199·8
Chromium trichloride	5·47	158·56	Cr : 52·45	17·48	52·45
Ferric chloride	4·32	161·99	Fe : 55·88	27·94	55·88
Vanadium chloride	6·69	192·6	V : 51·1	12·8	—
Molybdenum chloride	9·46	272·7	Mo : 95·9	19·2	95·9
Tungsten pentachloride	12·7	360·4	W : 183·6	36·7	183·6
Tungsten hexachloride	13·2	395·8	W : 183·6	36·7	183·6
Uranium tetrachloride	13·33	380·5	U : 239·0	59·75	239·0
Niobium chloride	9·6	270·5	Nb : 93·7	19·74	—
Tantalum chloride	12·9	358·8	Ta : 182	36·4	—
Ruthenium tetroxide	5·77	163·3	Ru : 103·5	12·94	103·5
Osmium tetroxide	8·9	254·8	Os : 191	23·87	191
Cuprous chloride	7·05	197·1	Cu : 126·36	63·18	63·18

It is only in the case of a small number of elements that the chemical equivalent is identical with the atomic weight deduced from the molecular weight; as a rule, the chemical equivalent is a sub-multiple of the atomic weight, and is therefore entirely unsuited for the determination of atomic weights. The atomic weights coincide with the thermic equivalents and the latter agree with the crystallographic equivalents.

The smallest quantity of the element contained in the molecular weight of the compound is double the thermic equivalent only in the case of cuprous chloride. But even this case does not form an exception, if we assume that the molecule contains two atoms of copper. This shows that Cannizzaro was justified in the statement made in 1857 that the molecular weights can be determined by means of the vapour density and the atomic weights by the specific heat.

§ 26. **Possible Errors.**—It is obvious that the calculation of molecular weight from the density can only be made in the case of homogeneous gases. If it be attempted to apply this method to gaseous mixtures, the result obtained is only the mean value of all the molecular weights contained in the mixture (*vide* § 23). Mistaking such a mixture for a homogeneous gas may lead to grave errors.

The molecular weight calculated from the observed density of the vapour of ammonium chloride is

$$m' = d \times 28\cdot 87 = 0\cdot 89 \times 28\cdot 87 = 25\cdot 69,$$

which becomes after correction by the known combining weights of hydrogen, chlorine, and nitrogen:

$$m = 2 + 17\cdot 685 + 7\cdot 005 = 26\cdot 69.$$

The quantities of chlorine and nitrogen (17·685 and 7·005 parts by weight respectively) are only half as large as the amounts found in the molecular weights of other compounds. If these quantities really do occur in the molecular weight of this compound, they must be regarded as the atomic weights of these elements, and we must assume that at least two atoms of these elements are contained in all their other compounds. But Pebal has shown that ammonium chloride splits up into equal volumes of ammonia and hydrochloric acid when it is converted into vapour. Its density is therefore the arithmetical mean of the densities of these two gases, and only one-half of the molecules present in the vapours contain chlorine; the other half contain nitrogen. The densities of the constituents are

Ammonia	$d = 0\cdot 59$
Hydrochloric acid	$d = 1\cdot 25$
Mean	$0\cdot 92$

The molecular weights are

Ammonia	$m = 14\cdot 01 + 3 = 17\cdot 01$
Hydrochloric acid	$m = 35\cdot 37 + 1 = 36\cdot 37$
Mean	$26\cdot 69$

Other ammonium salts, certain compounds of phosphorus, and other substances also exhibit abnormal vapour densities. These compounds cannot be used for molecular or atomic weight determinations.

On the other hand, if the vapour density is determined at too low a temperature the resulting molecular weight may be too high. Many substances when volatilised at the lowest possible temperature give a vapour the density of which, compared with air or other gases, is high, but at higher temperatures yield a relatively light vapour. If the vapour density is determined for a series of temperatures, it is found to decrease as the temperature rises until a point is reached above which it remains nearly constant. The chlorides of aluminium, gallium, and iron behave in this way. To explain this behaviour it is assumed that when these compounds are first converted into vapour they do not at once separate into isolated particles, but into aggregations of molecules, generally consisting of two molecules. These aggregations gradually break up as the temperature rises. Their dissolution may also be aided by reduction of pressure or by admixture with an indifferent gas.

§ 27. **Molecular Weights of the Elements.**—The molecular weights of the elements can be determined in the same way as the molecular weights of compounds. Some are identical with the thermic atomic weights, but as a rule they are larger than the latter. The following table gives a list of all the molecular weights of the elements known at the present time. The first column contains the names, the second the density in the state of gas or vapour at the temperature mentioned in the third column, the fourth the molecular weight calculated from the density and corrected by the results of analysis, and the fifth the atomic weight determined by Avogadro's (Av) or by Dulong and Petit's (D P) method.

Most of the elements contained in this table are either non-metals or semi-metals. Only a few of the metals are embraced in it, as they are, as a rule, difficult to volatilise; on the other hand, only a small number of non-metals are absent. There is a wonderful difference between the two groups; the semi-metals and non-metallic elements contain two or more atoms in the molecule; the molecules of the true metals only contain one atom

It is probable that the ductility and other properties of the metals are in some way determined by this peculiarity.

I	II Density	III t	IV Molecular Weight	V Atomic Weight	VI
Hydrogen	0·06926	0° C.	$H_2 =$ 2	$H =$ 1	Av
Nitrogen	0·9713	0°	$N_2 =$ 28·02	$N =$ 14·01	Av
Oxygen	1·10563	0°	$O_2 =$ 31·92	$O =$ 15·96	Av
Sulphur	2·24	940°	$S_2 =$ 63·96	$S =$ 31·98	Av DP
Zinc	2·36	1400	$Zn_1 =$ 65·10	$Zn =$ 65·10	Av DP
Chlorine	2·450	200°	$Cl_2 =$ 70·74	$Cl =$ 35·37	Av DP
Cadmium	3·94	940°	$Cd_1 =$ 111·7	$Cd =$ 111·7	Av DP
Phosphorus	4·35	500°	$P_4 =$ 123·84	$P =$ 30·96	Av DP
Bromine	5·54	100°	$Br_2 =$ 159·52	$Br =$ 79·76	Av DP
Selenium	5·68	1420	$Se_2 =$ 157·74	$Se =$ 78·87	Av DP
Mercury	6·98	446°	$Hg_1 =$ 199·8	$Hg =$ 199·8	Av DP
Iodine	8·72	940°	$I_2 =$ 253·08	$I =$ 126·54	Av DP
Tellurium	9·00	1440°	$Te_2 =$ 250	$Te =$ 125	Av DP
Arsenic	10·2	746°	$As_4 =$ 299·6	$As =$ 74·9	Av DP

The behaviour of sulphur is very remarkable. It has already been mentioned in § 17 that the vapour density at 500° is greater than at higher temperatures. This density corresponds to a molecular weight $S_6 = 191\cdot 88$, although it has not been decided with certainty whether the vapour of sulphur at a temperature a little above its boiling point (446° C.) is really composed entirely of hexatomic molecules. The density of the vapour changes as the temperature rises in a similar way to that exhibited by the compounds mentioned in § 26.

On the other hand the density of iodine (and in a lesser degree of bromine and of chlorine) is abnormally low at very high temperatures. This is explained by assuming that some of the molecules are split up by the action of heat into individual atoms, and that more molecules are split up as the temperature rises.

The density of iodine vapour is

8·76 at 115°
7·01 ,, 1043°
5·82 ,, 1275°
5·06 ,, 1470°

If the decomposition of the iodine molecules into atoms were complete, the original density would be halved. Bromine and chlorine exhibit similar peculiarities.

§ 28. **Nascent State.**—The necessity of distinguishing between atoms and molecules of elements has been but slowly recognised; it has proved of great service in providing an explanation of certain apparently inexplicable phenomena. It has frequently been observed that many elements which, as a rule, do not readily enter into combination easily unite if brought together at the moment of their liberation from other compounds. In this specially active condition the elements are said to be in the 'nascent state.' The peculiar behaviour of elements in the nascent state is accounted for by assuming that they are then present as isolated atoms. Naturally these isolated atoms are more ready to enter into combination than they would be if they were already united to similar atoms in the form of molecules.

Hydrogen offers a striking example of the activity of elements in the nascent state. It is only at a high temperature that free hydrogen burns in oxygen, forming water, but both elements will unite at the ordinary temperature, or even at a lower temperature, at the moment of their liberation from other compounds. It is more difficult to combine free nitrogen with oxygen or hydrogen, but if the elements are in the nascent state combination readily takes place. It is easy to understand that isolated atoms at once unite when they meet each other, but when an atom is united to one or more atoms to form a molecule, it must first of all be detached from this molecule before it can form a new compound. In the case of nitrogen the tendency of the two atoms to combine and form the free molecule appears to be very strong.

§ 29. **Determination of the Stœchiometric Values.**—Having considered the grounds on which the determination of the atomic weights is based, we must now proceed to the description of the methods employed in the exact determination of these highly important values. The process is far from simple. In the first place it is necessary to know, with the utmost degree of accuracy, the proportions by weight with which the given element unites with other elements. This knowledge can only be acquired by careful analyses or syntheses of compounds. But all our methods of analysis and synthesis are vitiated by certain errors, which can never be entirely avoided, but must be reduced to the narrowest limits. Those methods alone are to be used which can be carried out with the minimum amount of error. In analysis a certain definite weight of a compound is decomposed and the weight of its constituents determined. A distinction is made between partial and complete analyses, according as one or all the constituents are determined; and a similar distinction is drawn between partial and complete syntheses When practicable, complete or total analyses or syntheses are preferred, as in these cases we have a guarantee that nothing has been lost or gained during the operations, when the sum of the weight of the constituents is equal to the weight of the compound. In many cases it is only possible to make a partial analysis or synthesis, as some substances cannot be brought into a form in which their weight can be ascertained with a sufficient degree of accuracy.

As to the means for determining the weight and therewith the mass of a body, the balance and weights have been developed to a point of such great accuracy that the error has been reduced to $\frac{1}{100000}$, or even $\frac{1}{1000000}$. But such accuracy can only be attained in weighing stable bodies, which occupy a very small space in proportion to their weight, and do not possess a very large surface; for large volumes and large surfaces increase the possible errors in weighing.

As weighings are generally made in atmospheric air, the substance weighed appears lighter than it really is by the weight of air it displaces. This loss of weight can be calculated and allowed for, but the error increases as the volume of air displaced increases. Air and other gases and moisture condense on the surfaces of the body weighed as well as of the vessels containing it, and in this way the error of weighing increases with the surface. This source of error can be diminished, but cannot be entirely avoided.

In atomic weight determinations we avoid, as far as possible, weighing gases or liquids on account of the error introduced by the use of large vessels for holding them. This can be accomplished by measuring instead of weighing these bodies, if the weight of the unit of volume, i.e. the density, has been once determined.

The use of substances which easily oxidise, absorb moisture

from the atmosphere, or in other ways change, should be avoided if possible; if it is necessary to employ them they must be weighed in air-tight vessels, which have either been exhausted by the air-pump or filled with an indifferent gas.

It frequently occurs that an element in the free state is unsuitable for weighing. In this case it is converted into a suitable compound, which is weighed, the amount of the element in the compound having been previously accurately determined Chlorine is weighed as silver chloride, sulphur as barium sulphate, &c.

Great care must be taken to insure the purity of the substance investigated and of the other substances used in the various operations, in order that the bodies which are weighed may really have the composition they are supposed to possess. If these precautions are neglected very grave errors will follow.

§ 30 **Relation of Stœchiometric Determinations to each other.**—As hydrogen has been selected as the unit of equivalent and atomic weights, it is desirable to compare all determinations with this standard. Unfortunately hydrogen only unites with about a dozen other elements, and these compounds are mostly gaseous like hydrogen, and consequently difficult to determine quantitatively. Berzelius determined the atomic weights of nearly all the elements with which he was acquainted with wonderful accuracy, using as his unit the hundredth part of an atom of oxygen, regarding the atomic weight of oxygen as 100. He did this instead of using Dalton's unit, hydrogen = 1, on account of the difficulty involved in accurately determining the composition of the gaseous compounds of hydrogen. He also occasionally made use of Dalton's unit, calculating out his results in terms of this standard. At the present day we are frequently compelled to adopt this indirect method. This indirect method involves the knowledge of the proportion by weight in which hydrogen and oxygen unite to form water, and as a natural consequence this determination has been made with the greatest care The ratio 1 : 7 98 has been obtained as the mean of numerous concordant results arrived at by different methods. Water contains 1 part by weight of hydrogen to 7·98 of oxygen, and according to Avogadro's law (§ 19) we consider that water contains two atoms of hydrogen, but does not contain two or more atoms of oxygen.

Therefore

$$H_2 : O = 1 : 7{\cdot}98, \text{ or } H : O = 1 : 15{\cdot}96.$$

There may be an error of one or more units in the second place of decimals: that is, an error of some thousandths of the total value. The practice of representing the atomic weight of oxygen as a whole number, 16, is unwarrantable. Where great accuracy is not necessary the round number may be used as a matter of convenience, and the calculated result will be nearly accurate; but when scientific accuracy is required such arbitrary alterations in the experimental results are not permissible.

Having determined the atomic weight of oxygen in this way, we can now compare a large number of atomic weights of other elements, many metals in particular, with the atomic weight of hydrogen. The amount of oxygen in the oxides is determined by analysis or synthesis. The quantity of the element which unites with an atom of oxygen is equivalent to two atoms of hydrogen. Whether this quantity represents the atomic weight or a multiple or sub-multiple is ascertained by means of Avogadro's law, by the law of Dulong and Petit, or by isomorphism.

An example will explain the method. Berzelius obtained 4·2835 grams of oxide by oxidising 2·9993 grams of pure iron, or 1·42817 gram of oxide from 1 gram of iron, or making the necessary corrections for weighing in air 1·42836 gram of oxide from 1 gram of iron. One part by weight of the metal united with 0·42836 of oxygen. The quantity of metal A oxidised by one equivalent $= 7{\cdot}98$ parts by weight of oxygen is

$$1 : A = 0{\cdot}42836 : 7{\cdot}98;$$
$$A = 18{\cdot}629$$

This number cannot be the atomic weight of iron, for on multiplying it by the specific heat of the metal, $c = 0{\cdot}114$, it yields the product $A \cdot c = 2{\cdot}13$, whilst treble the value, i.e. 55·89, yields 6·4. The latter number also represents the quantity of iron contained in the molecular weight of ferric chloride

(§ 25); this must therefore be regarded as the atomic weight of iron compared with hydrogen as unity. Similar determinations by other chemists yield almost identical results The mean of the most trustworthy results gives 55 88 as the atomic weight of iron

The oxides of many elements are difficult to prepare in a state of perfect purity. This is true of many of the light and of some of the noble metals, but the chlorides, bromides, &c. of these elements are admirably adapted for weighing. In such cases the comparison of the atomic weight with that of hydrogen is made by a more indirect method than the preceding. The compounds of silver with chlorine, bromine, and iodine are quite insoluble in water, and are therefore well adapted for analytical determinations. The proportions by weight with which these elements unite with silver have been very carefully estimated In fact, the most correct of all the stœchiometrical determinations that have ever been made are those which fixed the combining proportions of silver and iodine—

$$Ag : I = 1 : 1\cdot 17534.$$

This determination was carried out by Stas with the utmost care and dexterity; the experimental error is about 1 in 100,000. As oxide of silver is too unstable to permit of correct analysis the proportion of silver to oxygen had to be determined by several indirect methods, all of which yielded similar results.

The analysis of potassium chlorate, $KClO_3$, gave the relative quantities of potassium chloride, KCl, and oxygen in the salt:

$$KCl : O = 4\ 6616 : 1.$$

By converting weighed quantities of potassium chloride, KCl, into silver chloride, AgCl, the following ratio was obtained:

$$Ag : KCl = 1 : 0\cdot 69104$$

Hence it follows that

$$Ag : O = \frac{Ag}{KCl} \times \frac{KCl}{O} = \frac{4\ 6616}{0\ 69104} : 1 = 6\cdot 7458 : 1.$$

The same result was obtained in a similar way by the synthesis of silver sulphide, Ag_2S, and its oxidation to silver sulphate

Ag_2SO_4 Finally Stas analysed the chlorate, bromate and iodate of silver, $AgClO_3$, $AgBrO_3$, and $AgIO_3$. The results of these analyses, and of the syntheses of AgCl, AgBr, and AgI, lead to the ratio:

$$Ag : O = 6·7456 : 1$$

which agrees closely with the former result. Compared with hydrogen, the atomic weight of silver is 107·66,

$$Ag : H = 6·7456 \times 15·96 : 1 = 107·66 : 1$$

Many other methods have been suggested for the indirect determination of the atomic weights of elements in terms of hydrogen. The preceding examples will suffice to illustrate the methods employed.

§ 31. **Selection from Different Determinations.**—Although no method of determination is free from error, the amount of error is very variable. Consequently the values for the atomic weights obtained by different methods do not coincide absolutely. But as Stas has proved by experiments, specially made for this purpose, that the atomic weights are constant and invariable values, under all known conditions, it follows that only one value can be accepted as correct. It is necessary to select this, the exact value, from the others. This problem is one frequently associated with difficulties, and requires much care and consideration.

The analytical or synthetical methods employed must be submitted to a critical examination for the purpose of ascertaining the extent and the sources of error.

The results of the method which is most free from error are naturally preferred. The magnitude of the error involved in a particular method can often, but not always, be ascertained by making several determinations by the method and comparing the results. This cannot, however, be done when all the determinations contain a common error, a so-called 'constant' error; e.g. if in a case of oxidation the reaction is not quite complete, a definite quantity of the element will always yield too little oxide, and in all such experiments the atomic weight will be found too high

If the precipitation of an element is accompanied by a certain loss, the total weight of the element will not be obtained, and the atomic weight will be too low in all the determinations.

The constant errors are more to be feared than the casual errors, because they lead us to believe in a degree of accuracy which in reality does not exist. This explains why Gauss's method of least squares is seldom used in atomic weight determinations, although, as a rule, it is well adapted for determining the extent of errors of experiment.

A complete analysis or synthesis offers a certain guarantee against constant or occasional errors. If the sum of the constituents is very nearly equal to the weight of the compound, this indicates that no considerable loss has taken place, or that the loss is exactly balanced by a gain of foreign matter taken up during the analysis. The loss of constituents exactly balancing the gain in foreign matter is a very rare occurrence. A partial decomposition may be mistaken for a complete one, and thus occasion serious mistakes. Berzelius attempted to determine the atomic weight of vanadium by reducing its highest oxide in hydrogen. Roscoe afterwards proved that only $\frac{3}{5}$ of the oxygen in the oxide is removed and that $\frac{2}{5}$ remains in the residue, which Berzelius regarded as the pure element. The true atomic weight V is 51·1, but Berzelius calculated it to be 137— *i.e.* V_2O_2.

The best guarantee against error of all kinds is secured when the atomic weight of an element has been determined by several distinct methods, and the results are found to agree.

§ 32. **Accuracy of the Atomic Weights.**—An examination of the numerous atomic weight determinations shows that there is an extraordinary difference in their degree of accuracy. The ratio between a small number of the atomic weights has been determined to the $\frac{1}{100000}$ part of their value (*e.g.* between iodine and silver), and for a somewhat larger number of elements to the $\frac{1}{10000}$ part. The error in the case of other elements amounts to $\frac{1}{1000}$ of their value, and in the case of a few it is not less than one per cent. The relation between the atomic weights of hydrogen and oxygen, which is taken as the standard by which all other atomic weights are measured, may contain an error of one or two thousandths of its value. This possible error affects all the other atomic weights which are referred to this standard. But this uncertainty does not vitiate the acccuracy of the stœchiometric calculations, as they are independent of the standard chosen. If we express the other possible errors in terms of this unit, then the error is not greater than 0 1 H for one third of the elements, and does not exceed 0 5 H for a second third. In the case of the remaining elements the error will amount to from 0·5 to 1, and in some cases, which require re-determining, may amount to two or more units.

§ 33. **Prout's Hypothesis.**—It has already been pointed out in § 31 that our investigations indicate that the atoms of one and the same element are alike in all respects, but that the atoms of two or more different elements are dissimilar. Up to the present day, it has never been possible to convert one element into another. At the same time, it is improbable that the elements which have been discovered, or are yet to be discovered, are really primal forms of matter. Their large number and other reasons induce us to believe that just as the elements are the basis of the composition of all the compounds derived from them, so they in turn will prove to be combinations of units of a higher order. This idea originated almost at the same time as the atomic theory, but, in spite of much experimental and theoretical effort, it has never advanced beyond the stages of conjecture.

In 1815 an English chemist, Prout, published (at first anonymously) a conjecture of this kind. He observed that the atomic weights of many of the elements appeared to be rational multiples of the atomic weight of hydrogen, and might be represented by whole numbers. Prout's hypothesis is tempting in its simplicity, and for a time was favourably received by chemists, excepting by those who had made exact and accurate atomic weight determinations. This hypothesis has never received experimental confirmation; on the contrary, many atomic weights may be nearly but not exactly represented by whole numbers, and in all the cases which have been accurately examined the deviations from the whole numbers have proved to be greater than the possible or probable experimental error. This hypothesis has attracted a considerable amount of attention, but is opposed to the best atomic weight determinations of Berzelius, Marignac, Stas, and others.

§ 34. **Dobereiner's Triads.**—Another relation between the atomic weights, discovered by Döbereiner in 1829, has led to better results. This chemist noticed that it frequently happens that one member of a group of three analogous elements possesses an atomic weight which is approximately the mean of the other two. In other cases, three elements bearing a close resemblance to each other in their properties have nearly the same atomic weights.

Examples of the first class.

Lithium	Li = 7·01
Difference	15·99
Sodium	Na. = 23·00
Difference	16·03
Potassium	K. = 39·03
Sulphur	S. = 31·98
Difference	46·89
Selenium	Se. = 78·87
Difference	46·13
Tellurium	Te. = 125
Calcium	Ca. = 39·9
Difference	47·4
Strontium	Sr. = 87·3
Difference	49·6
Barium	Ba. = 136·9
Chlorine	Cl. = 35·37
Difference	44·39
Bromine	Br. = 79·76
Difference	46·77
Iodine	I. = 126·53

Examples of the second class.

Iron	. . . . .	Fe.=55·88
Cobalt	. . . . .	Co.=58·6
Nickel	. . . . .	Ni.=58·6
Ruthenium	. . . .	Ru.=101·4
Rhodium	. . . .	Rh.=102·7
Palladium	. . . .	Pd.=106·3
Osmium	. . . . .	Os.=191
Iridium	. . . . .	Ir.=192·5
Platinum	. . . .	Pt.=194·3

Döbereiner believed that in these relations might be found the basis of a systematic classification of the elements, but it was long before this idea received development. It was impossible for the attempts which were made in this direction by Pettenkofer (1851), Dumas (1859), and others to be successful, as at this time the atomic weights had not been systematically deduced from the analytical results. When this had once been accomplished, it was found possible to arrange all the elements in groups of 3, 4, or 5 members, in all of which groups the differences were approximately the same. In these groups of elements, arranged in the order of the atomic weights of their members, is to be found the realisation of the systematic classification of the elements which Döbereiner had striven to accomplish.

The development of this system was brought about by the labours of Newlands, Mendeléeff, Lothar Meyer, and others. The following tables contain some of the elements arranged in groups of four and five members each. The corresponding members of the different groups form a continuous series of elements arranged in the order of their atomic weights.

I

				Li 7·01	Be 9·1	Bo 10·9	C 11·97
Diff.				16	15·2	16·1	16·3
	N 14·01	O 15·96	F 19·06	Na 23·00	Mg 24·3	Al 27·0	Si 28·3
Diff.	16·95	16·02	16·31	16·13	15·6	17·0	19·7
	P 30·96	S 31·98	Cl 35·37	K 39·03	Ca 39·9	Sc 44·0	Ti 48
Diff.	43·9	46·89	43·39	46·2	47·4	44·9	42·4
	As 74·9	Se 78·87	Br 79·76	Rb 85·2	Sr 87·3	Y 88·9	Zr 90·4
Diff.	44·7	46·1	46·77	47·5	49·6	49	49·5
	Sb 119·6	Te 125·0	I 126·53	Cs 132·7	Ba 136·9	La 138	Ce 139·9

II

	Ti 48	V 51·1	Cr 52·45	Mn 54·8	Fe 55·88	Co 58·6
Diff.	42·4	42·6	43·45		45·6	44·1
	Zr 90·4	Nb 93·7	Mo 95·9		Ru 101·4	Rh 102·7
Diff.	—	88·3	87·7		89·6	89·8
	—	Ta 182	W 183·6		Os 191	Ir 192·5
Diff.	—		55·4			
	Th 232		U 239·0			

In the four last groups the second member is nearly the arithmetical mean of the first and third; the fourth is the mean of the third and fifth. In the first three groups, the elements corresponding to the first members are missing. The differences are nearly the same as in the other families.

The second table embraces a number of similar groups, in which the difference between the first and second members is only half the difference between the second and third members. The first and last groups of this second table occur at the beginning and end of the first one, so that both tables may be united into a continuous one.

§ 35. **Arrangement of the Elements in the Order of their Atomic Weights.**—Most of the groups in the second table are related to one of the groups in the first table by analogies in the properties of their members, and especially by the isomorphism of their compounds. Vanadium, V, is associated with phosphorus, P, and arsenic, As, by isomorphism; in the same way chromium, Cr, and molybdenum, Mo, are related to sulphur, S, and selenium, Se; by the isomorphism of the permanganates with the perchlorates, manganese, Mn, is associated with chlorine, Cl. The first table does not contain any elements analogous to iron, nickel, cobalt, and the six platinum metals; but copper, Cu, and silver, Ag, are related to sodium, Na; and zinc, Zn, to magnesium, Mg, and calcium, Ca; indium, In, to aluminium, Al; and tin, Sn, is isomorphous with silicon, Si, and titanium, Ti. We are therefore not only justified in joining these two tables together, but in uniting them to form the following table. The perpendicular columns contain not only closely-allied elements, but also others which only bear an analogy to them in certain respects, but differ from them widely in other points.

II.—continued

Ni 58·6	Cu 63·18	Zn 65·1	Ga 69·9	Ge 72·3	As 74·9
47·7	44·48	45·6	43·7	46·5	44·7
Pd 106·3	Ag 107·66	Cd 111·7	In 113·6	Sn 118·8	Sb 119·6
88·0	89·0	88·1	90·1	87·6	87·7
Pt 194·3	Au 196·7	Hg 199·8	Tl 203·7	Pb 206·4	Bi 207·3

Atomic Weights of the Elements

—	I	II	III	IV	V	VI	VII	—
	Li 7·01	Be 9·06	B 10·9	C 11·97	N 14·01	O 15·96	F 19·06	
Diff.	15·99	15·2	16·1	16·3	16·95	16·02	16·31	
	Na 23·0	Mg 24·3	Al 27·04	Si 28·3	P 30·96	S 31·98	Cl 35·37	
Diff.	16·03	15·6	16·93	19·7	20·0	20·47	19·4	Fe 55·88
	K 39·03	Ca 39·91	Sc 43·97	Ti 48·0	V 51·1	Cr 52·45	Mn 54·8	Co 58·6
Diff.	24·15	25·2	25·9	24·3	23·8	27·42	25·0	Ni 58·6
	Cu 63·18	Zn 65·10	Ga 69·9	Ge 72·3	As 74·9	Se 78·87	Br 79·76	
Diff.	22·0	22·2	19·0	22·1	18·8	17·0	18 ?	Ru 101·4
	Rb 85·2	Sr 87·3	Y 88·9	Zr 90·4	Nb 93·7	Mo 95·9	— 98 ?	Rh 102·7
Diff.	22·5	24·4	24·7	26·4	25·9	29·1	28 ?	Pd 106·35
	Ag 107·66	Cd 111·7	In 113·6	Sn 118·8	Sb 119·6	Te 125·0	I 126·54	
Diff.	25·0	25·2	24·4	21·1				
	Cs 132·7	Ba 136·9	La 138	Ce 139·9				
			34·6					
	—	—	Yb 172·6	—	Ta 182	W 183·6	—	Os 191
			31·1		25·3			Ir 192·5
	Au 196·7	Hg 199·8	Tl 203·7	Pb 206·4	Bi 207·3			Pt 194·3
				25·6				
				Th 232·0		U 239·0		

In the horizontal rows of this table the elements are arranged in the order of their atomic weights. If the right side of each row is connected with the left side of the following row a single continuous series of all the elements will be produced. In this arrangement the nature and properties of the members will be represented as periodic functions of the atomic weights, changing systematically as the atomic weight increases from member to member, and returning to the beginning after a certain number of members. The periodicity may be more clearly indicated by means of the table at the end of this book. The table must be pasted on a wooden or pasteboard cylinder of suitable dimensions, so that the right and left sides meet.

The first two periods or series each embrace seven elements.

	1	2	3	4	5	6	7
I	Li	Be	B	C	N	O	Fl
II	Na	Mg	Al	Si	P	S	Cl

The corresponding members closely resemble each other—e.g. lithium and sodium, beryllium and magnesium

This resemblance continues in the third and fourth periods, so far as the first members are concerned; the following members do not exhibit corresponding properties, and it is not until we reach the seventeenth member after potassium that another alkali metal, rubidium, recurs. The next alkali metal, caesium, is again the seventeenth element after rubidium. Both metals are preceded by elements which are closely related to the last members of the first and second periods. On closer consideration, these large periods are found to split up into two smaller periods, in which some of the properties of the elements recur at a shorter interval. This is seen in the following table:

	1	2	3	4	5	6	7	8	9	10
III.	K	Ca	Sc	Ti	V	Cr	Mn	Fe	Co	Ni
	Cu	Zn	Ga	Ge	As	Se	Br			
IV.	Rb	Sr	Y	Zr	Nb	Mo	—	Ru	Rh	Pd
	Ag	Cd	In	Sn	Sb	Te	I			
V.	Cs	Ba	La	Ce						

The elements in the same column all have certain properties in common, but only the alternate elements bear a close resemblance to each other. After cerium, Ce, there is a gap of about forty units. This will probably be filled by the rare earth metals, which have not yet been sufficiently well investigated. Then comes ytterbium (the atomic weight of this metal has not been accurately determined) and tantalum; they are followed by elements resembling the former members, in the same order as in the preceding periods, but leaving some gaps and spaces:

1	2	3	4	5	6	7	8	9	10
—	—	Yb	—	Ta	W	—	Os	Ir	Pt
Au	Hg	Tl	Pb	Bi	—				
—	—	—	Th	—	U				

The gaps in this and the preceding tables will probably be filled by elements which remain yet to be discovered. Several of the gaps which existed when the periodic system of the elements was first promulgated have been filled up by the discovery of scandium, gallium, and germanium, and by the correction of the atomic weights of indium, yttrium, cerium, and lanthanum.

It appears from the table on page 55 that a dozen elements are yet to be discovered. The majority of these gaps will probably be filled by rare earth metals with atomic weights lying between 140 and 180.

§ 36. **Periodicity of the Physical Properties of the Elements.**—If we examine the long series of elements from member to member, we find a change in the properties, sometimes gradual and sometimes sudden, which recurs in the following periods in a similar way, so that almost every property of an element occurs again in a similar way in one or more of the later members, so that the properties of each individual element are determined by its position in the series. This is not only true of the chemical and physical properties of the elements, but also of the compounds.

This recurrence of the physical properties is very striking in the case of density, which regularly increases and decreases in each period. The connection between density and atomic weight is best exhibited by taking the atomic volume instead of the density—*i.e.* the volume occupied by the atomic weight instead of the weight of the unit volume. The simplest expression for the atomic volume is obtained by dividing the atomic weight by the density.

These quotients represent the volume of the atoms in the solid state compared with the volume occupied by the unit weight of liquid water as unity. As the absolute weight of an atom of hydrogen is not known, the unit of atomic weights is not known, and this unit of volume must remain an unknown quantity. But these quotients may be compared by means of another standard—*e.g.* the atomic weight of an element, expressed in grams, occupies in the solid state the same number of cubic centimetres as the value of the atomic volume. For example, the atomic volume of silver is 10 2, and therefore 107 66 grams of silver occupy 10·2 c.c.

In the table on p. 58 the density D and the atomic volume V are given under the symbol of each element. The density begins at a minimum with the alkali metals, lithium, sodium, rubidium, caesium, and ascends from here in the first two periods to carbon and silicon ; in the following periods the density continues to increase after passing the homologues of these elements till it reaches the metals copper, ruthenium, osmium, and then sinks. In the atomic volumes the position is reversed— the maximum is at the alkali metals, and the minimum occurs at carbon, aluminium, nickel, ruthenium, osmium.

DENSITY AND ATOMIC VOLUMES OF THE ELEMENTS

—	I	II	III	IV	V	VI	VII	VIII		
D V	Li *0·59* 11·9	Be *1·85* 4·9	B *2·68* 4·0	C *3·3* 3·6	N *3 (?)* 5 (?)	O *2 (?)* 8 (?)	F *1·5 (?)* 13 (?)			
D V	Na *0·97* 23·7	Mg *1·74* 13·9	Al *2·56* 10·6	Si *2·49* 11·4	P *2·3* 13·5	S *2·04* 15·7	Cl *1·38* 25·6			
D V	K *0·86* 45·4	Ca *1·57* 25·4	Sc *2·6 (?)* 17 (?)	Ti *3·7 (?)* 13 (?)	V *5·5* 9·3	Cr *6·8* 7·7	Mn *8·0* 6·9	Fe *7·8* 7·2	Co *8·5* 6·9	Ni *8·8* 6·7
D	Cu *8·8* 7·1	Zn *7·13* 9·1	Ga *5·96* 11·7	Ge *5·47* 13·2	As *5·67* 13·2	Se *4·6* 17	Br *2·97* 26·9			
D V	Rb *1·52* 56·1	Sr *2·50* 34·9	Y *3·6 (?)* 25 (?)	Zr *4·15* 21·7	Nb *7·06* 13·0	Mo *8·6* 11·1	—	Ru *12·26* 8·3	Rh *12·1* 8·5	Pd *11·5* 9·2
D V	Ag *10·5* 10·2	Cd *8·65* 12·9	In *7·42* 15·3	Sn *7·29* 16·3	Sb *6·7* 17·9	Te *6·25* 20·2	I *4·94* 25·6			
D V	Cs *1·88* 70·6	Ba *3·75* 36·5	La *6·2* 22·5	Ce *6·7* 21·0						
D V					Ta *10·8* 16·9	W *19·13* 9·6	—	Os *22·48* 8·5	Ir *22·42* 8·6	Pt *21·50* 9·1
D V	Au *19·3* 10·1	Hg *14·2* 14·1	Tl *11·86* 17·2	Pb *11·38* 18·1	Bi *9·82* 21·1					
D V				Th *11·2* 20·9	—	U *18·69* 12·6				

The relation between the atomic volume and atomic weight is more clearly depicted by the accompanying graphic representation. In this table the elements are arranged on the

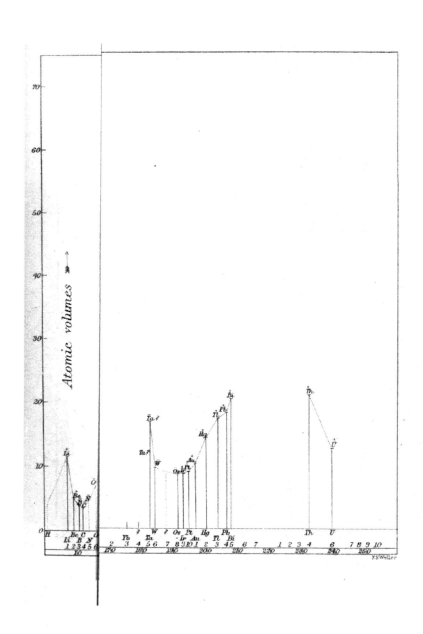

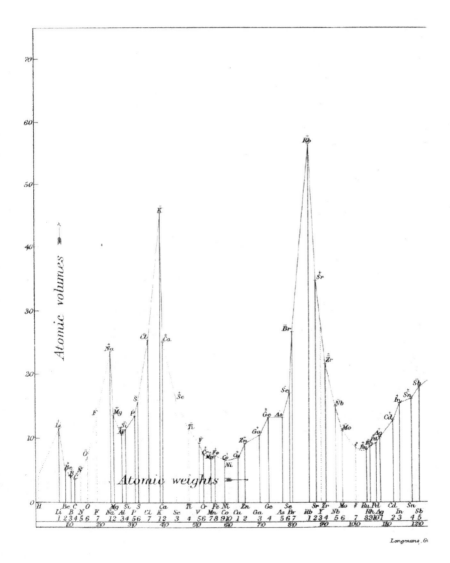

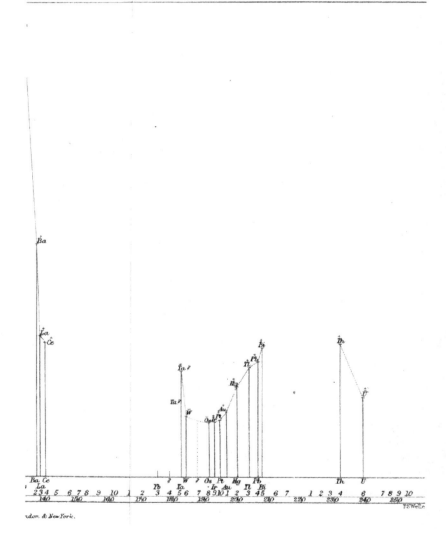

horizontal axis of the abscissae at distances from zero proportional to their atomic weights. The position of each element is denoted by the corresponding symbol, and from each of these points an ordinate is drawn, which is proportional in length to the atomic volume of the element. By connecting the summits of all the ordinates by lines, we obtain a curve which clearly illustrates the relation of the atomic volume to the atomic weight. The alkali metals occupy a striking position at the five maxima. Those portions of the curve between the maxima resemble chains, which are broken at certain points, because the elements which should occupy these positions are either unknown or have not yet been sufficiently investigated. The great regularity in the course of the curve indicates that the curve will, without doubt, closely follow the dotted course. On this account the probable values, in round numbers, of the density and atomic volume of these elements have been inserted in the preceding table. In order to distinguish the real from the hypothetical values, notes of interrogation are affixed to the latter.

It is very remarkable that the properties of all the elements appear to be determined by their position on this curve. The descending portions of the curve from the maximum to the minimum, and a little beyond, are entirely occupied by difficultly-fusible and non-volatile elements, and, as a rule, the lower the element is on the curve the less fusible it is found to be. Only easily-fusible, and as a rule volatile elements occur on the ascending portions of the curve.

In the first period, nitrogen, oxygen, and fluorine are gases, in the second period chlorine; but phosphorus and sulphur are easily fusible and volatile. In the next period the series of volatile elements begins with zinc (or perhaps even with copper). In the following period, the volatile elements begin with silver, which can be distilled by means of the oxyhydrogen blowpipe, and in the last incomplete period mercury is the first volatile element. This relation may be expressed in general terms by saying that when the atomic volume decreases with an increasing atomic weight the elements are refractory and non-volatile; but when the atomic volume increases as the atomic weight increases the elements are easily fusible and volatile.

Other properties change twice in these larger periods. This is the case with the metallic nature of the elements as exhibited by their malleability. The elements at the maximum of the curve and their immediate successors are metals. They are followed by brittle elements down to the minimum. These are succeeded by malleable metals, which are separated from the metals at the maximum by brittle non-metals and semi-metals—*e.g.*

    K, Ca, (Sc ?), malleable ;
    Ti, V, Cr, Mn, brittle ;
    Fe, Co, Ni, Cu, Zn, Ga, malleable ;
    Ge, As, Se, Br, brittle or non-metallic.

The malleability is the same in the following periods. Other physical properties change in a similar way, but some of these properties have not yet been sufficiently investigated. The elements on ascending portions of the curve are without exception diamagnetic, those on the falling part of the curve are magnetic. The optical properties, crystalline form, and expansion by heat exhibit similar regularities.

§ 37. **Periodicity of the Electro-chemical Properties.**—The intimate connection between the chemical properties and the atomic weight proceeds from the fact that the whole system of arrangement consists in bringing together the natural families of elements which have been developed from Dobereiner's triads.

The chemical elements and their compounds exhibit certain contrasts in their nature. These are indicated by the terms 'positive' and 'negative.' The use of these terms arises from the close relation between chemical and electrical properties. As a rule, when two or more bodies of different composition are brought in contact with each other, both are electrified—one becoming positive, the other negative. The greater the difference between the composition of the two substances the greater the electrical excitement will be. The difference which exists between the two bodies is called the electro-chemical difference. The direct measurement of the electric charge produced by the contact of heterogenous bodies is difficult. But the electro-chemical nature of the substances can be determined by another method. Many liquids and some solids are decomposed by the electric current.

In this act of electrolysis, those constituents which are positive on contact are liberated with the positive electricity and those which become negative with the negative electricity, so that the electro-chemical nature of the constituents is easily recognised. The difference in the electro-chemical nature of a substance is not absolute, but merely relative, so that one element can be positive with regard to a second element and negative to a third. It has also been observed that a positive element in a compound can generally be replaced by a more positive and a negative by a more negative. This replacement of one element by another, affords another means of ascertaining the electro-chemical nature of an element. The oxides and hydroxides of the positive elements have basic properties (*i.e.* they neutralise acids); the oxides, hydroxides, and some of the hydrides of the negative elements are acids.

If the elements are divided into the two classes—electro-negative and electro-positive—these properties are regularly divided in the periods. In the atomic volume table, the positive elements are denoted by * and the negative by —. The positive nature changes in the same way as the metallic nature and malleability, *i e.* twice in the large periods of atomic volumes.

The first family in the table on page 55 consists of positive elements, the alkali metals, Li, Na, K, Rb, Cs; the positive character increases with the atomic weight, and caesium is not only the most electro-positive metal of this group but of all the elements. The metals Be, Mg, Ca, Sr, Ba, in the second family, closely resemble these metals in their electro-positive nature; again, we find the metal with the highest atomic weight, barium, is the most electro-positive. In the third family, containing Bo, Al, Sc, Y, La, Yb, the electro-positive nature is much feebler. The hydroxide of boron is a feeble acid, and aluminium hydroxide exhibits the properties of a weak acid as well as of a strong base: here again the negative character grows feebler and the positive stronger, as the atomic weight increases. In the fourth family C, Si, and Ti yield acids, but the higher members Zr, Ce and Th have a more positive character. The elements in all these four families have one property in common: they form very stable compounds with oxygen, and consequently their oxides are difficult to reduce

The four sub-groups, which are entirely composed of heavy metals, are of an opposite character;

I.	II.	III.	IV.
Cu	Zn	Ga	Ge
Ag	Cd	In	Sn
Au	Hg	Tl	Pb

These elements are easily obtained from their oxides and analogous compounds by reduction. In the two first groups, the facility with which the compounds are reduced increases with the atomic weight. In the first and second family the positive character decreases as the atomic weight increases. This is exactly opposite to the behaviour of the difficultly-reducible light metals of this family. Nothing is known of the third group in this respect, but in the fourth group lead (Pb) is more positive than tin (Sn); the positive character, as usual, increasing with the atomic weight.

The same contrasts occur in the following three families, only with this difference, that the first members do not belong to the difficultly, but to the easily reducible, elements; with the exception of phosphorus, which is not so easily reducible as arsenic, antimony, and bismuth, but more easily than vanadium, niobium, and tantalum. The chief group is here formed of the easily reducible elements:

V.	N	P	As	Sb	Bi
VI.	O	S	Se	Te	—
VII.	Fl	Cl	Br	I	—

The sub-group is composed of the difficultly-reducible elements:

V.	V	Nb	Ta	—
VI.	Cr	Mo	W	U
VII.	Mn	—	—	—

The three groups generally embraced in family VIII. are easily reducible:

Fe	Ru	Os
Co	Rh	Ir
Ni	Pd	Pt

A comparison of the chemical properties with the position on the curve of atomic volumes shows that the difficultly-reducible elements occur on the descending, and the easily-reducible elements on the ascending, portions of the curve, but the change from positive to negative is seen on both portions of the curve.

§ 38. **Theoretical Prediction of Properties.**—The close connection between atomic weights and properties renders it possible to predict the unknown properties of an element as soon as its atomic weight is ascertained, and, on the other hand, the atomic weight can be deduced approximately from the chief properties of an element.

When the 'Periodic Law' was first propounded, scandium, gallium, and germanium were unknown, and the position these elements now occupy was represented by blank spaces. Mendeléeff ventured to predict the properties of these undiscovered elements, and his predictions were afterwards verified when the elements were discovered and investigated. The speedy recognition of the value of this systematic arrangement of the elements was, to a great extent, the result of this happy verification of Mendeléeff's predictions. On the other hand, some atomic weights had been incorrectly determined, and attention was called to this fact by the circumstance that these elements did not fit into the system.

The atomic weight of caesium was ten units too low; indium was only two-thirds of the value now in use. Earlier determinations placed platinum before iridium and iridium before osmium, but the properties of these metals indicated that the order should be reversed, and this has been confirmed by the new atomic weight determinations of K. Seubert. The question whether the atom of beryllium corresponds to two or three equivalents—that is, whether the atomic weight is $2 \times 4\cdot 54 = 9\cdot 08$ or $3 \times 4\cdot 54 = 13\cdot 62$—has been decided by the followers of the periodic system in favour of the first assumption, because there is no space for an element with the atomic weight, 13·6, between carbon ($C = 11\cdot 97$) and nitrogen ($N = 14\cdot 01$), and an element possessing the properties of beryllium would be out of place in such a position. The question was definitely settled by the determination of the vapour density of beryllium chloride by Nilson and Pettersson. This result has also materially influenced the recognition of the Periodic System.

§ 39. **Periodicity of Valency.**—The elements differ widely in their combining power. The atoms of some elements can only combine with a single atom, but the atoms of other elements can each unite with two, three, four, or more other atoms. They have double, treble, &c., the power of the other atom, and are said to be di-, tri-, tetra-, penta- or hexa-valent, or they are said to have two, three, or more affinities. Hydrogen again forms the standard of comparison, as it does in the case of the equivalent and atomic weights. The combining powers of the chemical elements vary regularly with the atomic weights.

All those elements are called 'monovalent' that have an atomic weight equivalent to one atom of hydrogen; if their atoms unite with or displace two atoms of hydrogen, they are said to be divalent.

The determination of this property of chemical valency is simple enough in principle. For, if the atomic weight of an element is equal to its equivalent weight (§ 11), the element is monovalent; if the atomic weight is double the equivalent weight, it contains two equivalents and the element is divalent.

Generally speaking, the chemical valency is determined by the number of equivalent weights contained in the atomic weight. The chemical valency determined by this method is a periodic function of the atomic weight. Before studying this relationship, it is necessary to consider the methods of determining valency.

§ 40. **Determination of Chemical Valency.**—The valency of an element is most easily determined from the composition of the molecule of its hydrogen compounds. These hydrides are not numerous; they may be divided into four types:—

I	II.	III.	IV.
HF	H_2O	H_3N	H_4C
HCl	H_2S	H_3P	H_4Si
HBr	H_2Se	H_3As	—
HI	H_2Te	—	—

As the hydrogen atom can only unite with a single atom of its own class to form the molecule H_2, we must assume that the hydrogen atoms contained in the compounds under II., III., and IV. are united to the other constituents. These compounds may be represented graphically by the formulæ—

$$H-F \qquad H-O-H \qquad H-\underset{\underset{H}{|}}{N}-H \qquad H-\underset{\underset{H}{|}}{\overset{\overset{H}{|}}{C}}-H$$

The dashes indicate the manner in which the atoms are supposed to be united together. As the elements in the four types are incapable of combining with a larger number of hydrogen atoms, we regard fluorine, chlorine, bromine, and iodine as monovalent; oxygen, sulphur, selenium, and tellurium as divalent; nitrogen, phosphorus, arsenic, antimony as trivalent; carbon, silicon as tetravalent; in their compounds with hydrogen.

As F, Cl, Br, and I are monovalent in the compounds in the first group and have the same valency as hydrogen, they may be used like hydrogen, for the purpose of determining the valency of other elements. This is very desirable, as their compounds are much more numerous than those of hydrogen. A comparison of the fluorides, chlorides, bromides and iodides of the first four families shows that their compounds correspond to the four types which have just been mentioned, e g. :

I.	II.	III.	IV.
LiCl	BeCl$_2$	BCl$_3$	CCl$_4$
NaCl	MgCl$_2$	AlCl$_3$	SiCl$_4$
KCl	CaCl$_2$	ScCl$_3$	TiCl$_4$
CuCl	ZnCl$_2$	GaCl$_3$	GeCl$_4$
RbCl	SrCl$_2$	YCl$_3$	ZrCl$_4$
AgCl	CdCl$_2$	InCl$_3$	SnCl$_4$
CsCl	BaCl$_2$	LaCl$_3$	(CeCl$_4$?)
AuCl	HgCl$_2$	TlCl$_3$	(PbCl$_4$?)

The chemical valency is constant for each family, and, with an increasing atomic weight, rises from one family to the next, by one unit.

The following families behave in a similar way, but at first sight the relationship appears somewhat more complicated, the composition of the typical hydrides indicating that the valency decreases, thus :—

V.	VI.	VII.
NH_3	OH_2	FH
PH_3	SH_2	ClH

Certain chlorine compounds of these elements have an analogous composition:

V.	VI.	VII.
NCl_3	OCl_2	$ClCl$
PCl_3	SCl_2	ICl

But these and similar compounds do not contain the maximum amount of chlorine or other monovalent atoms, with which the elements are capable of uniting. Compounds of the following composition are known:

V.	VI.	VII.
NH_4Cl	SCl_4	ICl_3
PCl_5	$SeCl_4$	—
PF_5	$TeCl_4$	—
VCl_4	$CrCl_3$	—
$NbCl_5$	$MoCl_6$	—
$SbCl_5$	WCl_6	—
$TaCl_5$	—	—

Some of these compounds are very unstable: ammonium chloride, phosphorus pentachloride, and iodine trichloride decompose on volatilisation, e.g.: $NH_4Cl = NH_3 + HCl$; $PCl_5 = PCl_3 + Cl_2$; $ICl_3 = ICl + Cl_2$; others can be converted into vapour without decomposition, e.g.: PF_5, $NbCl_5$, and $TaCl_5$, $TeCl_4$, $MoCl_6$, WCl_6. This difference in the behaviour of the compounds is explained by the fact that the affinity of the negative elements for chlorine and its analogues is feeble, and consequently the chlorine atoms are easily separated from the compound. The behaviour of sulphur is very remarkable: the tetrachloride SCl_4 can only exist at $-20°$ C.; even at $0°$ C. it begins to decompose into SCl_2, and on distillation half the residual chlorine is lost. Sulphur does not form any definite compounds with bromine and iodine. Phosphorus combines with five atoms of fluorine to form a stable compound. PCl_5 and PBr_5 easily part with two atoms of chlorine or bromine respectively: but phos-

OXIDES AND HYDROXIDES 67

phorus can only unite with three atoms of iodine; as a rule it only combines with two, forming PI_2.

We may assume that the difference in the behaviour of the elements belonging to families V. and VI towards the non-metals is not due to a difference in their valency, but is probably caused by a difference in the force with which they attract the monovalent elements.

This assumption is confirmed by an examination of the oxygen compounds. As an atom of oxygen is equivalent to two atoms of hydrogen and is divalent, any other atom which has the power of uniting with one atom of oxygen is also divalent. One trivalent atom could combine with oxygen in the proportion of one to one and a half, or, more correctly, two trivalent atoms can unite with three atoms of oxygen. The radical hydroxyl —OH is formed by the union of one atom of hydrogen with one atom of oxygen; as the oxygen still has the power of uniting with a second atom, the radical is monovalent. The valency of an element is represented by the number of hydroxyls with which an atom combines, or by twice the number of oxygen atoms which in its oxide would be united with one atom. In order to permit of a uniform comparison, the formulæ of the oxides in the following table are given as though they contained two atoms of the other element, even where the molecule may only contain one atom.

Oxides

I. Monovalent	II. Divalent	III. Trivalent	IV. Tetravalent	V. Pentavalent	VI. Hexavalent	VII. Heptavalent	VIII. Octovalent
Li_2O	Be_2O_2	B_2O_3	C_2O_4	N_2O_5	—	—	—
Na_2O	Mg_2O_2	Al_2O_3	Si_2O_4	P_2O_5	S_2O_6	Cl_2O_7	—
K_2O	Ca_2O_2	Sc_2O_3	Ti_2O_4	V_2O_5	Cr_2O_6	Mn_2O_7	—
Cu_2O	Zn_2O_2	Ga_2O_3	Ge_2O_4	As_2O_5	Se_2O_6	Br_2O_7	—
Rb_2O	Sr_2O_2	Y_2O_3	Zr_2O_4	Nb_2O_5	Mo_2O_6	—	Ru_2O_8
Ag_2O	Cd_2O_2	In_2O_3	Sn_2O_4	Sb_2O_5	Te_2O_6	I_2O_7	—
Cs_2O	Ba_2O_2	La_2O_3	Ce_2O_4	Ta_2O_5	W_2O_6	—	Os_2O_8
Au_2O	Hg_2O_2	Tl_2O_3	Pb_2O_4	Bi_2O_5	U_2O_6	—	—

This table shows the remarkable relation which exists between valency and atomic weight. The number of each family indicates its valency. In families I. to VII. only oxygen and fluorine are missing; no oxide of the latter element has as yet been prepared. In VIII. iron is omitted; the highest oxide, the anhydride of ferric acid, is unstable and has not been satisfactorily investigated. The same is true of the highest oxides of Co, Ni, Rh, Pd, Ir, Pt.

A few examples of the hydroxides will suffice:—

	Hydroxides		Valency	Hydrides
I.	$NaOH$	$= Na(OH)$	$1 \times 1 = 1$	—
II.	MgO_2H_2	$= Mg(OH)_2$	$2 \times 1 = 2$	—
III.	AlO_3H_3	$= Al(OH)_3$	$3 \times 1 = 3$	—
IV.	SiO_4H_4	$= Si(OH)_4$	$4 \times 1 = 4$	SiH_4
V.	PO_4H_3	$= PO(OH)_3$	$3 \times 1 = 3$	PH_3
VI.	SO_4H_2	$= SO_2(OH)_2$	$2 \times 1 = 2$	SH_2
VII.	ClO_4H	$= ClO_3(OH)$	$1 \times 1 = 1$	ClH

Here again the valency is indicated by the number of the family.

It is to be noted that families V., VI., VII. do not exhibit the same valency towards hydrogen and the metals that they do towards oxygen. Beginning with family IV., the valency increases one unit for oxygen and other negative elements, but decreases one unit for hydrogen and the positive elements as we pass on to families V., VI., &c.

§ 41. **Possible Errors in the Determination of Chemical Valency.**—There are many other compounds, besides those mentioned in the preceding section, which can be used for determining the chemical valency of an element. Most of these yield a smaller value, but some give a larger value for the valency.

The valency is always too low when the element in question is not combined with the maximum number of atoms; that is to say, when some of its affinities remain unsaturated. The tetravalent carbon atom can unite with four monad atoms, such as hydrogen or chlorine, or two divalent oxygen atoms:—

$$\begin{array}{c} H \\ | \\ H-C-H \\ | \\ H \end{array} \qquad \begin{array}{c} Cl \\ | \\ Cl-C-Cl \\ | \\ Cl \end{array} \qquad O=C=O$$

Marsh Gas   Carbon Tetrachloride   Carbon Dioxide

When a limited supply of oxygen is passed over an excess of red-hot charcoal, then the carbon atoms cannot take up the maximum amount of oxygen, but form carbon monoxide.

The molecule of this compound is represented by the formula

$${}^*_*{=}C = O.$$

Here the asterisks are intended to show that two affinities are unsaturated; this is proved by the fact that the compound unites with two atoms of chlorine, forming phosgene gas,

$$\begin{matrix}Cl\\Cl\end{matrix}\!\!\!>\!\!C = O.$$

Nitric oxide (NO), nitrogen peroxide (NO$_2$), and nitrosylchloride (NOCl) are similar compounds: they are known as unsaturated compounds or as compounds containing unsaturated affinities. Those metals which only contain one atom in the molecule (§ 27), e.g. mercury, cadmium, and zinc, belong to this class.

There is another class of compounds which cannot be regarded as unsaturated. In these compounds the number of monovalent atoms does not correspond to the valency of the polyvalent atom.

In addition to marsh gas CH$_4$, we are acquainted with hydrocarbons which only contain three, two, or one atom of hydrogen for each atom of carbon. A determination of the molecular weight shows that each of these compounds contains more than one atom of carbon, e.g. ethane C$_2$H$_6$, ethylene C$_2$H$_4$, acetylene C$_2$H$_2$. The two latter unite with hydrogen with some difficulty, forming ethane; but they combine more readily with chlorine. Ethylene takes up two, and acetylene four, atoms of chlorine, but not more.

The compounds C$_2$H$_6$, C$_2$H$_4$Cl$_2$, C$_2$H$_2$Cl$_4$ must be regarded as saturated, although they only contain three monovalent atoms for each carbon atom. This is explained by the fact that one affinity of each carbon atom is required for the purpose of attaching it to the other carbon atom, so that only three affinities are free to unite with hydrogen or chlorine:—

$$\begin{array}{cc} \text{H} & \text{H} \\ | & | \\ \text{H—C—C—H} \\ | & | \\ \text{H} & \text{H} \end{array}$$

that is, one less than corresponds to the chemical valency.

A correct determination of the valency may be attempted by taking into account the affinities required for the purpose of linking together the polyvalent atoms: but this process may lead to erroneous conclusions. If we apply it to ethane we obtain the correct result: 6 affinities for H and 2 for C; total 8 But in the case of ethylene we only obtain 2 for C and 4 for H; total 6: and for acetylene 2 for H and 2 for C; total 4. According to these results carbon might erroneously be considered as only di- or tri-valent

It was formerly assumed that some of the affinities in ethylene and acetylene were unsaturated: this hypothesis is unnecessary and is even regarded as improbable at the present day. The fact that the carbon is combined with less hydrogen in these compounds than it is in ethane, may be due to the carbon atoms being attached to each other by more than one affinity, thus :—

$$H_3{\equiv}C{-}C{\equiv}H_3 \qquad H_2{=}C{=}CH_2 \qquad H{-}C{\equiv}C{-}H$$
Ethane   Ethylene   Acetylene

It follows from these considerations that the chemical valency can only be deduced with certainty from the composition of those compounds which only contain one atom of the polyvalent element in the molecule. If more than one polyvalent atom is present, we do not know how many affinities are used in uniting the several polyvalent atoms together. We must carefully ensure the absence of unsaturated affinities in the compound.

It is often difficult to decide whether this is the case, as the compound will not contain the full number of monovalent atoms if the element has feeble affinities

The determination of the valency is a problem requiring great care in its solution, and it is not surprising that in the case of many elements the valency has not always been correctly determined.

§ 42. **Irregularities of the Chemical Valency.**—There are exceptions to the great regularity in the relation of chemical valency to atomic weight. Certain compounds undoubtedly contain more chlorine, bromine, or oxygen than corresponds to their chemical valency. Many of these compounds may be regarded as molecular aggregations, formed by several complete molecules crystallising together. The beautiful crystalline compound PCl_3Br_4 may be regarded as $PCl_3Br_2 + Br_2$, or as $PCl_3 + Br_2 + Br_2$; in the same way the unstable tri-iodide of potassium may be considered to be $KI + I_2 = KI_3$. But all such compounds cannot be regarded in this light. Auric chloride, $AuCl_3$, is undoubtedly a true chemical compound; and gold must be trivalent, not monovalent, as we should expect from its being a member of the first family. The molecular weight of cupric oxide, CuO, is not known, as the oxide is non-volatile. Its formula may be $Cu—O—O—Cu$; but cupric chloride, $CuCl_2$, could not have an analogous formula. Copper is isomorphous with divalent zinc, and must therefore be divalent. It is shown to be a member of the first family by the fact that the chloride, $CuCl_2$, is not volatile, but is decomposed by heat, losing half its chlorine, yielding cuprous chloride. The molecular weight deduced from the vapour density determination of Victor Meyer corresponds to Cu_2Cl_2, $Cl—Cu—Cu—Cl$, in which copper is again divalent. At present we can only point out these exceptions without attempting to offer any explanation.

§ 43. **Theoretical Significance of Chemical Valency. Nature of Affinity.**—As science is not satisfied with a simple knowledge of facts, but endeavours to investigate their causal connection, theoretical chemistry has attempted to solve the problem of explaining the remarkable fact, that the chemical valency of different elements undergoes a systematic variation. It is very difficult to find this explanation, as very little is known as to the cause of the formation of chemical compounds. The cause is termed affinity, because the old chemists held that only those bodies are capable of uniting with each other, which possess a certain likeness or affinity for each other. Exactly the opposite view now prevails: namely, that the more unlike two bodies are, the more readily will they combine together; but the term affinity still survives.

Affinity is generally considered to be an attractive force existing in the atoms. This hypothesis is not the only one possible, nor is it, indeed, the most probable, but it is the most convenient, and consequently the most generally accepted. This hypothesis will be used for the present, and the consideration of other hypotheses (still imperfectly developed) which do not require the assumption of an attractive force, will be postponed. Affinity is probably closely allied to, if not identical with, electrical attraction; but no definite statement on this point can be made at present.

Affinity only acts at short distances; for bodies combine or decompose each other only when in direct contact. It is not in any way directly identical with the attraction which is produced by the ordinary electric charge or by magnetisation, which work at relatively large distances. We may imagine such a division of the magnetic or electric masses in the atom, as to produce an attractive force which could only be effective at a very small distance. But at present the state of our knowledge is not yet ripe for speculations of this nature.

Leaving aside the question of the true nature of affinity, we may still be able to draw some conclusions from the differences of chemical valency.

There is no doubt that the effect of affinity is to keep the atoms in a compound at a definite distance from each other, for the space which a compound occupies in the solid or fluid state is fixed and definite. It varies regularly with the temperature and pressure, but depends on the nature of the constituents. The atoms cannot be immovable in the positions which the affinities have caused them to assume; for, according to the mechanical theory of heat, not only the molecules as such, but also the atoms in the molecules, are in a state of active motion, oscillating or rotating round points of equilibrium.

In the solid state the molecules of most bodies arrange themselves systematically, forming crystals. The form of the crystal is determined by the composition of the molecules and the nature of the atoms contained in the molecule, and is characteristic of both. As the different parts of a crystal exhibit certain points of difference, and the nature of this difference depends on the composition of the molecules and the nature of the atoms, it seems probable that these points of difference must already exist in the atoms and molecules themselves. The attractive force of affinity is active at these points. It endeavours to attract the other atoms and keep them in positions, which lie in these lines of force at a definite distance from the centre of gravity of the first atom. The distances between the centres of gravity may vary considerably for different atoms. There will be only one such position in the vicinity of a monovalent atom, in which a second atom can be fixed; but there will be two such points for a divalent and three for a trivalent atom, &c.

We may also venture to determine the position of these points in space. In the case of a compound consisting of two monovalent atoms only the distance between the atoms is fixed; the system will be in a state of equilibrium in any position. This may be the reason why compounds formed of two monovalent atoms generally crystallise in the regular system. A polyvalent atom requires a number of points corresponding to its chemical valency; these positions must be symmetrically arranged, at equal distances from the centre of gravity of the polyvalent atom. If this is not the case an exchange in the position of the atoms will produce 'isomeric' compounds—that is, compounds possessing the same composition, but exhibiting dissimilar properties. For example, there would be two potassium hydroxides, $K-O---H$, and $H-O---K$, and two amides of potassium, $\begin{smallmatrix}H\\H\end{smallmatrix}-N---K$, and $\begin{smallmatrix}H\\K\end{smallmatrix}-N---H$.
Apparent examples of this kind of isomerism have from time to time been discovered, but on closer investigation they have invariably been proved to be spurious. It is, therefore, exceedingly probable that the points are symmetrically arranged at equal distances round the surface of a sphere. In a divalent atom the points will be diametrically opposite each other; in a trivalent atom the points will be arranged in a circle, at angles of 120°; in a tetravalent atom the points will be arranged in space like the angles of a regular tetrahedron; in a hexavalent atom the points will occupy the solid angles of an octahedron,

or the centres of the faces of a cube; in an octovalent atom the points are arranged like the corners of a regular cube, or the centres of the faces of an octahedron. A perfectly symmetrical arrangement of five or seven points on the surface of a sphere is not possible, but it is probable that in this case the arrangement will be as symmetrical as possible.

Starting from these assumptions, it is easy to represent the configuration of the molecules, which are composed of monovalent atoms and only one polyvalent atom. A compound consisting of two monovalent atoms, or two monovalent and one polyvalent atom, is represented by a formula lying in a straight line.—

$$H - - - Cl \qquad H - - - O - - - H$$

One trivalent and three monovalent atoms lie in a plane:—

One tetravalent and four monovalent atoms are arranged round the centre of a tetrahedron, at the solid angles. In fact, physical investigations of such compounds have made it exceedingly probable that their molecules really possess this form.[1]

It is difficult to follow this hypothesis when the monovalent atoms are wholly or partly replaced by polyvalent atoms, for one atom cannot occupy several positions at the same time. Attempts to overcome this difficulty are made by assuming that the atom alternately occupies the different positions moving between them like a pendulum, or rotating about them. This view receives support from the observation that compounds containing polyvalent atoms attached to each other by multiple linkings occupy a larger space than those compounds do in which the polyvalent atoms are united together by a single linking. Again, it is observed that those carbon compounds which contain doubly or trebly linked carbon atoms easily split

[1] Conclusions drawn from the friction of gases, with reference to the size of the section of molecules, appear to confirm these views

up at the points where the double or treble linking exists. Great importance must not be attached to speculations of this nature at present, as they are much too hypothetical; but they serve a useful purpose by enabling us to survey a variety of observations from a common standpoint.

§ 44. **Investigation of the Constitution of Chemical Compounds.**—The chemical valency of the elements and the composition of their compounds are intimately related. Not only the number of the atoms, but their arrangement in the molecule, depends on the valency of the elements. The possibility of investigating and ascertaining the manner in which the atoms are arranged, was for a long time a disputed question. Although some chemists attempted to investigate the arrangement of the atoms, others looked upon such investigations as absolutely valueless But even the followers of the latter school could not avoid holding certain views regarding the manner in which the atoms combine together to form compounds, for they rejected as unwarranted the doubts which existed as to the correctness and permissibility of their views. This dispute lasted more than twenty years, and, strange to say, it ended in the overthrow of these old dogmas by new hypotheses, by means of which we have acquired an unexpected insight into the nature of chemical compounds. At the present day the investigation of the 'constitution' or 'structure' of the chemical compounds is one of the chief problems of the science; more particularly is this the case in organic chemistry, which treats of the compounds of carbon. In the course of the last fifty years these investigations have been brought to such a state of perfection, that it is now usual to dogmatically insert the results of such investigations in text-books as the fixed truth, without giving any exact account of the methods which have led to the attainment of such intimate knowledge

It is desirable to know the exact grounds on which our knowledge rests, not only in the interests of those who specially devote themselves to such subjects, but also in the interests of the general history of civilisation and the history of science in particular. These investigations form one of the most striking examples of the power of the human mind to penetrate into things which are as a sealed book to our senses alone. The path which the science of chemistry pursued, to attain its present position, was long, and not entirely free from error. But in looking back we can separate the essential from the non-essential and gain without difficulty a clear idea of the chief features of this development.

The chief difference between our present views and the older conceptions consists in this: formerly it was more or less explicitly assumed that a chemical compound was held together by the total attractive force of the affinities of all the atoms contained in it, but as our knowledge increased it was gradually recognised that the connection is between atom and atom and that the atoms are attached to each other like the links in a chain, the continuity ceasing if even a single link of the chain is removed. This kind of combination is termed 'atomic linking'; the idea involved was not suddenly realised, but was the gradual outcome of previous conceptions.

The necessity of studying the atoms themselves was clearly stated by A. Kekulé in 1857, and by A. S. Couper in 1858. The doctrine of atomic linking is the outcome of the investigation of organic compounds, and at the present day it is chiefly applied to organic bodies; but numerous conclusions with regard to the constitution of inorganic compounds have been deduced by its aid.

The theory of atomic linking first gave a satisfactory explanation of the common observation that two or more chemical compounds having the same composition may exhibit widely different properties. This remarkable phenomenon has long been known as 'isomerism,' from ἴσος, same, and μέρος, the part. Isomeric bodies are those which contain the same constituents, ἴσα μέρη. We distinguish between 'metamerism' and 'polymerism'; metamerism embraces those cases in which the constituents are present in exactly the same number and quantity, but are differently arranged: the grouping of the constituents, has been altered by a change of position, 'metastasis.' 'Polymerism,' or, better, 'pleomerism,' applies to those compounds in which the relative proportion between the constituents is the same, but the absolute number of atoms contained in the molecular weight of one compound is double or treble the number contained in the other.

There are several methods of investigating atomic linking which mutually support and supplement each other. In the first place, in many simple cases the atomic linking can be deduced on purely theoretical grounds from the composition and molecular weight of the compound and the chemical valency of its constituents. But this can be done only when a single form of combination is possible, and the composition only permits of one interpretation. When the conditions are not so simple we make use of analysis and synthesis, assuming that those constituents which remain combined together when a compound is decomposed were previously united, and inversely in building up a compound, the parts which were united before remain united after the combination has taken place. Finally, we have a very important aid to such investigations, in the connection which has been established by innumerable comparisons between the chemical and physical properties of a body and its atomic linking.

§ 45 **Theoretical Determination of the Possible Forms of Combination.**—After the composition of the molecular weight of a compound has been empirically determined, the next question is to ascertain the manner in which the atoms are linked together. This is a purely mathematical problem and the answer can, when necessary, be calculated by permutations. It is obvious that any indefinite number of atoms cannot unite together to form distinct compounds : for instance, the number of monovalent atoms is limited, as each monovalent atom can only unite with one other atom, and cannot lengthen the chain to any greater extent. Compounds composed entirely of monovalent atoms can only exist in the form represented by type I. (§ 40). Compounds composed of one polyvalent atom and several monovalent atoms exhibit forms exemplified by types II to VIII. The number of monovalent atoms which can enter into combination corresponds to the valency of the polyvalent atom. If a second or third polyvalent atom is added, then two valencies are required for the linking of each additional polyvalent atom, and are, therefore, not available for union with monovalent atoms. The number of monovalent atoms is increased by a number equal to two less than the valency of the new polyvalent atom. If n_1, n_2, n_3, n_4, represent the number of mono-, di-, tri- and tetra-valent atoms, then the maximum number of monovalent atoms will be

$$n_1 = 2n_2 + 3n_3 + 4n_4 + 5n_5 + 6n_6 + 7n_7 + 8n_8$$
$$- 2(n_2 + n_3 + n_4 + n_5 + n_6 + n_7 + n_8 - 1)$$
$$= 2 + 1n_3 + 2n_4 + 3n_5 + 4n_6 + 5n_7 + 6n_8$$

In organic compounds, which usually contain only mono-, di-, tri-, and tetra-valent atoms,

$$n_1 = 2 + 1n_3 + 2n_4.$$

The number of divalent atoms has no influence on the number of monovalent atoms. Each trivalent atom increases the number of possible monovalent atoms by one, and each tetravalent atom by two. As no compounds are known in which the number n_1 of monovalent atoms is greater than is here indicated, this is regarded as a confirmation of the theories of valency and of atomic linking.

If there is only one polyvalent atom in the molecule then only one constitution is possible, even when the monovalent atoms differ in their nature, because the valencies of one and the same atom must be held to be equivalent (§ 43), and it is, consequently, immaterial which atom is united to a given affinity. The following formulæ admit of only one interpretation:

CH_4	CH_3Cl	CH_2Br_2	$CHBr_3$	CH_2ClBr
Methane	Methylchloride	Methylenebromide	Bromoform	Chlorobromomethane

It is an open question (§ 54) whether the formulæ only admit of one signification when all four monovalent elements are different. When two polyvalent atoms combine, the formula has only one meaning when all the affinities are satisfied by monovalent atoms of the same element. For example:—

$C_2H_6 =$ $H_3C - - CH_3$ $CNH_5 =$ $H_3C - - NH_2$
              Ethane   Methylamine

Three similar polyvalent atoms can unite with one kind of monovalent atom to form saturated compounds, which can only exhibit one form of structure, e.g. propane:—

$$CH_3 - - CH_2 - - CH_3.$$

Again, one structure alone is possible in a compound containing

INVESTIGATION OF ATOMIC LINKING   79

two polyvalent atoms where one of the monovalent atoms differs from the others, *e.g.*:

$$H_3C--CH_2Cl \qquad H_3C--CH_2I \qquad Cl_3C--CHCl_2$$
Ethyl Chloride   Ethyl Iodide   Pentachlorethane

But this is no longer the case when a second monovalent atom of another element enters the compound. The entrance of the first of these two atoms, puts an end to the equality between the two polyvalent atoms, and consequently the particular polyvalent atom with which the second monovalent atom unites is now of material importance. Isomeric compounds are now possible, and the number of such compounds theoretically possible are actually known. When there are only two atoms of the new kind present, it does not matter whether they are alike or dissimilar. Only two forms are possible for the compounds

$$C_2H_4Cl_2 \text{ and } C_2H_4ClBr$$

$$H_3C--CHCl_2 \text{ and } H_2ClC--CH_2Cl$$
Ethylidene chloride   Ethylene chloride

$$H_3C--CHClBr \text{ and } H_2ClC--CH_2Br$$
Ethylidene chlorobromide   Ethylene chlorobromide

But if the number of different monovalent elements increases the number of isomerides will increase. If all six monovalent atoms are different, then there will be 10 isomerides, as can be calculated by permutation. If the six monovalent atoms are numbered 1, 2, 3, 4, 5, 6, then we have the following combinations:

The first C atom			The second C atom		
1	2	3	4	5	6
1	2	4	3	5	6
1	2	5	3	4	6
1	2	6	3	4	5
1	3	4	2	5	6
1	3	5	2	4	6
1	3	6	2	4	5
1	4	5	2	3	6
1	4	6	2	3	5
1	5	6	2	3	4

or $(4+3+2+1) = 10$ combinations.

In the case of three similar or two dissimilar polyvalent atoms, isomerism occurs as soon as a single atom of a second monovalent element enters the compound :—

$$CNH_4Cl = CH_2Cl--NH_2 \text{ or } CH_3--NHCl$$
Chloromethylamine   Methylchloramine

$$C_3H_7Cl = CH_3--CH_2--CH_2Cl \text{ or } CH_3--CHCl--CH_3$$
Propylchloride   Isopropylchloride

The number of isomeric compounds increases rapidly as the number of polyvalent atoms and the variety of monovalent elements increase. Three carbon atoms and eight similar monovalent atoms can only be arranged in one manner, but if the 8 monovalent atoms are all different, then no less than 280 forms of combination are possible. It is clear that the atomic linking in a given compound can only be determined by calculation in the very simplest cases.

§ 46 **Determination of the Linking by Synthesis and Analysis** The decomposition and building up of compounds afford a valuable means of determining the atomic linking. The conclusions based on these methods depend on the assumption that those atoms which are united together before the union of two compounds remain united together after the act of combination, and that, on the other hand, those atoms which remain joined together after the decomposition of a compound were previously united in the said compound. This deduction was made use of long before the doctrine of atomic linking was known, but, strange to say, the conclusions arrived at in this way were proved to be untenable by the knowledge of atomic linking and were abandoned after a prolonged discussion.

The very ancient observation that a salt is formed from an acid and a base, and can again be decomposed into these constituents, led to the view that the acid and base are present as such in the salt. Calcium carbonate decomposes into lime and carbon dioxide, $CaCO_3 = CaO + CO_2$; from this it was inferred that calcium carbonate contained the proximate constituents CaO and CO_2, and that its formula was CaO,CO_2.

Analogous formulæ were given to other salts, e.g —

CaO,SO_3 K_2O,SO_3 $3\ CaO,P_2O_5$
Calcium Sulphate   Potassium Sulphate   Calcium Phosphate

And similar formulæ were used for the acids :—

$$H_2O.SO_3 \qquad\qquad 3H_2O,P_2O_5$$
Sulphuric Acid Phosphoric Acid

and so on.

It is evident that formulæ of this description are not permissible, for the compounds are represented as composed of groups of atoms: these groups are already saturated and therefore have no free affinities available for mutual combination.

$$H--O--H, \quad Ca\!=\!=\!O, \quad K--O--K, \quad O\!=\!=\!C\!=\!=\!O$$

$$O\!=\!=\!S\!=\!=\!O, \quad O\!=\!=\!P\!=\!=\!O\!=\!P\!=\!O$$
$$\quad\;\;\|\quad\qquad\quad\;\|\qquad\quad\;\;\|$$
$$\quad\;\;O\quad\qquad\quad O\qquad\quad\;\;O$$

These formulæ are called dualistic, on account of their separation into two parts. They have been replaced by others in which the groups are united together by means of their oxygen atoms :—

$$Ca\begin{matrix}.O.\\ \;\\ .O.\end{matrix}C\!=\!=\!O \qquad H--O--\overset{\overset{O}{\|}}{\underset{\underset{O}{\|}}{S}}--O--H$$

The principle underlying these old formulæ, viz. the assumption that those atoms which were united in a compound, must be regarded as remaining combined, still remains in force, but in its application due care is taken to comply with the law of atomic linking.

For example, the action of hydrochloric acid on alcohol is represented by the equation—

$$C_2H_6O \quad + \quad HCl \quad = \quad C_2H_5Cl \quad + \quad HOH$$
Alcohol   Hydrochloric Acid   Ethyl Chloride   Water

In this case two of the carbon atoms and at least four of the hydrogen atoms remain together; we may assume, therefore, that these atoms are contained in alcohol and in ethyl chloride also—

$$C_2H_4,H_2O \qquad\qquad C_2H_4,HCl$$
Alcohol   Ethyl Chloride

The two groups H_2O, water, and HCl, hydrochloric acid, are closed groups, in which all the affinities are saturated. We must therefore assume, that not more than one hydrogen atom in alcohol is united to oxygen; that is to say, that alcohol contains the monovalent 'hydroxyl' group, — O — — H, and that this group and the five hydrogen atoms, must be directly attached to the carbon thus: C_2H_5— — O— — H.

By the action of hydrochloric acid, oxygen is split off; there is no doubt about this taking place, as the oxygen ceases to be united to carbon. The oxygen atom takes away with it the atom of hydrogen to which it was previously united. Where does the second atom of hydrogen come from? Is it taken away from the carbon or the chlorine? Since the monovalent chlorine must detach itself from the hydrogen, before it can unite with the carbon, it is more than probable that the hydrogen atom from the hydrochloric acid, combines with the hydroxyl. As there is only one interpretation for a group containing two carbon atoms, the formula must be

$$CH_3—CH_2—O—H + H—Cl = CH_3—CH_2Cl + H—O—H$$
$$\text{Alcohol} \qquad\qquad\qquad\qquad \text{Ethyl Chloride}$$

The groups of atoms which remain united together in these reactions are termed 'radicals,' as they were considered to be the roots from which the peculiarities of the compounds arose: this expression dates back to the time of Lavoisier. Alcohol and ethyl chloride have the same root, the radical ethyl, C_2H_5.

Further conclusions as to atomic linking may be deduced from the decomposition and the mode of formation of substances. If an atom or a radical replaces another in a compound, we assume that it takes the place previously occupied by the latter. The chlorine, from the hydrochloric acid, takes the place of the hydroxyl and the hydroxyl takes the place of the chlorine and unites with the hydrogen atom. This replacement of one atom or radical by another is termed 'substitution,' and is distinguished from 'addition,' *i.e.* the simple union or combination of two radicals or atoms; *e.g.*

$$C_2H_4 \ + \ Br_2 \ = \ C_2H_4Br_2$$
$$\text{Ethylene} \quad \text{Bromine} \quad \text{Ethylene Bromide}$$

The formation of addition compounds is frequently used in determining atomic linking, it being assumed that the addition takes place at those points where the available affinities are situated.

§ 47 **Determination of Atomic Linking from Physical Properties.**—Numerous observations show that the atomic linking exercises a marked influence on the properties of substances, and it often happens, that two isomeric compounds containing exactly the same constituents, possess totally different properties, solely in consequence of the different linking of their atoms; *e.g.* ethyl acetate has a pleasant ethereal odour and butyric acid has a rancid, offensive smell When the constitution of a series of substances has been investigated, the influence of the atomic linking on their properties is soon apparent, and we are now able to determine the atom linking by a study of the properties. The following physical properties chiefly come into consideration · density, fusibility, volatility, colour, solubility, crystalline form, smell, taste, physiological action, &c. The relation of all these properties to atomic linking, has not yet been sufficiently investigated. These relations grow clearer day by day, and by this knowledge it is now possible to make new substances possessing certain desired properties. The recent syntheses of dyes and colouring matters offer a brilliant example of our power to accomplish this object.

The application of physical properties to the investigation of atomic linking depends chiefly on the fact that the physical properties change regularly, when a certain definite alteration in the atomic linking is repeatedly made and the rest of the compound is left unchanged. If we examine a series of organic compounds, the members of which differ from each other in their molecular weights by increments of 1C and 2H it is often observed that the boiling points of these bodies exhibit a certain fixed difference for each CH_2 group. This is not always the case, but only when the constitution and linking remain the same, with the exception of the slight difference in composition due to the introduction of the group CH_2. When we find that there is a regular increase in the boiling point with the molecular weight, we conclude that the bodies have the same or similar atomic linking. Numerous examples of these relations are found in the text-books on organic chemistry.

§ 48. **Determination of Atomic Linking from the Chemical Behaviour.**—The chemical properties are even more dependent on the atomic linking than the physical properties. The influence which certain groups of atoms exert on chemical behaviour, is first determined in compounds of comparatively simple structure, such as those, for instance, in which only one arrangement of the atoms is possible or such as permit their atomic linking to be easily ascertained. More complicated compounds exhibiting similar properties are assumed to contain the same groups of atoms. If large or small deviations occur, the origin of these is investigated by increasing the number of observations and comparing them with one another. In this way a rich collection of rules has been obtained, which enable us to deduce the structure of compounds from their chemical properties.

In the case of each of the frequently occurring combinations of atoms, such as hydroxyl, OH, amide, NH_2, imide, NH, &c., we have not only determined which properties of the compounds indicate their presence, but we have also ascertained the differences in their behaviour caused by the nature of the atoms or radicals with which they are combined. For example, we are not only acquainted with a whole series of tests for identifying the presence of hydroxyl, but we can also ascertain, from the peculiarities in the behaviour of the substance, whether this hydroxyl is attached to carbon or nitrogen or whether the carbon atom united to the hydroxyl is combined with hydrogen, or oxygen, or only another carbon atom. In other words, we have the means of discriminating between the following formulæ:

CH_2—OH, =CH—OH, ≡C—OH, —CO—OH,

and many others.

If a compound contains nitrogen we can ascertain from its chemical character whether the nitrogen is directly combined with oxygen, oxygen and carbon, hydrogen and carbon, or with carbon only.

The relations between atomic linking and chemical properties are, at the present time, amongst the chief objects of investigation in the field of organic chemistry, and are generally discussed in connection with this branch of the science. Unfortunately this subject seldom meets with systematic and comprehensive treatment.[1]

§ 49. **History of the Development of the Theory of Atomic Linking.**—Our present knowledge of atomic linking has not been gained by a peaceful, gradual development. On the contrary, in proportion as the number of organic compounds which had been investigated and analysed increased, the number of new formulæ in use increased, and these formulæ were changed when they apparently ceased to answer their purpose. Much was left to individual caprice, and formulæ were used of which it is scarcely possible at the present day to discover the meaning. It is only natural that under these conditions differences of opinion were frequent, and disputes arose, which were carried on with increasing bitterness, as the difficulty of proving the correctness of one view or the other increased. Gradually these points of difference were smoothed away, and widely divergent views were brought into concord. At the present time all chemists, with very few exceptions, agree in recognising as correct those formulæ which have been established in accordance with the laws of the theory of atomic linking.

As a result of this gradual development, the correct expression of the composition of most substances was discovered, before the theory, on which the formulæ are based, was known. The theory is still of great value, and is used in determining the formula of every newly discovered substance; it is also useful in testing and correcting those constitutional formulæ already in use; and, finally, it forms the philosophical basis for the theories with which the experienced chemist is so familiar that he scarcely notes the foundations on which they rest, but which prove difficult for the beginner to understand if he has not received systematic instruction in these matters.

We will now take a few examples of the method pursued in determining the constitution of an organic compound.

§ 50. **Examples of the Determination of the Atomic Linking.** We will assume that the constitution of that class of organic bodies termed 'alcohols' (from the Arabic name for spirits of wine)

[1] The relationship is systematically treated in E. Lellman's *Principien der organischen Synthese*, Berlin, 1887.

is unknown and has to be determined. These bodies are composed of carbon, hydrogen, and oxygen, and are characterised by certain properties common to all members of the class, more particularly by their power of reacting with acids, with elimination of water, to form ethereal salts. On hydrolysis the ethereal salts yield the original acid and alcohol. The alcohols are mono-, di-, or poly-acid, that is, they can combine with one, two, or more equivalents of an acid. The mono-acid contain at least one, the di-acid two, the tri-acid three oxygen atoms, from which we may conclude that there is a close connection between the equivalence of the alcohol and the quantity of oxygen it contains. We will confine our attention to the mono-acid alcohols, and only consider those mono-acid alcohols containing the maximum number of hydrogen atoms, which have the general formula $C_nH_{2n+2}O$, in which n may represent any whole number; its value generally lies between 1 and 30. Some of these alcohols are liquid at the ordinary temperature, others are solid but easily fusible. They are all volatile, and can be distilled; in the case of the higher members of the series the distillation must be carried on under reduced pressure. The volatility generally diminishes as the molecular weight increases, but a larger molecular weight is not always accompanied by a higher boiling point. Isomeric alcohols have, without exception, different boiling points.

In order to determine the atomic linking it is best to begin with the lowest member of the series—that is, with the member having the lowest molecular weight. This is wood spirit, CH_4O, in the formula for which $n=1$. It is obvious that only one arrangement of the atoms is possible in this case :—

$$\begin{array}{c} H \\ | \\ H-C-O-H \\ | \\ H \end{array}$$

As no other mode of combination is possible, the alcohol must be a compound of methyl (CH_3) and hydroxyl (HO). This view is confirmed by the behaviour of the compound, e.g.

$$CH_3-OH + H-I = CH_3-I + HOH$$

ATOMIC LINKING OF ALCOHOLS

As this and analogous reactions are common to all alcohols, it is probable that they all contain hydroxyl. If $n=2$, the formula is that of spirits of wine, C_2H_6O. In this case two different modes of arranging the atoms are possible —

$$CH_3\text{—}CH_2\text{—}OH \quad \text{and} \quad CH_3\text{—}O\text{—}CH_3$$
$$\text{Ethyl hydroxide} \qquad\qquad \text{Methyl oxide}$$

But the alcohol must have the first formula, because the radical ethyl, C_2H_5, can be expelled unchanged from this compound by the action of acids and other substances, and this shows that the two carbon atoms are united together. The second combination represents the formula of a well-known compound (methyl oxide) which may be prepared by the following reaction:—

$$CH_3\text{—}O\text{—}Na + CH_3\text{—}I = CH_3\text{—}O\text{—}CH_3 + NaI$$
$$\text{Methyl Alcoholate} \quad \text{Methyl Iodide}$$

There is not a second alcohol isomeric with ethyl alcohol, but when $n=3$, two isomeric alcohols are possible. Both contain the group of atoms C_3H_7, propyl; but the compounds which these two radicals form are only isomeric, and not identical. It is evident, then, that the radicals are not identical, but merely isomeric. Now, three carbon atoms can only be linked together in one way; the difference must therefore be due to the different manner in which the hydrogen atoms are distributed. Taking this into account, we can only have two formulæ for the alcohols:—

$$CH_3\text{—}CH_2\text{—}CH_2\text{—}OH \quad \text{and} \quad CH_3\text{—}\underset{\underset{OH}{|}}{CH}\text{—}CH_3$$

The hydroxyl is either united to one of the end carbon atoms, which is also combined with two hydrogen atoms, or it is attached to the middle carbon atom, which is united to one hydrogen atom. Now the question arises, which formula is to be ascribed to each of the two known alcohols, C_3H_7OH. One is formed together with ethyl alcohol in the process of fermentation, and occurs in fusel oil, and boils at 97°C.; the other boils at 83°, and was first prepared by Friedel by the action of nascent hydrogen on acetone, C_3H_6O.

If we compare these formulæ with that of ethyl alcohol we find that the formula of ethyl alcohol bears a closer resemblance to the first than it does to the second formula, for the hydroxyl is attached to a carbon atom which is united to two hydrogen atoms, and only *one* other carbon atom. It is therefore probable that the first formula belongs to that alcohol which bears the closest resemblance to ethyl alcohol.

This is without doubt the fermentation propyl alcohol boiling at 97°. Without going into detail, we may point out that, like ethyl alcohol, this alcohol on oxidation loses two atoms of hydrogen, forming an aldehyde (alcohol dehydrogenatus), and this by taking up oxygen is converted into an acid. On oxidation isopropyl alcohol, boiling at 83°, yields the acetone C_3H_6O, from which it was obtained by reduction, but it does not yield any acid. Other isomeric alcohols exhibit a similar difference of behaviour on oxidation. It is consequently important to ascertain the atomic linking of the aldehydes, acids, and acetone. The aldehydes and acids have the molecular weights represented by the following formulæ :—

CH_2O	C_2H_4O	C_3H_6O
Formaldehyde	Acetaldehyde	Propionaldehyde
CH_2O_2	$C_2H_4O_2$	$C_3H_6O_2$
Formic Acid	Acetic Acid	Propionic Acid

As these bodies are derived from alcohols, all their carbon atoms must be united together. But as the number of hydrogen atoms does not attain the maximum value for n, given in § 45, the question arises: Are we to assume the existence of unsaturated affinities or of double linking? This question is difficult to decide experimentally in the case of the aldehydes. With regard to the acids, the answer is decidedly in the negative. We consider that the hydroxyl of the alcohol remains in the acid, as it is easy to simultaneously expel from an acid one atom of oxygen and one of hydrogen. If we make use of this supposition, only one of the theoretically possible formulæ for formic acid derived from methyl alcohol is available, viz H—CO—OH

The radical HCO, which is combined with the hydroxyl, is called 'formyl'; it is composed of carbonyl, CO, and hydrogen, H.

On comparing this formula with that of methyl alcohol, it is seen that in addition to the hydroxyl, the acid contains an atom of oxygen attached to the carbon atom instead of two atoms of hydrogen in the alcohol. The close resemblance which exists between acetic and propionic acids and formic acid makes it highly probable that these acids are formed from the alcohols in a similar way, and contain instead of two atoms of hydrogen, one atom of oxygen, united to the carbon atom to which the hydroxyl is attached. According to this hypothesis the formulæ for the acids would probably be

$$\text{Formic acid, } H—CO—OH$$
$$\text{Acetic acid, } CH_3—CO—OH$$
$$\text{Propionic acid, } CH_3—CH_2—CO—OH$$

If these formulæ are correct the group of atoms termed 'carboxyl,' CO—OH, is characteristic of these acids and determines their properties. Formic acid is therefore hydrogen carboxyl; acetic acid, methyl carboxyl; and propionic acid, ethyl carboxyl. This supposition is confirmed by the behaviour of the acids; for in reactions in which formic acid and its salts give off hydrogen, acetic acid yields methyl and propionic acid yields ethyl.

$$H—CO—ONa + HONa = H—H + NaO—CO—ONa$$
$$CH_3—CO—ONa + HONa = CH_3—H + NaO—CO—ONa$$
$$C_2H_5—CO—ONa + HONa = C_2H_5—H + NaO—CO—ONa$$

All three acids are decomposed by heating with an excess of caustic soda, yielding sodium carbonate and hydrogen, methyl hydride or methane, ethyl hydride or ethane respectively.

These views are confirmed by many reactions of these acids, and the investigation of many other acids proves that wherever the carboxyl group of atoms occurs the compound has the properties characteristic of an acid.

When this was once recognised it became evident why some alcohols do not yield acids. Only those alcohols can yield acids which contain a carbon atom, which is united to two hydrogen atoms and the hydroxyl group.

The group —CH$_2$—OH is as characteristic of these 'primary' alcohols (as they are called) as the carboxyl group is of the acids.

In the same way it can be shown that the group =CH—OH is characteristic of the second class, the 'secondary' alcohols, which yield acetone or kindred bodies on oxidation. The 'tertiary' alcohols which yield neither acids nor ketones, but lose carbon on oxidation, contain the group $\equiv$C—OH.

After ascertaining these characteristic points of difference for a large number of alcohols, the other chemical and physical properties of the alcohols were investigated. The result showed that, in a group of isomeric alcohols, the primary boil higher than the secondary, and these again higher than the tertiary, but the latter have, on the other hand, a higher melting point. The three classes of alcohols can be distinguished by means of their boiling points. Although it is unnecessary to use this method for this particular purpose, it proves of great value in discriminating between isomeric alcohols of the same class. For example, four isomeric butyl alcohols ($C_4H_{10}O$) are known: two of these are primary, and consequently contain the group HO—CH_2—. The difference between them must consist in a difference in the arrangement of their other carbon atoms. According to theory, two modes of linking are possible :—

HO—CH_2—CH_2—CH_2—CH_3 and HO—CH_2—CH—CH_3
$\qquad\qquad\qquad\qquad\qquad\qquad\qquad\qquad\quad$ |
$\qquad\qquad\qquad\qquad\qquad\qquad\qquad\qquad\ CH_3$

Which of these formulæ belongs to the alcohol boiling at 116°, which is obtained by the reduction of butyric acid, and which formula must be ascribed to the alcohol boiling at 109° and contained in fusel oil? This problem may be solved in different ways. By depriving each alcohol of the elements of water a hydrocarbon, butylene (C_4H_8), is obtained. Each butylene unites with hydriodic acid, forming a butyl iodide (C_4H_9I), in which the iodine can be replaced by hydroxyl. The original alcohols are not reproduced by this process. The alcohol boiling at 116° yields a secondary alcohol (boiling point 99°), and the alcohol boiling at 109° yields a tertiary alcohol boiling at 83°. Only one formula is possible for each of these alcohols :—

CH_3——CH——CH_2——CH_3 $\qquad$ CH_3——C——CH_3
$\qquad\ \ \ $|$\qquad\qquad\qquad\qquad\qquad\qquad$|
$\qquad\ \ OH\qquad\qquad\qquad\qquad\qquad\quad$OH
$\ \ \ \ $Secondary$\qquad\qquad\qquad\qquad\quad$Tertiary

(with CH_3 above the central C in the tertiary structure)

The difference from the original alcohols, can only be due to the fact, that the new hydroxyl does not take up the position previously occupied by the old hydroxyl. Imagine that they are reconverted into primary alcohols, then we get the preceding formulæ again, and we see that the first formula, in which no carbon atom is directly united to more than two others, belongs to the alcohol boiling at 116°; the other, in which one carbon atom is united to three others and one hydrogen atom—is consequently in a 'tertiary' position—belongs to the fusel oil alcohol boiling at 109° The first kind of linking is termed 'normal' to distinguish it from the abnormal 'branched' or 'side-chain' linking.

Experience has shown that the normal compounds always have a higher boiling point than those with side chains, and that the boiling point of the latter falls as the number of side chains increases. In the case of bodies having a similar constitution, the addition of CH_2 raises the boiling point from 18° to 22°. This fact may be used for determining the constitution or for testing and confirming the accuracy of a constitution determined by other methods.

§ 51. **Aromatic Compounds.**—Benzene and the so-called aromatic compounds[1] derived from it offer a remarkable example of the manner in which the atomic linking has been investigated. Benzene is a hydrocarbon which contains the same number of carbon and hydrogen atoms. Its composition is represented by the formula $C_n H_{3n}$, where n stands for a whole number. Its molecular weight is therefore

$$m = n(C+H) = n(11 \cdot 97 + 1) = n \times 12 \cdot 97.$$

Faraday found that the density of its vapour is 2·752 times that of air; m will therefore be approximately 79·43.

$$m = 28 \cdot 87 \times 2 \cdot 752 = 79 \cdot 43,$$

or, for the corrected value,

$$m = 6 \times 12 \cdot 97 = 77 \cdot 82 = C_6 H_6.$$

[1] The name 'aromatic compounds' has its origin in the fact that the members of this group which were first investigated possess an aromatic odour, a property not shared by all the members.

A very large number of combinations is possible for the twelve atoms contained in this molecular weight, and, at first sight, it appears perfectly hopeless to attempt to investigate the constitution of benzene.

An ingenious interpretation of the behaviour of this substance led Kekulé to propose an hypothesis which explains all its peculiarities in the simplest way. This hypothesis has maintained itself to the present day, in spite of all the criticism to which it has been exposed for a quarter of a century. The hypothesis is based on the observation that, when an atom of hydrogen in benzene is replaced by another atom or radical, only one single derivative is produced. It does not matter which of the hydrogen atoms is replaced; isomeric compounds are never formed. That it is not always one and the same hydrogen atom that is replaced, but that in reality different hydrogen atoms are displaced, can be shown in the following way. Nitro-benzene is formed by the action of nitric acid on benzene:—

$$C_6H_6 + HO-NO_2 = C_6H_5-NO_2 + H_2O$$
$$\text{Benzene} \quad \text{Nitric acid} \quad \text{Nitro-benzene} \quad \text{Water}$$

Chloro-benzene (C_6H_5Cl) can be prepared in several ways from this nitro-benzene, in which the nitro-group (NO_2) has replaced an atom of hydrogen. We may either reduce the nitro-group to NH_2 and replace the latter by chlorine, or we may replace a hydrogen atom in nitro-benzene by chlorine (in this case it is evident a different hydrogen must be displaced). The nitro-group is eliminated from the chloro-nitro-benzene ($C_6H_4NO_2Cl$) and replaced by hydrogen. Experiments of this kind have been conducted in widely different forms, but they all yield one and the same chloro-benzene. From this behaviour of benzene we conclude that all the hydrogen atoms in benzene are equivalent to each other in every respect, and that each hydrogen atom is combined in exactly the same way as each of the others. These conditions are satisfied by Kekulé's hypothesis that all six carbon atoms are united together forming a closed ring,[1] and the hydrogen atoms are uniformly distributed amongst the carbon atoms as is shown by the following formula:—

[1] The ring formula does not indicate that the atoms are arranged in a plane circle, but only that they form a closed chain

ISOMERIC BENZENE DERIVATIVES

```
      H
      |
  H   C   H
   \ / \ /
    C   C
    |   ||
    C   C
   / \ / \
  H   C   H
      |
      H
```

In order that all four affinities of each carbon atom may come into play, it is assumed that the linking in the ring is alternately by one and by two affinities. In recent times this comparatively minor detail of the hypothesis has given rise to much discussion.

Kekulé's formula explains the whole behaviour of benzene and its derivatives in a remarkably satisfactory manner. In the first place it indicates that each 'mono-substitution product' obtained by the replacement of one of the hydrogen atoms can exist in one form only, and that isomerides cannot exist. But if a second atom or radical is substituted for a hydrogen atom, the perfect symmetry of the molecule is changed, and the second atom may take one of three positions, namely, next to the first or separated from it by one or by two carbon atoms. If the first atom takes the position at 1, the second may occupy the position at 2 and 6 (which are identical), or at 3 and 5, or finally at 4.

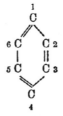

Strictly speaking, the positions 2 and 6 are not absolutely identical on account of the double linking; this has led some authors to assume that the fourth affinities are free or else united to the opposite carbon atoms. These modifications of the hypothesis have not up to the present acquired any particular practical signification

In spite of the repeated endeavours of many chemists to discover four isomeric di-substitution products of benzene, e g. dichloro-benzenes, not more than three have ever been discovered. It is this circumstance which has gained for Kekulé's hypothesis a general recognition of its value. The three isomeric di-substitution products are distinguished by the prefixes 'ortho,' 'meta,' and 'para'

The problem now arises, Which of the three positions 1 . 2, 1 . 3, and 1 . 4, or which of the three formulæ

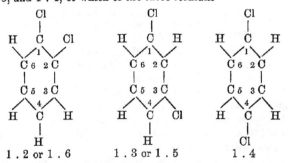

is to be assigned to each of these compounds?

Owing to the inherent difficulties of the problem, this question was debated for years, and our views on the subject have frequently been altered. One remarkable fact is, that on further substitution the para-derivative only yields one tri-substitution product, but both of the other derivatives yield more than one tri-substitution product. As it is only in the third formula that the four remaining hydrogen atoms occupy similar positions, this formula has been assigned to the para-compounds 1 . 4. In the first formula, 1 . 2, the four remaining hydrogen atoms are in two different relations to the chlorine atoms, 3 and 6 are adjacent to the chlorine atoms, 4 and 5 are separated from them by a carbon atom In the second formula, 1 . 3, the third chlorine atom may occupy three different positions—e g. 2, between the two chlorine atoms; 4 and 6, adjacent to the chlorine atoms;

and 5, separated by a carbon atom. As it has been proved by experiment that an ortho-di-substitution product can only yield two tri-substitution products, and the meta-compound yields three tri-substitution products, the formula 1 . 2 is assigned to the ortho- and 1 . 3 to the meta-derivatives.

Numerous comparisons have fully confirmed these hypotheses, and it is now seventeen years since the accuracy of these views was disputed.

These examples suffice to give an idea of the methods by which our intimate knowledge of the constitution of organic compounds has been acquired.

We may in this see a confirmation of the saying of Bacon:

Nec manus nuda, nec intellectus sibi permissus ad inveniendam veritatem multum valet Instrumentis et auxiliis res perficitur, quibus opus est non minus ad intellectum quam ad manum

§ 52. **Physical Isomerism. Allotropy.**—As the investigation of the constitution of organic compounds was extended, many instances were observed in which a larger number of isomeric bodies were discovered than could be accounted for by means of the formulæ derived according to the laws of atomic linking. In most of these cases the isomeric substances differed less in their chemical than in their physical properties, such as density, melting point, crystalline form, &c.

Such cases of isomerism which cannot be explained by chemical formulæ are termed 'physical isomerides' to distinguish them from the 'chemical isomerides,' which are caused by a difference in the mode of linking. This physical isomerism is very closely related to and is almost identical with 'allotropism.' The latter expression was introduced by Berzelius, and applied by him to describe the occurrence of elements in different forms or conditions, or 'allotropic modifications.' Before the molecules of elementary bodies were regarded as compounds of similar atoms, the existence of one and the same element in different modifications could not be explained in the same way as the isomerism of compounds. Hence the necessity of a special term to be applied to this class of phenomena. At the present time the expression 'allotropism' is also applied to compounds, and is synonymous with physical isomerism. There are several kinds of physical isomerism.

§ 53. **Polymorphism.**—Dimorphism and polymorphism are common forms of physical isomerism. When one and the same substance crystallises in two or more distinct forms, it is said to be dimorphous or polymorphous. Both elements and compounds exhibit this peculiar phenomenon. Well-known examples of polymorphism are exhibited by carbon, which crystallises in the regular system as the diamond, and in the hexagonal system as graphite. Sulphur is deposited from fusion in monoclinic crystals and from solution in carbon bi-sulphide in rhombic crystals. Calcium carbonate ($CaCO_3$) occurs in rhombohedral crystals as calcite and in rhombic crystals as arragonite. Silica is met with in two distinct hexagonal forms as quartz and tridymite. Titanium dioxide (TiO_2) exists in three distinct forms as rutile, brookite, and anatase. Stannic oxide (SnO_2), which is isomorphous with titanium dioxide, assumes the same forms as rutile and brookite, and perhaps anatase. These bodies are consequently 'isodimorphous' or 'isotrimorphous.'

There are many other examples of isodimorphism, such as that of the oxides of arsenic and antimony, As_4O_6 and Sb_4O_6, the sulphides of copper and silver, Cu_2S and Ag_2S. Many organic compounds are also dimorphous.

The form that a di- or poly-morphous body assumes on crystallisation depends chiefly on the temperature, and also on certain other external conditions. If the crystallisation takes place from a solution, the nature of the solvent, the presence of other substances, especially of such as are isomorphous with one of the forms of the body in question, influence the form that body assumes.

The conditions under which many forms are produced are entirely unknown. We do not know under what conditions carbon crystallises as diamond, in spite of the numerous attempts which have been made to produce this valuable gem. In the case of many organic compounds one modification has been accidentally obtained, but the conditions under which it is formed still remain unknown.

The allotropic modifications of a substance differ considerably in their stability. Some modifications when once formed are very stable, but others can only exist within narrow limits of the conditions under which they are produced. As examples of the first class we have carbon as diamond or graphite; sulphur is an example of the second class.

The diamond and graphite can exist unaltered side by side, and it is only at a very high temperature that the diamond is converted into graphite. On the other hand the rhombic form of sulphur is only stable below, and the monoclinic form above, a temperature of 95° 6 C.; both modifications can exist unchanged for some time outside these limits But they are in a state of unstable equilibrium, which is easily upset by heating, or shaking, or more particularly by contact with a crystal of that modification which is stable at the prevailing temperature, and the whole mass is converted into this form.

Many dimorphous organic compounds behave like sulphur in this respect, and as a rule only one modification is stable, and the other unstable above and below a certain definite temperature

This kind of physical isomerism is supposed to be due to a difference in the arrangement of the particles or molecules, which are in themselves identical. The accuracy of this hypothesis cannot be proved, as we do not possess any method by which the nature, or even the size, of the molecules of solid bodies can be ascertained. But when we see that under suitable conditions crystals of both modifications can be obtained from one and the same liquid, it seems probable that these modifications are composed of similar molecules, just as different kinds of buildings can be constructed from the same kinds of bricks. This class of isomerism may be termed 'isomerism of aggregation'

§ 54. **Physical Isomerism of the Molecules.**—There are also cases of physical isomerism caused by a difference in the molecules. The examples of real polymerism belong to this class, *e.g.* when a body has different molecular weights in the gaseous and liquid states. In the case of sulphur the molecules at temperatures near the boiling point consist of six atoms, S_6, which are split up at higher temperatures into molecules consisting of two atoms, S_2. Many organic and inorganic compounds, such as certain aldehydes, acetic acid, nitrogen peroxide, &c , exhibit analogous behaviour.

The allotropic modifications of phosphorus are probably due to differences in the number of atoms composing the molecules

H

If phosphorus be heated above 210° in a closed vessel too small to permit the element being completely converted into vapour, it passes from the gaseous state into a red solid modification, from which the colourless variety is regenerated, if sufficient space be offered for complete volatilisation. The red modification is produced from the compressed and the colourless from the expanded vapour at the same temperature (210–300°) It is therefore probable that both modifications already existed in the state of vapour as isolated molecules. A difference in the vapour can only be due to a difference in the molecules. It is not yet known whether this difference is to be ascribed to polymerism.

§ 55. **Optical Isomerism.**—The most remarkable form of isomerism, is that in which the isomeric bodies crystallise in forms which are identical in all their individual parts, such as angles and faces, and are symmetrical but not superposable, and bear the same relation to each other that an object bears to its reflected image in a mirror, or that a right-hand glove bears to a glove for the left hand. This peculiar behaviour is generally associated with another remarkable property, viz. the bodies are optically active. One turns the plane of polarised light to the right, to the same extent that the other does to the left. The bodies thus acting on polarised light are divided into two classes. Some substances are optically active only when they are in a solid and crystalline state; others are optically active as liquids, either in solution or in a molten state; and a few gases or vapours are optically active. The members of the first class either crystallise in the regular form or are uniaxial and crystallise in the quadratic or hexagonal systems. If the two kinds of crystals are placed in parallel lines it is noticed that certain hemihedral faces which occur on the right side of the one set of crystals are found on the left side of the other crystals.

Cinnabar, quartz in the form of rock crystal, chlorates, bromates, periodates, thiosulphates, sodium sulphantimoniate, and some organic bodies belong to this class.

As the rotation of light by these substances depends on their crystalline form and ceases when the substances are brought into the liquid state by fusion or by solution, it is evident that the rotation is not due to the nature of the molecules, but is caused by a peculiarity in their arrangement. It is assumed that the molecules are arranged in a spiral form, and that in one form of crystal the spiral turns to the right and in the other to the left.

The second class of optically active compounds exhibits this property in the liquid state. In these cases the molecules are free to move about and do not take up fixed positions. Hence it appears that the rotation of light is not due to the relative position of the molecules, but to their peculiar nature.

Of course this does not exclude the possibility of these substances (if they are capable of crystallising) exhibiting a peculiar arrangement of the molecules. This is indeed the case with many compounds; e.g. tartaric acid ($C_4H_6O_6$) crystallises in two different forms, which are non-superposable and bear the same relation to each other that an object does to its reflected image. Only a few of these compounds crystallise in the regular system (amylamine alum) or are optically uniaxial (strychnine sulphate): these bodies rotate the plane of polarised light in the crystalline state.

Most of these substances belong to the rhombic, monoclinic, or triclinic systems, and form optically biaxial crystals, which do not exhibit the phenomenon of rotation.

§ 56. **Asymmetrically linked Carbon Atoms.**—In investigating the cause of the rotation of light due to the nature of the molecules, it is important to notice that this peculiar phenomenon is only observed in organic compounds, and only a comparatively small number of carbon compounds exhibit this property. This observation led to the hypothesis that the phenomenon is due to a peculiarity in the linking of the atoms. In fact, in 1874 two different investigators, Van t' Hoff and Le Bel, independently discovered the connection existing between the rotation of light and atomic linking and offered a perfectly satisfactory explanation of this optical isomerism.

As stated in § 43, the four affinities of a carbon atom are uniformly arranged in space, and consequently the four atoms united to the carbon atom are arranged round it like the four corners of a tetrahedron round its centre. If these four atoms all differ from each other either in their nature or in being combined with different atoms, then two forms of combination are possible. These are sketched in perspective and numbered I and II.

The four atoms or radicals, a, b, c, d, are attached to the carbon

100   OUTLINES OF THEORETICAL CHEMISTRY

atom in such a way that the two figures are non-superposable, and one is the reflected image of the other. Imagine your eye is placed in the position of one of the atoms, say a, and directed towards the other three atoms; then it sees $b\ c\ d$ in I. in the direction in which the hand of a clock moves, but in II. in the reverse direction.

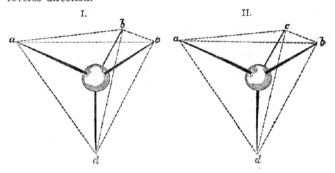

A carbon atom in this condition is said to be an unsymmetrically linked carbon atom, or briefly an asymmetrical carbon atom. A careful examination of all those compounds which can in the liquid state rotate light shows that each of these bodies contains at least one asymmetrical carbon atom; several contain more than one. The property of rotation depends on the presence of an asymmetric carbon atom.

Let $a=$H, $b=$HO, $c=$COOH, $d=$CH$_2$; these groups are contained in malic and tartaric acids: both of these acids exist in two symmetrical forms.

$$\begin{array}{cc} \text{H} & \text{H} \\ | & | \\ \text{HO—CO—C—CH}_2\text{—} & \text{—CH}_2\text{—C—CO—OH} \\ | & | \\ \text{OH} & \text{OH} \end{array}$$

According to the formulæ generally in use, only one form of malic acid is possible, viz.—

$$\begin{array}{c} \text{HO—CO—CH—CH}_2\text{—CO—OH} \\ | \\ \text{OH} \end{array}$$

But if we take into consideration the fact that the carbon atom attached to the HO group is asymmetrical, then two formulæ are possible. Starting from the hydroxyl, the sequence of the other atoms or radicals is in the direction of the hands of a clock in one formula—

$$H,CO—OH,CH_2—CO—OH$$

and in the reverse direction in the other—

$$H,CH_2—CO—OH,CO—OH.$$

The two formulæ are non-superposable.[1]

§ 57. **Active and Inactive Forms.**—The rotatory power of a compound ceases when the asymmetrical carbon atom disappears; for example, malic acid is converted by reduction into succinic acid—

$$HO—CO—CH_2—CH_2—CO—OH$$

which is inactive.

The rotatory power also ceases when equivalent quantities of both modifications unite and crystallise together. For example, the two optically active malic acids unite and form an inactive acid because the rotatory power of the one neutralises that of the other. In such cases the components may be separated by means of suitable agents; for example, one constituent may combine more readily with other dextrogyrate bodies; the other may unite more easily with other lævogyrate compounds We are acquainted with two optically active malic acids which unite together, forming an inactive modification.

If a compound contains two asymmetrical carbon atoms which are united to similar atoms or radicals, then there can exist two optically active and two inactive forms. This is the case with regard to tartaric acid; we have dextro- and lævo-tartaric acid. One inactive acid (racemic) is a compound of the two active forms, but the second acid owes its inactivity to the

---

[1] To make this point perfectly clear, divide the surface of two wooden balls of the same size into eight equal spherical triangles or quadrants by means of three circles cutting each other at right angles. Bore a hole down to the centre of the globe in the middle of each alternate quadrant. Insert four rods of equal length, one in each hole: these indicate the direction of the forces of affinity Fix four balls of different colours to the free ends of the rods, and you have a representation of an asymmetrical carbon atom. According to the sequence of the coloured balls, the groups will be either identical or symmetrical, i e. the reflected image of each other

fact that the position of the other atoms at one carbon atom is unsymmetrical with the dextrogyrate and at the other carbon atom unsymmetrical with the lævogyrate modification.

This second form cannot be split up into two active modifications. If the two asymmetric carbon atoms are united to different atoms and radicals, the effect of one is not, as a rule, counterbalanced by that of the other, and consequently all four modifications may be optically active, but in different degrees.

The number of possible isomerides increases with the number of asymmetrical atoms. A large number of isomerides can exist in the series of sugars, and the terpene derivatives.

§ 58. **Physical Isomerism, with Double Linking.**—When an asymmetric carbon atom loses one of the four atoms or radicals with which it is combined, and attaches itself to a neighbouring atom by a double linking, the optical activity of the compound is lost, but the possibility of physical isomerism still continues. Malic acid ($C_4H_6O_5$) affords one of the best known examples of this class. It loses water ($HO + H = H_2O$), forming the isomeric, fumaric, and maleic acids ($C_4H_4O_4$). The latter again loses water, yielding the anhydride $C_4H_2O_3$, but fumaric acid does not form an anhydride. There is only one formula[1] for the two acids in the system in general use, viz.

$$HO-CO-CH-CH_2-CO-OH$$
$$|$$
$$OH \quad \text{Malic Acid}$$

$$HO-CO-CH=CH-CO-OH$$
$$\text{Fumaric and Maleic Acids}$$

But if we take into consideration the arrangement of atoms in space, then we can have two different formulæ,

$$\begin{array}{cc} H \quad H & H \quad CO-OH \\ \diagdown C = C \diagdown & \diagdown C = C \diagdown \\ HO-CO \quad CO-OH & HO-CO \quad H \\ \text{Maleic Acid} & \text{Fumaric Acid} \end{array}$$

---

[1] The only other formula, $HO-CO-C(=)-CH_2-CO-OH$, cannot be correct, as fumaric and maleic acid unite with Br_2, forming one and the same dibromosuccinic acid, $HO-CO-CHBr-CHBr-CO-OH$.

which Van t' Hoff and Wislicenus have shown are perfectly capable of explaining the difference in the behaviour of the two acids.

It is obvious that the first formula represents maleic acid, as the proximity of the carboxyl groups —CO—OH facilitates the formation of an anhydride.

$$\begin{matrix} H & & H \\ \diagdown & & \diagup \\ & C{:}C & \\ \diagup & & \diagdown \\ CO{-}O\;\boxed{H\;\;HO}{-}CO & & \end{matrix} \;=\; \begin{matrix} H & & H \\ \diagdown & & \diagup \\ & C{:}C & \\ \diagup & & \diagdown \\ CO{-}O{-}CO & & \end{matrix} \;+H_2O$$

In fumaric acid the carboxyl groups are diametrically opposite each other.

Both acids combine with the elements of water, forming inactive malic acid, which can be split up into two optically active isomerides. The addition of the elements of water takes place in each of the two possible ways.

The introduction of the idea of a difference in the arrangement of the atoms in space into the constitutional formulæ of organic compounds has provided a satisfactory explanation for numerous cases of isomerism which could not be formerly accounted for. It has also led to the discovery of numerous relations between the arrangement of the atoms and the properties of compounds. The hypothesis of asymmetrically linked carbon atoms was first propounded in 1874, and it now ranks as one of the most firmly established of the doctrines of chemistry.

§ 59. **The Absolute Dimensions of Molecules and Atoms.**—The molecules, the constitution of which has been discussed in the preceding paragraphs, are not indefinitely small, although much smaller than any magnitude perceptible to our unaided or even to the aided senses. As to the magnitude of the molecules themselves, it is at present impossible to give any exact determinations; still the limits within which the dimensions must lie can be approximately determined. Such approximations may, as was shown by Sir William Thomson in 1871, be arrived at by the aid of various physical phenomena; his conclusions have been confirmed and extended by other investigators. From certain optical phenomena, for instance, from the dispersion accompanying the refraction of light, it may be concluded, with some degree of probability, that the molecules of transparent materials, such as glass, water, and the like, are greater than the ten-thousandth part of a wave-length of light, which latter amounts again to only a few ten-thousandth parts of a millimetre Similar conclusions may be drawn also from the destruction of colouring matters on solution, and again from the contact electricity of metals, and the heat produced by the attraction of metallic plates oppositely electrified, from the minimum thickness which soap bubbles can attain without bursting, and especially from the properties of gases and the liquids produced by their condensation

The highly developed kinetic theory of gases shows, for instance, that certain relationships exist between the dimensions of gaseous particles, their velocity, and the path which they traverse before they come in contact with one another. From these relationships approximations may be made as to the weight and the mass of the molecules, and at the same time also of the atoms.

All these investigations have proved with approximate agreement that the diameters of the molecules of different substances are smaller than the ten-millionth part of a millimetre, but at the same time not indefinitely smaller than this.

These approximations agree fairly well with the determination of the weights of the atoms mentioned in § 21, which also show that certain limits exist within which the value of these extremely small quantities must lie.

§ 60 **Aggregation of the Molecules.**—The particles of matter of which we are cognisant by our senses are produced by the heaping together of the molecules. These, according to the foregoing, must exist in enormous numbers, even in the smallest visible and ponderable mass.

The mode of aggregation of these molecules must vary, and these differences will give rise to the different states of matter. In the solid condition the particles are held together in an unalterable position; in the liquid state they are so held that the particles move easily among one another in such a manner that no two particles remain neighbours for any length of time. Between these two conditions, forming as it were the passage between the extremes, we have the soft, plastic, and viscous states of matter in which the particles may move with greater or less difficulty, under the influence of the force of gravity or pressure, without destroying the continuity of the whole mass.

In the gaseous state the attraction of the particles for one another ceases, so that these separate particles move away into space unless they are prevented from doing so by impassable boundaries.

§ 61. **The Effect of Heat**—In no one of these conditions can we assume that the particles are in a state of absolute rest; we must rather imagine that in each one the particles possess a certain motion, which is perceptible to us as heat, and this movement becomes the more active the greater the amount of heat the bodies take up. The form of this motion is not fully understood; still in the solid state each particle can only move round a certain fixed position of equilibrium, this motion being either vibratory or rotatory.

In liquids the particles must be imagined as moving over one another, so that they leave no spaces between them, whereas in the gaseous or vaporous condition the particles are so far separated from one another that they move into space along rectilinear paths until they come in contact with some hindrance. by which they are diverted from their path. A consequence of an accelerated motion of the particles is to be found in the expansion of bodies by heat, because more space is required for these extended movements.

It is, however, a remarkable fact that in the passage from one state of aggregation to another bodies take up the heat which disappears as such, so that it is no longer recognised by the senses or by the thermometer. This so-called latent heat serves, doubtless in a great part, to produce those movements of the particles which are characteristic of the new condition; in part, perhaps, also to overcome the forces of attraction between the particles, assuming such forces to exist

The expansion exhibited by the majority of substances in melting may also be attributed to the increase of these external movements

In addition to the motion of the molecules we must also assume that the atoms constituting these molecules are likewise in a state of motion, and this again would be altered by the application of heat. In monatomic molecules, consisting only of one atom, as, for instance, in the case of the molecule of gaseous mercury, which has been proved to be monatomic by Kundt and Warburg, such atomic movements will not occur.

§ 62. **Homogeneous Solid Bodies.**—When similar molecules collect together to form a solid aggregate, a solid body is produced, which will have a structure determined entirely by the relative position of the particles. In the formless, or amorphous, condition the arrangement of the particles would be similar in each direction throughout the mass of the body, whilst in the case of crystals in certain directions it would be found to be different from others, and these differences are shown not only in the relation of the external boundaries of the crystals by plane surfaces, but also in any piece of crystal taken from any part of the interior. These differences are shown in the solidity, the hardness, the cleavage of the crystals in certain directions, the expansion by heat, the conduction of heat, the velocity and refraction of light, the colour of the same, and in some cases also in certain peculiar electrical phenomena produced by heating or cooling. Such differences can only find their explanation in a different arrangement of the molecules. We may assume that the molecules are brought nearer together in one direction than they are in another; but the reason for such an arrangement of the molecules must be sought for in the molecules themselves; so we must assume that in these, certain directions are different from others, and that the particles arrange themselves near one another, so that the directions or axes are parallel in all or are otherwise regularly arranged.

All possible regularities with regard to the disposition of points in space have been geometrically investigated by Leonard Sohncke, and their relations to the different systems of crystals established. The greater the symmetry of the distribution of such points, the simpler is the crystal system; and in full accord with this it is found that substances of the simplest composition, as, for instance, the elements and the compounds composed of a few atoms, form, as a rule, crystals belonging to the regular and hexagonal systems; whereas molecules composed of many atoms—for instance, the majority of organic compounds—yield aggregates which in a few cases crystallise with little or no evidence of symmetry. In amorphous substances the particles must be imagined as arranged irregularly, for this is the only way in which the particles could be arranged so that in any finite mass all sections would be the same. In many of their properties, e.g. behaviour with polarised light, amorphous bodies resemble the substances crystallising in the regular system; but this is not the case for other properties, such as cohesion, hardness, and cleavage.

§ 63. **Heterogeneous Solid Molecular Aggregates.**—A solid body may also be produced by the grouping together of different kinds of molecules. Many substances crystallise with water of crystallisation; still these compounds would appear rather to be homogeneous aggregates, for every molecule is united with a definite number of molecules of water, and the molecules so produced are regularly grouped into new and larger ones. A few only of the compounds containing water crystallise in the regular system · as, for instance, the alums, the twenty-four molecules of water being so arranged around the salt molecule as to produce an aggregate homogeneous in all directions. The so-called double salts are similarly constituted to the compounds containing water of crystallisation, and these must be reckoned amongst the homogeneous aggregates, and also all other combinations produced in accordance with the laws of stœchiometry.

The mixed crystals of isomorphous bodies in which the constituents occur in varying and changing proportions must, on the other hand, be considered as heterogeneous aggregates. Thus, for example, the so-called vitriols, that is, the sulphates of magnesium, copper, zinc, iron, manganese, nickel, and cobalt, crystallising with water of crystallisation, may be crystallised together in any proportions, which is true also of other isomorphous substances. This crystallisation together takes place only when the compounds are of analogous constitution, and when the isomorphous constituent is able to take up approximately the same space. If this condition is not exactly satisfied, then an angle of the crystal of one substance would be altered to a greater or less extent by the entrance into that crystal of another body. For instance, calcspar ($CaCO_3$) crystallises in rhombohedra, the angle being 105° 5', whereas magnesite ($MgCO_3$) crystallises in the same form, the angle of which is 107° 25'. When both crystallise together in the form of dolomite the angle is 106° 15'. This difference in angle of these crystals arises from the fact that the quantity of calcium carbonate represented by its formula occupies a greater space than the quantity of magnesium carbonate represented by its formula, and the increase of volume in consequence of this results in an extension of the crystal along its chief axis.

The expansion of the crystal by heat takes place chiefly in this same direction, and brings about also a reduction of the terminal angle of the crystal.

In addition to these mixed crystals there are also amorphous heterogeneous aggregates, which are produced by the solidification of a mixture in a molten state.

§. 64. **Density of Solid Bodies.**—Great variations are exhibited by the densities of solid bodies; substances are known, *e.g.* certain metals, which are forty times as heavy as the lightest known solid, and more than twenty times as heavy as an equal bulk of water, with which liquid solids are usually compared. The apparent irregularities observed in the densities of various solids to a large extent disappear and certain regularities become apparent when in the case of compounds the volumes occupied by their molecular weights or the stœchiometric quantities represented by their formulæ are considered, as has already been done in the case of the elements in § 36. Investigations of this kind have been carried out by H. Kopp, H. Schroeder, and others.

The inexactitude of the determinations, and also the doubts as to the temperature at which the determination should be made, have combined to retard the realisation of the laws to which these quantities are doubtless subservient

The simplest way of looking at this problem is to compare the space occupied by a compound with that filled by the constituent elements in the free state. When this is done it is found, as a rule, that the volume of the compound is approximately equal to the sum of the volumes of the constituent elements.

According to the table in § 36, the volumes of zinc and sulphur are—

$$V (Zn) + V (S) = 9\cdot1 + 15\cdot7 = 24\cdot8.$$

The volume of the compound zinc sulphide formed by the union of these elements is obtained by dividing the stœchiometric quantity ZnS by the density of zinc sulphide (blende), thus:—

$$V(ZnS) = \frac{Zn + S}{d} = \frac{65·1 + 31·98}{4·05} = \frac{97·1}{4·05} = 24·0.$$

Thus it is seen that the volume of the compound is approximately equal to that of the sum of the constituents. Other monosulphides show the same relation, as is exhibited in the following table, in which under the sign Σ the sum of the volumes of the constituents are given for the sake of comparison:—

		Σ	Difference	V(S) calculated
$V(MnS) = \frac{86·8}{4·0}$	= 21·7	22·6	−0·9	14·8
$V(FeS) = \frac{87·9}{4·8}$	= 18·3	22·9	−3·6	11·1
$V(NiS) = \frac{90·6}{4·6}$	= 19·7	22·4	−2·7	13·0
$V(CuS) = \frac{95·2}{4·16}$	= 22·9	22·8	+0·1	14·8
$V(ZnS) = \frac{97·1}{4·05}$	= 24	24·8	−0·8	14·9
$V(CdS) = \frac{143·7}{4·8}$	= 29·9	28·6	+1·3	17·0
$V(HgS) = \frac{231·8}{8·0}$	= 29·0	29·8	−0·8	14·9
$V(SnS) = \frac{150·8}{5·0}$	= 30·2	32·1	−1·9	13·8
$V(PbS) = \frac{238·4}{7·5}$	= 31·8	33·8	−2·0	13·7
			Mean	14·2

The agreement exhibited here is satisfactory, considering the difficulties surrounding the exact determination of the density. Consequently, no very great error would be made if the volumes of sulphur were calculated by subtracting from the volume of each sulphide the volume of the metal contained in it, thus :—

$$V (ZnS) - V (Zn) = 24·0 - 9·1 = 14·9 = V (S)$$

In this manner the values under the heading V (S) in the above table have been obtained. The mean of these is 14·2 instead of 15·7. This difference appears to indicate that the combination is attended by a slight contraction.

The marked analogy exhibited by the elements sulphur and oxygen is sufficient to justify a calculation in a similar manner of the atomic volume of solid oxygen from the molecular volumes of the oxides If this be done the following values are obtained, which agree fairly well with one another. In the following table in the first column are placed the stœchiometric values; under d in the second the density; under V in the third the volume of the oxide is given, and in the fourth under V (R) the volume of the metal; finally under V (O) the volume of oxygen, which is the difference between the two preceding sets of numbers.

	d	V	V (R)	V (O)
MnO = 70 8	5·4	13·1	6 9	6·2
CoO = 74·6	5 75	12 4	6·9	6 0
NiO = 74·6	6·4	11 7	6·7	5·0
CuO = 79·17	6·4	12·4	7·1	5·3
ZnO = 81·1	5·7	14·3	9·1	5·2
CdO = 127 7	6 95	18 3	12 9	5·4
SnO = 134 8	6 3	21·4	16 4	5·0
HgO = 215·8	11·3	19·1	14·1	5·0
PbO = 222·4	9 4	23 7	18·1	5 6

Similar values may be obtained from the so-called sesquioxides R_2O_3.

	d	V	V (R_2)	V (O_3)	V (O)
Cr_2O_3 = 152 8	5 2	29·0	15·4	13·6	4·5
Mn_2O_3 = 157·5	4·8	32·7	13 8	18·9	6·3
Fe_2O_3 = 159 6	5 3	30·1	14·4	15·7	5·2
Co_2O_3 = 165 1	5·6	29 5	13·8	15·7	5·2
Ni_2O_3 = 165·1	4·9	33·7	13·4	20 3	6·8

These results show the space filled by the three atoms of oxygen to be nearly three times that occupied by one atom in the first series of oxides.

The values obtained for the atomic volume of oxygen are not always identical with those given in the above tables; thus, in the case of the oxides of the composition R_2O, e.g Ag_2O, Cu_2O, Hg_2O, the space filled by the oxygen is much greater, whilst it is much smaller in the oxides RO_2; such as SnO_2 and SbO_2, e.g.

$$V(Cu_2O) - V(Cu_2) = 24\cdot4 - 14\cdot2 = 10\cdot7 = V(O)$$
$$V(SnO_2) - V(Sn) = 21\cdot7 - 16\cdot3 = 5\cdot4 = V(O_2)$$

In cuprous oxide the atom of oxygen would appear to occupy twice the space occupied by it in cupric oxide. In stannic oxide, on the other hand, the volume is only half as great. In the case of the compounds of the lighter metals still more remarkable relationships obtain. The production of the majority of these compounds is apparently attended by a considerable contraction; so much so indeed is this the case that the volume of the compound is smaller than that of the constituent metal; thus, for example:—

$$V(Na_2O) = 22\cdot1, \; V(Na_2) = 47\cdot4$$
$$V(K_2O) = 35\cdot5, \; V(K_2) = 90\cdot4$$
$$V(MgO) = 12\cdot5, \; V(Mg) = 13\cdot9$$

It is needless to remark that in these and similar cases the method of interpretation employed in the case of the oxides cannot be used. Still some regularities amongst these compounds do become evident when a comparison is instituted between the volumes of analogous compounds of elements belonging to the same natural family or elements following one another in the periodic system. Still such relationships, despite the energy expended in their investigation, are at the present time but ill understood.

Of necessity the space filled by a solid body is not constant. Alterations in pressure, and more especially of temperature, affect this to a greater or less degree. When heat is applied to a solid body the volume increases. The expansion in the case of crystalline solids, save those crystallising in the regular system, is different in different directions; in fact, it appears probable that an expansion in one direction is accompanied by a contraction in another.

§ 65. **Fusion and Solidification.**—When heat is applied to a solid body, provided no chemical change is produced, then sooner or later the coherence of the particles is so far reduced that the solid melts; the individual particles are then able to move freely around one another, but still their coherence has not been completely overcome.

In many instances other changes of solidity precede the liquefaction, whilst in others, as soon as a definite temperature, the melting point, is attained the solids suddenly and completely liquefy. Others again soften or become pasty before melting, passing, in fact, through a state intermediate between the solid and the liquid. In this plastic condition particles can be welded together by pressure, as is the case with metals like iron and platinum. Some metals and some of the semi-metals, such as zinc, bismuth, and tellurium, before melting become brittle at a certain temperature, whilst at other temperatures they are malleable and ductile, and can then be either rolled into sheets or drawn into wire.

The change in the state of aggregation is associated with a greater or lesser absorption of heat. When the temperature of a solid is very much below its melting point, a definite amount of heat is required to produce a certain rise in temperature for each part by weight of the substance, and this is approximately the same for every degree of temperature. This amount of heat so required is styled 'the specific heat.' When the body begins to soften under the application of heat, the amount of heat required to produce a given rise in temperature increases more and more, until when the body melts the amount of heat absorbed is considerable, and is no longer perceptible as such, becoming, in fact, latent heat. The heat so absorbed serves in all probability to give an accelerated motion to the particles, and being thus converted into motion is no longer perceptible as heat. The fusion proceeds only in proportion as the heat is applied, and as this serves only for melting, the temperature remains stationary until the whole mass is fused. On the other hand, when a molten mass gives up the heat to surrounding objects its temperature is not necessarily lowered below the melting point, for the part solidifying will give out its latent heat of fusion. Nor is it until the whole has solidified that the temperature begins to sink. A molten body may, however, be frequently cooled below its melting point without solidifying. In this state of superfusion the particles are in a condition of unstable equilibrium, such that the slightest change suffices to bring about solidification. This solidification is more easily produced by contact with the minutest fraction of the solid itself. At the moment of solidification the temperature rises to that of the melting point but no further: this rise in temperature is produced by the liberation of the latent heat. This acceleration in the rate of motion of the particles, corresponds to considerable increase in volume, which, as a rule, appears to take place suddenly on fusion or in part during the softening, this increase amounting in some cases to 12 or more per cent. of the volume of the solid Yet in the case of some substances, especially water, cast iron, bismuth, and some of its compounds and alloys, and perhaps also in the case of other metals, contraction is known to attend the fusion, which can perhaps be explained as arising from an altered arrangement of the atoms in the molecules. In water this contraction amounts to nearly 10 per cent. of the volume. The change in the state of aggregation produced by pressure depends upon whether fusion be attended by an expansion or contraction, and in such a way that by sufficiently great pressure that condition is produced in which the material fills the smallest space. Ice can be liquefied by pressure, whilst by its aid the majority of other solid substances can be retained in the solid state at temperatures much above their melting points.

§ 66. **Melting Points of the Elements** —The temperatures at which different substances melt are specific and characteristic for each, and serve, therefore, as important aids for their identification. In § 36 it has already been mentioned that the fusibility of the elements is a periodic function of their atomic weights. This relationship, so far as it has been in any way ascertained, is exhibited in the following table. The melting points of many elements are still unknown, because the temperature at which they melt is either too high or too low to be accurately determined; in some other cases the rarity of the element or the difficulties surrounding its isolation have prevented the exact determination. In the following table the abbreviations used are: a = approximation, b = above, c = very low, d = very high, e = not melted, rh = red heat, drh = dull red heat, brh = bright red heat, wh = white heat.

MELTING POINTS OF THE ELEMENTS

I	II	III	IV	V	VI	VII	VIII
Li	Be	B	C	N	O	F	
180°	brh	d	e	c	c	c	
Na	Mg	Al	Si	P	S	Cl	
96°	a 430°	a 700°	a 1500°	*44°*	114°	*−105°*	
K	Ca	Sc	Ti	V	Cr	Mn	Fe Co Ni
63°	drh	?	c	e	d	wh	a1600° a1500° a1450°
Cu	Zn	Ga	Ge	As	Se	Br	
1054°	433°	30°	a 900°	a 500°	a 680°	*−7°*	
Rb	Sr	Y	Zr	Nb	Mo	?	Ru Rh Pd
39°	drh	?	a 1500°	d	d	?	a 2000° a1800° a1500°
Ag	Cd	In	Sn	Sb	Te	I	
954°	321°	*176°*	233°	423°	455°	114°	
Cs	Ba	La	Ce	Ta	W	?	Os Ir Pt
26°	drh	a 800°	a 800°	d	d	?	a2500° a1950° a1775°
Au	Hg	Tl	Pb	Bi			
1045°	*−39°*	294°	326°	268°			
			Th		U		
			d		brh		

The elements are arranged in the horizontal lines in the order of their atomic weights. With these the melting point rises suddenly and falls suddenly; the minima of the melting points are printed in italics, the maxima in block print.

The periods of fusibility do not coincide with those of other physical properties—in fact, are less regular than these, but are nearly related, as has already been shown in § 36, to those of the atomic volumes.

It is remarkable that in every family the members of one group are difficultly fusible, whilst those of the other are easily fusible; *e.g.* lithium, sodium, potassium, rubidium, cæsium are easily fusible, whilst copper, silver, and gold melt at high temperatures, and similar relationships are found to exist in other families. In separate groups the melting point changes with the atomic weight, but not in the same manner. In some families the melting point falls with increase in atomic weight, thus:—

Li 180°, Na 96°, K 63°, Rb 39°, Cs 26°,
Zn 433°, Cd 321°, Hg − 39°;

in others, again, it rises with increase in atomic weight; for example:—

Ga 30°, In 176°, Tl 294°,
Cl −105°, Br −7°, I + 114°;

whilst in some families it rises at first to fall again, or falls first and then rises.

§ 67. **Melting Points of Compounds.**—In the melting points of compounds we have similar differences to those exhibited by the elements. By the introduction into a compound of certain elements the fusibility is in some cases raised, in other cases lowered. The oxides of metals, e.g., are much more difficultly fusible than the metals themselves; the majority of the oxides of the non-metals are more easily fusible than the elements; in one and the same group of elements these changes are, as a rule, found to be of the same character, but even in this case also there are exceptions. Whilst, for example, the infusible element carbon yields an oxide (CO_2) which melts at −60°, the corresponding oxide (SiO_2) of the difficultly fusible silicon is almost as difficultly fusible as the element itself. Fluorides, chlorides, bromides, iodides, melt, as a rule, much more easily than the oxides, and usually the iodide of an element is more easily fusible than the bromide, and this than the chloride, whilst the fluoride has the highest melting point. Thus, for example, the melting points of halogen compounds of the alkali metals are, according to Carnelley, as follows:—

—	Li	Na	K	Rb	Cs
F	801°	902°	789°	753°	?
Cl	598°	722°	734°	710°	631°
Br	547°	708°	699°	683°	?
I	466°	628°	634°	642°	?

The melting point falls, therefore, with increased atomic weight of the halogen, and similar relationships are to be found in other families of the elements.

Many similar regularities are to be found amongst organic compounds; still our knowledge of the general laws in this province is much less extensive than might be imagined from the thousands of melting-point determinations which have been made.

It is, however, to be observed that in many cases the repeated introduction of a given atom or a group of atoms in an organic compound is accompanied by alternate raising and lowering of fusibility. This is the case, as was first shown by Baeyer, in the normal primary fatty acids of the general formula $C_nH_{2n}O_2$. In these compounds the atom linkage is represented as follows:

$$HO-CO-CH_2- \quad \ldots \quad CH_2-CH_2-H$$

in accordance with which, the several members of the series differ from one another only in the number of CH_2 groups introduced between the carboxyl group, COOH, and hydrogen. The relationships are shown in the following table:—

Name	Formula	Melting Point	
Formic Acid	CH_2O_2		$+8°·4$
Acetic Acid	$C_2H_4O_2$	$+17°$	
Propionic Acid	$C_3H_6O_2$		$-24°$
Butyric Acid	$C_4H_8O_2$	$+1°$	
Valerianic Acid	$C_5H_{10}O_2$		below $-16°$
Caproic Acid	$C_6H_{12}O_2$	$-2°$	
Heptylic Acid	$C_7H_{14}O_2$		$-10°·5$
Caprylic Acid	$C_8H_{16}O_2$	$+16°·5$	
Pelargonic Acid	$C_9H_{18}O_2$		$+12°·5$
Capric Acid	$C_{10}H_{20}O_2$	$+30°$	
Undecylic Acid	$C_{11}H_{22}O_2$		$+28°·5$
Lauric Acid	$C_{12}H_{24}O_2$	$+43°·6$	
Tridecylic Acid	$C_{13}H_{26}O_2$		$+40°·5$
Myristic Acid	$C_{14}H_{28}O_2$	$+58°·8$	
Quindecylic Acid	$C_{15}H_{30}O_2$		$+51°$
Palmitic Acid	$C_{16}H_{32}O_2$	$+62°$	
Margaric Acid	$C_{17}H_{34}O_2$		$+60°$
Stearic Acid	$C_{18}H_{36}O_2$	$+69°$	
—	$C_{19}H_{38}O_2$		?
Arachic Acid	$C_{20}H_{40}O_2$	$+75°$	
Medullinic Acid	$C_{21}H_{42}O_2$		$72°·5$
Behenic Acid	$C_{22}H_{44}O_2$	$+73°$	

From the above it is seen that the first introduction of the group

CH₂ between the carboxyl and hydrogen raises the melting point, whereas the introduction of the second group lowers the melting point; consequently those members in this series of acids' which contain an uneven number of carbon atoms melt at a lower temperature than either of their neighbours containing an even number of carbon atoms. As the molecular weight increases this difference gradually disappears. The melting point of the dibasic acids of the formula,

$$C_nH_{2n-2}O_4 = HO-CO-(CH_2)_m CO-OH,$$

consisting of oxalic, malonic, and succinic acids, &c., exhibit similar relationships.

The melting points of many hydro-carbons, e.g. of benzene, as shown by Jungfleisch, is alternately raised and lowered by the replacement of the hydrogen by chlorine.

—	Melting Points	
C_6H_6	+3°	
C_6H_5Cl		−40°
$C_6H_4Cl_2$	+53°	
$C_6H_3Cl_3$		+17°
$C_6H_2Cl_4$	+139°	
C_6HCl_5		+86°
C_6Cl_6	+228°	

Still, it is only when the chief products of the action of chlorine upon benzene are compared with one another that such regularities are observed. In addition to these, several isomeric compounds are formed, but in much smaller quantities, and these again have different melting points. In fact, it is found that the melting point of a compound is influenced by the positions which the chlorine atoms occupy relatively to one another

As a general rule, it may be stated that of the three isomeric di-substitution products which may be obtained by replacing two atoms of hydrogen in benzene by two other atoms or radicals, the para- compound has a melting point much higher than the ortho- and the meta-. Which of the latter has the higher melting point depends upon the nature of the atom or radical replacing the hydrogen. If one of these is the carboxyl group, COOH, then the meta- compound has a higher melting point than the ortho-, otherwise the ortho- compound will melt at the higher temperature. Still these rules are not without exceptions; in the presence of the nitro- group, NO_2, it sometimes happens that the ortho- is more easily fusible than the meta-, and in some cases the reverse obtains. The following examples will serve to illustrate these points:—

—	—	—	Para-	Meta-	Ortho-
C_6H_4	Cl	Cl	53°	under −15°	below −14°
,,	Br	Br	89°	−28°	−1°
,,	I	I	127°	40°	94°
,,	Cl	I	56°	?	liquid
,,	Cl	Br	67°	liquid	?
,,	Br	I	92°	liquid	liquid
,,	OH	OH	172°	99°	112°
,,	NH_2	NH_2	140°	63°	99°
,,	,,	Br	64°	18°	31°
,,	,,	I	60°	25°	?
,,	CH_3	CH_3	15°	−54°	−28°
,,	COOH	OH	210°	200°	156°
,,	,,	OCH_3	175°	106°	99°
,,	,,	Cl	234°	152°	137°
,,	,,	Br	250°	155°	148°
,,	,,	I	267°	185°	159°
,,	,,	NH_2	187°	174°	144°
,,	NO_2	NO_2	171°	90°	118°
,,	,,	I	171°	36°	49°
,,	,,	Cl	83°	44°	32°
,,	,,	Br	126°	56°	42°
,,	,,	NH_2	146°	110°	71°

When a third atom of hydrogen in benzene is replaced, then the melting point is altered still more; as a rule, the melting point of a para- compound is lowered, and indeed often very considerably; whilst those of the other isomeric di-substitution products are raised. Still, even in this case the change in the melting point is determined, not only by the nature of the replacing radical, but also by their relative positions. In the most symmetrical arrangements of these several groups in the position 1 . 3 . 5 (*vide* § 54) the melting point is found to attain the maximum.

§ 68. **Melting Points of Mixtures.**—Heterogeneous solid bodies melt either in such a way that only one portion is liquefied, whilst the other remains solid or all the several constituents become liquid simultaneously. In the last case the fusion always takes place at a fixed temperature, which may be below the melting point of the most difficultly fusible constituent, and is frequently found to be lower than the melting point of the most easily fusible component. In this we have an explanation of the observations so frequently made in laboratory practice that even very small impurities suffice to effect a considerable reduction in the melting point of a substance. Such a mixture can frequently be distinguished from a pure homogeneous substance by the fact that the temperature does not remain stationary during the fusion. As a rule, the constituent with a lower melting point melts first, and with it only a part of the higher melting constituent, the remainder of the latter continuing in the solid state, and not melting until a higher temperature has been reached. If one were to separate the liquid portion from the solid before this had occurred, then each portion when separately examined would be found to possess a higher melting point, because it contains a smaller portion of impurity. An excellent method for the purification of solids is based upon this difference.

§ 69. **Homogeneous Liquids, Cohesion, Capillarity, Friction.** As has already been pointed out in § 60, the liquid state of aggregation is distinguished by the fact that the particles, although held together, can move easily over one another. In consequence of this, liquids under the influence of the force of gravity assume the form of the vessel containing them; whilst the surface assumes a direction perpendicular to the line of the action of gravity, provided that other forces—*e.g.* the centrifugal force—do not tend to change this position. The space occupied by a liquid can only be reduced to a very small extent by great pressure; liquids are therefore only slightly compressible fluids.

The mobility of the particles is very different in different liquids. On the one hand we have liquids possessing a so-called syrupy consistence; on the other hand, those possessing a mobility approaching very nearly to that characteristic of gases. The resistance which they offer to movement is what is usually styled the internal friction or the viscosity of the liquids. This property may be determined from the velocity with which the liquid flows through a narrow tube (transpiration according to Graham), or by the retardation, which a body rotating round its axis, experiences when set in motion in such liquids. The friction is dependent upon the nature and the composition of the liquid; still, too little is known of the connection between these properties to allow of any general statement being made

Nor is our knowledge of the manner in which the particles of a liquid are held together in a much more advanced state, the cohesion of liquids, which is especially exhibited in the phenomena of capillarity, *i.e.* the manner in which liquids rise in very narrow tubes, the walls of which are moistened by them, and is likewise shown in the formation of drops. The weight or volume of the liquid raised by capillarity is dependent upon the chemical nature and composition of the liquid; still, of this inter-dependence so little is known that it would not be advisable to discuss it further.

§ 70. **Density of Liquids** —The subject of the density or the specific gravity of liquids, *i.e.* the weight of a unit volume, is one which has been exhaustively investigated. Usually, however, it is not the density, but rather its reciprocal, the so-called specific volume—that is, the volume of the unit of weight—which is dealt with in these investigations. The product of these values into the atomic weights of elements and into the molecular weights of compounds gives the atomic and molecular volumes. Relationships have been recognised amongst these values similar to those found to obtain in the case of solids. As the majority of elements are only to be obtained in the liquid state, at either inconveniently low or high temperatures, their atomic volumes in the liquid state have been but little studied.

Inasmuch as for an equal rise in temperature liquids expand much more easily than solids, it is of much importance in the case of liquids that comparisons should be instituted at corresponding temperatures. Hermann Kopp proposed that this comparison should in the case of liquids be made at a temperature at which their vapour pressures are the same, viz. at the boiling point under the same pressure. The pressure usually taken as normal is the mean atmospheric pressure, viz. 760 millimetres, although in the light of the more recent investigations it would appear more desirable to choose a much smaller pressure. But even the molecular volumes of compounds compared at their boiling points under the atmospheric pressure, more especially those of organic compounds, exhibit numerous relationships, which, although they cannot be regarded as fixed natural laws, may at any rate be taken to represent approximations to such laws

The fundamental law of atomic volumes is that every atom in a compound at its boiling point occupies a given space which is chiefly determined by its nature, and only to a limited extent by the manner in which it is combined; so that the volumes occupied by the molecular weights of different compounds may be taken to be represented by the sum of the volumes of all the atoms contained in them.

Thus if V be this volume, then in the case of alcohol we have the following:—

$$V(C_2H_6O) = 2V(C) + 6V(H) + 1V(O);$$

and similarly in other compounds

The unit of volume in this case is the space which the unit weight of water at its maximum density occupies, and the unit of weight the weight of an atom of hydrogen. The value of this latter unit is unknown, but that does not signify, as in this case it is, as in all determinations of density, only a question of relative values. In fact, the same values for the molecular volumes are obtained if, instead of an atom, one gramme of hydrogen is taken as the unit of weight and one cubic centimetre as the unit of volume.

Expressed in these terms, according to Kopp's determinations, the volumes of the atoms of the following elements in their compounds at their boiling points would be approximately the following:—

$$V(H) = 5\cdot 5, \ V(C) = 11, \ V(O) = 7\cdot 8.$$

Accordingly in the case of alcohol, already cited, the following value must be obtained:—

$$2V(C) + 6V(H) + 1V(O) = 22 + 33 + 7\cdot 8 = 62\cdot 8;$$

whilst the actual determination at the boiling point 78° C. shows the molecular volume of alcohol to be 62·2.

From Kopp's law it follows, then, that a fixed difference in the composition must always be associated with a similar difference in the molecular volumes; thus, for example, the difference CH_2 in a homologous series of compounds must give rise to a difference in volume. This difference in volume for every addition of CH_2 has been found to be 22; and similar differences will be found in other cases. The correspondence between the calculated and the observed values is, however, only approximate, thus, e.g., for the first five members of the series of alcohols $C_nH_{2n+2}O$ the following values have been obtained:—

n	V calculated	Difference	V observed	Difference
1	40·8		42·7	
2	62·8	22	62·2	19·5
3	84·8	22	81·3	19·1
4	106·8	22	101·6	20·3
5	128·8	22	122·7	21·1

The deviations from this fundamental rule may in many cases be attributed to differences in the mode of linkage of the atoms. Thus, for instance, two polyvalent atoms occupy less space when united to each other by single affinities than when two or more combining units are used for their mutual combination. Thus the following relations are found to hold :—

$$V(-O-C\equiv) < V(O=C=)$$
$$V(-S-C\equiv) < V(S=C=)$$
$$V(=N-C\equiv) < V(N\equiv C-)$$
$$V(\equiv C-C\equiv) < V(=C=C=) \text{ &c.}$$

This and similar relationships have been frequently used in the investigation of atomic linkage; still, it must be remembered that conclusions drawn from such observations are always more or less uncertain, as there are many deviations from this rule which cannot be explained as due to variations in the mode of union of the atoms. In the meantime investigations of this kind are being steadily carried on. It has, for instance, been shown that when an atom of chlorine or of bromine replaces an atom of hydrogen in organic compounds, the space occupied by the atom of the halogen element is dependent upon the position it occupies, being greater when attached to one atom than when combined with another. In the case of benzene substitution products, the radicals replacing hydrogen in this hydrocarbon have a greater volume when they occupy the para- position than in the meta-, and in the meta- position a greater volume than in the ortho- position. All such results are of great importance as contributing to our knowledge of the properties of matter.

§ 71. **Expansion by Heat.**—The volume of a liquid varies with the temperature, and as a rule the alterations produced by given changes of temperature are greater in the case of liquids than for solids. Usually the volume increases with rise in temperature, and this expansion becomes greater and greater as the temperature rises. It is only in the neighbourhood of the solidifying point that some liquids, notably water (§ 65), are found to contract in volume as their temperature is raised.

Van der Waals has theoretically deduced the law which controls the expansion of liquids by heat, and has demonstrated the truth of the law by a comparison of the deductions made from it with the results of observation. For such comparisons a knowledge of the critical temperature of a liquid is required, which still remains unknown for the majority of those liquids the coefficients of expansion of which have already been determined.

The expansion of a liquid is attended by a considerable absorption of heat, which with one and the same substance is, for an equal interval of temperature, greater when in the liquid state than when in the solid condition. The heat capacity or the specific heat of a given substance is greater in the liquid state than in the solid, often twice as great, and is even greater in the liquid than in the gaseous state.

By multiplying the specific heat into the molecular weight the so-called molecular heat is obtained, which in the case of homologous organic compounds changes with tolerable regularity.

§ 72. **Refraction of Light by Liquids.**—The refraction of light by liquids has been very completely investigated. It has been found to be dependent upon the nature and the amount of the elements contained in the liquids, as also upon the manner of their union with one another. This interdependence has been specially studied and demonstrated for the compounds of carbon, the organic compounds, and for many others also.

If n be taken to represent the refractive index of a liquid, and d its density, then it can be shown theoretically that the quotient [1]

---

[1] Until recently the simpler expression $\frac{n-1}{d}$ was employed to represent the specific refractive index, instead of the expression deduced by H. A Lorentz and L. Lorenz. The simpler expression, which was arrived at empirically, explains satisfactorily the majority of observed facts, but is not, according to Brühl, so satisfactory in some cases.

$$\frac{n^2-1}{(n^2+2)d},$$

which is known as the specific refractive power, is practically unaffected by temperature, a conclusion which has been substantiated by actual observation. With the aid of this expression one may, as has been shown by Gladstone and Dale, by Landolt and his pupils, represent the specific refractive power of a liquid as made up of the sum of the refractive powers of its constituents. If the weight P of the liquid contains p_1, p_2, p_3, &c. weights of the constituents, then the following relation will obtain, in which N and D represent the refractive index and density of the liquid, and n_1, n_2, n_3, d_1, d_2, and d_3 are the refractive indices and densities respectively of the constituents:—

$$\frac{N^2-1}{(N^2+2)D} \cdot P = \frac{n_1^2-1}{(n_1^2+2)d_1} \cdot p_1 + \frac{n_2^2-1}{(n_2^2+2)d_2} \cdot p_2 + \frac{n_3^2-1}{(n_3^2+2)d_3} \cdot p_3 + \ldots$$

Landolt's investigations have shown that this expression applies equally to mechanical mixtures as well as to chemical compounds.

If, therefore, P be the molecular weight, M, made up of x atoms of A_1, of y atoms of A_2, &c. then, since

$$P = M = xA_1 + yA_2 + zA_3 + \ldots$$

it follows that

$$\frac{N^2-1}{(N^2+2)D} \cdot M = x\frac{n_1^2-1}{(n_2^2+2)d_1} \cdot A_1 + y\frac{n_2^2-1}{(n_2^2+2)d_2} \cdot A_2 + z\frac{n_3^2-1}{(n_3^2+2)d_3} \cdot A_3 + \ldots$$

Or that the molecular refractive power or the molecular refraction of a compound is the sum of the refraction equivalents of its constituents. The refraction equivalent of the elements, which is here represented by the expression

$$\frac{n^2-1}{(n^2+2)d} \; A,$$

may, in the cases in which these values are known, be calculated from the refractive index n, the density d, and the atomic weight A. It is, however, more convenient to deduce these values from the observed molecular refraction of compounds, which differ in composition by a definite number of atoms of one or other of the elements. Calculations of this kind have been carried out in numerous instances, and are based upon data supplied by a very extensive series of observations.

Since light of different colours is refracted differently, the index of refraction, n, must vary with the colour; consequently observations made with light of different colours yield different refraction equivalents for one and the same substance. Inasmuch as up to the present no formula has been discovered which enables one to eliminate satisfactorily this influence of colour, the index of refraction is determined for light of a fixed colour. For instance, that corresponding to Fraunhofer's line C in the sun's spectrum is frequently used for this purpose, and this is identical with the red line in the hydrogen spark spectrum. For this coloured light Landolt found the following to represent the molecular refractions (Mrf) of the compounds in the two following tables, each of which consists of a series of compounds differing from one another by constant difference (CH_2):—

Name	Formula	Difference	Mrf	Difference
Water	H_2O		3·69	
Wood Spirit	CH_4O	CH_2	8·16	4·47
Ethyl Alcohol	C_2H_6O	CH_2	12·71	4·55
*Propyl ,,	C_3H_8O	CH_2	17·28	4·57
Butyl ,,	$C_4H_{10}O$	CH_2	21·96	4·68
Amyl ,,	$C_5H_{12}O$	CH_2	26·59	4·63

Mean 4·58

Name	Formula	Difference	Mrf	Difference
Formic Acid	CH_2O_2		8·52	
Acetic Acid	$C_2H_4O_2$	CH_2	12·93	4·41
Propionic Acid	$C_3H_6O_2$	CH_2	17·42	4·49
Butyric Acid	$C_4H_8O_2$	CH_2	22·01	4·59
Valerianic Acid	$C_5H_{10}O_2$	CH_2	26·72	4·71
Caproic Acid	$C_6H_{12}O_2$	CH_2	31·22	4·50
Œnanthic Acid	$C_7H_{14}O_2$	CH_2	35·85	4·63

Mean 4·56

A difference in composition of one atom of carbon and two atoms of hydrogen is seen from the above to produce a difference of 4·56 in the molecular refraction. Similarly, the effect on the molecular refraction may be determined for other differences in composition, and from such results the refraction equivalents of individual elements may be calculated The following represent the refraction equivalents of some of the commoner elements, for the Fraunhofer line C, or the line a in the hydrogen spectrum.

		Refraction Equivalent
Carbon	C	2 48
Hydrogen	H	1·04
Oxygen	O	1·58
Chlorine	Cl	6 02
Bromine	Br	18 95
Iodine	I	3·99
Nitrogen	N	8 02

By the aid of such numbers the molecular refraction of a compound like ethyl alcohol, for instance, may be calculated, thus:

$$C_2H_6O = 2 \times 2·48 + 6 \times 1 04 + 1 \times 1·58 = 12·78.$$

The observed refraction for ethyl alcohol is 12·71. Similarly, the molecular refractions of other compounds may be calculated.

§ 73. **Influence of Atom-linkage on Refraction.**—Such agreement between the observed and calculated results does not obtain in all cases; as, for instance, in the following we have

Aldehyde, C_2H_4O, Mrf $= 2 \times 2·48 + 4 \times 1 04 + 1 \times 1·58$
$= 10 70$ (observed 11·50).

Acetic acid, $C_2H_4O_2$, Mrf $= 2 \times 2 48 + 4 \times 1·04 + 2 \times 1·58$
$= 12 28$ (observed 12·93).

Valerianic acid, $C_5H_{10}O_2$, Mrf $= 5 \times 2·48 + 10 \times 1·04 + 2 \times 1 58$
$= 25 96$ (observed 26·72).

In each of these three instances the experimental values are greater than the calculated, and the difference is very nearly the same in each case, thus :—

$$11·50 - 10·7 = 0 8; \ 12 93 - 12 28 = 0 65;$$
$$26 72 - 25 96 = 0·76.$$

The molecular refractions of acids, aldehydes, ketones,

ethereal salts, and those compounds derived from them are found to be greater than the calculated values, and in these compounds it is assumed for several reasons that they contain an atom of oxygen united to an atom of carbon by both its affinities If it be assumed that the refraction equivalent of oxygen when so combined is 2 34, that is, 0·76 greater than its refraction equivalent in the alcohols and other similar compounds, then we obtain calculated results exhibiting a satisfactory agreement with the results of observation.

Investigations undertaken at the suggestion of Landolt by J. Bruhl have shown that the so-called unsaturated carbon compounds, viz. such compounds as combine directly with chlorine, bromine, or even hydrogen, possess a molecular refraction greater than those obtained by calculation. From the numerous cases investigated it is found that a satisfactory agreement between the calculated and observed results is obtained when to the calculated molecular refraction 1·79 is added, for every pair of carbon atoms united by double combining units, and 1·97 must be added for every pair of carbon atoms united by three combining units.

After these rules had been established chemists sought by their aid to determine the mode of atomic linkage in various organic compounds, and more especially to fix the number of the groups of carbon atoms united by two or three combining units. It has thus been shown to be extremely probable that in benzene, toluene, and analogous hydrocarbons there are three pairs of carbon atoms united by two combining units, as is required to satisfy Kekulé's constitutional formula (§ 51) :—

The molecular refraction of benzene and its derivatives has been found to be about five units greater than the sum, S, of the refraction equivalents of the elements contained in them, as will be seen from the following examples :—

		Molecular Refraction	Sum S	Difference
Benzene	C_6H_6	25·93	21·12	4·81 = 3 × 1·60
Toluene	C_7H_8	30·79	25·68	5·11 = 3 × 1·70
Mesitylene	C_9H_{12}	40·33	34·8	5·53 = 3 × 1·84
Phenol	C_6H_6O	27·85	22·70	5·05 = 3 × 1·68
Benzyl Alcohol	C_7H_8O	32·23	27·26	4·97 = 3 × 1·66

This and similar applications have combined to make the molecular refraction a very important aid in the investigation of the mode of linkage of the atoms in different compounds.

§ 74. **Interaction of Liquids with other Substances. Wetting and Imbibition.**—If a liquid be brought into contact with another liquid or with a solid body upon which it has no chemical action, the change resulting from this contact will depend upon the material composition of both, and determined by this, mixing, or dissolution, or mere contact will result. Liquids which do not mix with one another will arrange themselves in accordance with their specific gravities, liquids of equal densities forming spherical drops in the mass of the other.

If one of the immiscible substances is a liquid and the other a solid, then one of two sets of phenomena will be produced; either the liquid wets or moistens the solid, and in that case we have the phenomenon of capillary attraction and the liquid is raised in the solid, or the liquid does not wet the solid, then at the point of contact a depression of the liquid surface is produced. Thus, as is well known, water, spirits of wine, oils, and many other liquids rise on the surfaces of glass, whilst mercury is depressed by glass, just as the surface of water is depressed by contact with fat. In such cases the nature of the solid body is of importance only so far as it determines whether it is moistened or not by the liquid; in other respects the capillary ascent or depression is dependent upon the nature of the liquid alone.

There is a class of solids which possess the remarkable property of absorbing liquids, by which they are moistened, without dissolving in these same liquids.

This absorption of liquids is usually accompanied by a considerable increase in the volume of the solid, and is described as 'Gelatinisation' or 'Imbibition.' Cellulose, starch, glue, coagulated albumen, and many other substances swell up when brought into contact with water, and caoutchouc behaves similarly when moistened by ether. To those substances which exhibit this phenomenon is ascribed a large molecular weight and an atom-linkage of such a character that the atoms form a species of network into the spaces between which the smaller molecules of liquids are able to penetrate without destroying the network It is worthy of remark that frequently phenomena such as diffusion (§ 80) can proceed in the interior of the absorbed liquid as well as in that portion which has not been so taken up. This power of absorption is very different for different substances; whilst in many cases the volume of a solid is considerably increased during the process of imbibition, in some cases the increase is scarcely perceptible. We are acquainted with all the intermediate stages exhibited by this class of bodies, and by substances such as burnt clay, hydrophane, &c. which, possessing a visibly porous structure, take up liquids into their pores, which serve simply to wet the interior of the pores.

§ 75. **Heterogeneous Mixtures of Liquids. Solutions.**—Many substances are able to form fluid mixtures with other bodies. Such mixtures are usually styled 'solutions' or 'dissolutions,' one constituent being distinguished as the solvent, the other as the dissolved substance. Such distinctions are entirely arbitrary and have no scientific import

Fluid mixtures may be produced in the following ways :—
(1) By solid bodies alone.
(2) By solids and liquids.
(3) By liquids alone.
(4) By liquids and gaseous bodies.
(5) By gases alone.
(6) By gases and solids.

The states of aggregation of the constituents of such liquids only affect the nature and properties of the mixture so far as the constituents assume these conditions or states on separating out from the mixture. So long as they exist in the mixture, they must be regarded as liquids.

The quantities of the constituents in such a fluid mixture or solution are either quite unlimited, the mixing taking place indefinitely in any proportions, or the proportions are so limited that the admixture takes place only within certain limits, beyond which it is not possible to pass

The first of these cases is represented by liquids such as water and alcohol, ethyl alcohol and methyl alcohol, or water and glycerol, which mix with one another in every proportion.

In those cases in which such mixing or solution takes place only within certain limits the maximum amount of one of the substances which is taken up by a definite proportion of the other, say 100 or 1000 parts by weight of this substance, is styled the 'solubility' of the first in the second. When both substances are liquids, then the proportion of one of these may be raised from zero to a certain fixed limit, but this latter cannot be exceeded. If more than this amount be added, then it remains in the liquid state and separates from the rest; it can, on its part, however, take up some of the other constituent. According to Schuncke, water at 20° C can take up 0·075 of its weight of ether, whilst this latter may take up as much as 0·027 of its weight of water. Mixtures of ether and water, therefore, can only be obtained containing from 0 to 7 or from 97 to 100 parts by weight of ether in 100 parts of the mixture. Consequently at 20° C. mixtures of ether and water can only be produced containing less than 7 or more than 97 parts by weight of ether.

When one of the bodies is a liquid and the other a solid, then, whilst the proportion of the former may be raised indefinitely, that of the latter is fixed within a certain maximum limit, any excess above this amount remaining undissolved and generally in the solid state, though in some cases, as with phenol and water, in a fluid condition. Solutions which are incapable of dissolving any more of the solid are said to be 'saturated'

When both constituents are solids, but the mixture formed by them a liquid, then, as in the case of salt and ice, there is for both of the constituents of the solution an upper and lower limit; neither of these limits must be exceeded if the mixture is to remain liquid.

§ 76. **Effect of Heat on Solubility.**—The dissolution and also the solubility of different bodies are considerably affected by heat, the effects being analogous to those produced on simple unmixed substances. With such simple bodies an increase of volume is associated with an absorption of heat: a reduction in volume, with a loss of heat; so also, as a rule, in the admixture of liquids, a contraction is attended by an evolution of heat, which may be, and often is, considerable

The changes in aggregation associated with dissolution are also frequently accompanied by considerable thermal disturbances.

Just as when a solid body is melted, heat is rendered latent, so also there is a reduction in temperature attending the dissolution of a solid. The reduction in temperature is especially great when both the bodies passing into solution are solids. Thus, by mixing salt and ice in suitable proportions, the temperature of the mass can be lowered by 20° C. The heat so disappearing or becoming 'latent' is used in the conversion of the solid into the liquid state. Many substances first combine chemically with a portion of the solvent, and the compound so produced is then dissolved. Thus, for instance, anhydrous calcium chloride when brought into contact with water combines with the latter with production of heat to form the crystallisable compound $CaCl_2, 6H_2O$, which dissolves in water with a considerable absorption of heat. For the production of cold, therefore, hydrated, and not anhydrous, substances are best adapted.

The limits of solubility are extended by changes of temperature, and in the majority of cases a rise in temperature increases the solubility. Still there are exceptions to this rule, and more especially in the case of liquids. Thus, for example, ether is less soluble in warm water than in cold, and consequently a cold saturated solution of ether in water becomes turbid when heated, owing to the separation of ether from the water.

According to Alexejeff, in the case of aniline and water the mutual solubility of each is increased by rise in temperature. At low temperatures solutions can be obtained containing only but little water and very little aniline. As the temperature rises their solubility in each other increases, so that at 167° C. these substances may be mixed with each other in any proportion.

A reduction in the solubility with rise in temperature has been observed only in the case of a few solids, and in these cases the substances undergo a change in their chemical composition; as, for instance, they may lose their water of crystallisation or some other similar change may take place. The degree of solubility is, as a rule, very considerably increased by a rise in temperature; in some cases, however, the alteration is but slight.

In consequence of this marked increase of solubility, a hot saturated solution when cooled must deposit a portion of the dissolved substance. This as a matter of fact does take place, accompanied by an evolution of the latent heat, which had disappeared in the dissolution. In the separation of solids from their hot saturated solutions we have an excellent means for purifying many substances; for, when the solution is saturated with one substance and not with the impurity, then the first of these alone separates out, unless there are special conditions which may cause the deposition of the impurity.

§ 77. **Crystallisation Supersaturation.**—A hot saturated solution may, when suitably protected from external influences, retain on cooling an excess of the dissolved substance, just as a fused substance may, if carefully cooled below its melting point, still be maintained in the liquid state (§ 65). Such solutions are described as 'supersaturated,' just as simple substances are said to be 'superfused.' These states of supersaturation and of superfusion are no doubt determined, more especially of crystals, by the circumstance that a certain impetus is needed for the formation of solid aggregates, without which they are not formed. Mechanical disturbance, such as shaking or contact with a solid, may bring about solidification, a particle of a crystal of the solid itself or of an isomorphous body is most effective in causing the separation of a solid from a supersaturated solution, or the solidification of a superfused liquid. The crystal acts on the particles surrounding it, in such a manner that by arranging themselves around it, and then by becoming attached to the crystal, they cause it to grow. It is not infrequent to obtain solutions which can only be induced to crystallise by making use of these facts. Crystals when introduced into supersaturated solutions, as a rule, only cause the separation of substances of the same composition as themselves, so that the solution may remain supersaturated for another solid. This does not obtain when the substances in solution are isomorphous, for then the introduction into the solution of a crystal of either of them would cause the crystallisation of both of the isomorphous bodies, whatever the proportion in which they exist in the solution. Consequently isomorphous bodies cannot be separated from one another by recrystallisation.

When the temperature of a solution falls below the freezing or melting point of the liquid constituent, $e.g.$ of water, then we have a phenomenon similar to that which in § 75 was described as characteristic for a fluid mixture formed by solids only. There is now, therefore, a lower limit of solubility as well as an upper limit, so that neither of the constituents must be present in less than certain proportions, if the other is not to solidify

The further the temperature sinks, so much the nearer do these limits come together and finally coincide; consequently at the lowest temperature only one liquid mixture can exist. A concentrated aqueous solution of common salt will deposit salt on cooling; whilst ice separates from a dilute solution cooled below the freezing point The further the temperature sinks the more nearly do both solutions approach one another in composition, until at $-22°$ C. they have the same composition and contain one part of salt to three parts of water.

Further cooling would effect a solidification of the whole; a liquid mixture of salt and ice cannot, therefore, exist below this temperature.

§ 78. **Relations between the Freezing Points of Solutions and the Molecular Weights of their Constituents.**—Rüdorff and De Coppet have found that the freezing point of a not too concentrated solution of salt sinks in proportion to the amount of salt present. One part of common salt dissolved in 100 parts of water reduces the freezing point of water from zero to $-0°6$ C, two parts reduce it to $-1°·2$ C., four parts to $-2°4$ C., six parts to $-3°·6$ C, and so on; for every further addition of salt a reduction of $0°·6$ C. is produced till the proportion of salt in the solution amounts to 14 in 100, when the solution freezes at $-8°·4$ C.

At first sight it would appear that below this temperature the relation between the proportion of salt and the reduction in the freezing point ceases. Further investigation has, however, shown that this relationship still exists even at this temperature, but no longer holds for anhydrous salt, but for the compound $NaCl + 2H_2O$, which is the compound crystallising from water at this lower temperature.

We may therefore conclude that below the limit between $-8°$ and $-9°$ C the solution contains this compound, and not the anhydrous salt.

In other cases, even with salts crystallising with water at higher temperatures, the reduction of the freezing point below zero is found to be proportional to the amount of the hydrated salt present in the solution. For instance, for sodium iodide the reduction is proportional to the compound $NaI + 4H_2O$ in 100 parts of water. This reduction of freezing point is therefore an excellent means of deciding the question as to whether a given salt, when dissolved in water, loses or retains its water of crystallisation. All that is necessary is simply to determine the freezing point of solutions of different concentration, and in this way ascertain whether the lowering of the freezing point is in proportion to the amount of the hydrated or of the anhydrous salt in solution.

The results obtained by this method of investigation have in many cases been confirmed by other observations, more especially of the colour of the solution, when the hydrated salt differs in colour from the anhydrous salt. For instance, anhydrous copper sulphate, $CuSO_4$, is colourless, whilst the hydrated blue vitriol, $CuSO_4 + 5H_2O$, is blue; so also is the solution; therefore the solution must contain the hydrated and not the anhydrous salt. This conclusion is confirmed by the results of the determination of the freezing point of its solutions.

If the reduction in the freezing point, instead of being calculated for one part by weight, is calculated for the stœchiometric amount represented by its formula, viz the quantity Q, then substances of analogous composition yield very nearly equal values. In the following table under Q are given the weights of each of the compounds dissolved in 1000 parts of water, the freezing points are given under E Q, and under E the depression in the freezing point produced by one part by weight of the salt:—

	Q	E	E Q
Sodium Chloride .	NaCl $= 58.4$	0°·0600	−3°·50
Potasssium Chloride .	KCl $= 74.4$	0°·0446	−3°·32
Ammonium Chloride .	NH$_4$Cl $= 53.4$	0°·0653	−3°·48
Sodium Bromide .	NaBr + 4H$_2$O $= 174.6$	0°·0189	−3°·30
Potassium Bromide .	KBr $= 118.8$	0°·0292	−3°·47
Sodium Iodide .	NaI + 4H$_2$O $= 221.4$	0°·0152	−3°·35
Potassium Iodide .	KI $= 165.6$	0°·0212	−3°·51

With such regularities as are here exhibited, there can be no doubt that if the amount represented by the formula NaCl is the true molecular weight of common salt, then the other quantities under Q must also represent the molecular weights of the several compounds.

But if Q be twice or thrice as great, a similar conclusion must be arrived at. This method, therefore, still leaves some room for doubt as to which value must be accepted, and this uncertainty becomes greater as in the case of some salts smaller and for others larger values for E Q are obtained; thus, for example, with the so-called vitriols, the following results have been obtained :—

	Q	E	E Q
Epsom Salts	MgSO$_4$ + 7H$_2$O $= 245.9$	0°·0072	1°·77
Zinc Sulphate	ZnSO$_4$ + 7H$_2$O $= 286.7$	0°·0058	1°·66
Nickel Sulphate .	NiSO$_4$ + 7H$_2$O $= 280.1$	0°·0055	1°·54
Copperas	FeSO$_4$ + 7H$_2$O $= 277.4$	0°·0055	1°·53
Blue Vitriol .	CuSO$_4$ + 7H$_2$O $= 248.8$	0°·0065	1°·62

By simply doubling the quantities Q, these results might be brought into agreement with those above. In the case of other compounds, however, such agreement could not possibly be brought about by these simple devices.

It has been found by F. M. Raoult that organic substances examined by this method give much more uniform results than inorganic salts. This knowledge is all the more valuable, as the molecular weights of many of these bodies can be determined in the state of vapour (§ 21). Thus, for example, the reduction of the freezing point, brought about by one part by weight of ether, $C_4H_{10}O = 73.84$, in 100 parts of water gives a value for E of 0°·23. If the molecular weight of ether (73·84) be dissolved in 1000 parts by weight of water, then the molecular depression

E Q is equal to $\cdot 023 \times 73\cdot 84 = 1°\cdot 7$; a number which agrees satisfactorily with the molecular depression for the vitriols. Similar values are obtained for many other organic compounds, as shown by the following examples:—

—	Q	E Q	—	Q	E Q
Glycerol	$C_3H_8O_3$	1°·71	Lactic Acid	$C_3H_6O_3$	1°·92
Mannitol	$C_6H_{14}O_6$	1°·80	Malic ,,	$C_4H_6O_5$	1°·89
Invert Sugar	$C_6H_{12}O_6$	1°·93	Tartaric ,,	$C_4H_6O_6$	1°·95
Milk ,,	$C_{12}H_{24}O_{12}$	1°·81	Citric ,,	$C_6H_8O_7$	1°·93
Cane ,,	$C_{12}H_{22}O_{11}$	1°·85	Urea	CH_4N_2O	1°·72

This discovery is of great importance, since by its aid we can determine, at any rate in terms of certain standards, the molecular weights of those substances to which on account of their lack of volatility Avogadro's law cannot be applied. Thus, for instance, for a long time some doubt existed as to whether the molecular weight of milk sugar was equal to or was double the molecular weight ascribed to grape or fruit sugar, the mixture of which forms inverted sugar. The above numbers, however, remove this doubt and show that the molecular weight of milk sugar cannot be represented by the formula $C_6H_{12}O_6$, for this amount would only correspond to a depression of 0°·9 C.

Raoult has also found that the solutions of other solvents besides water obey similar laws, and, as a matter of fact, the depression of the freezing point of a solvent by a given amount of dissolved substance is the greater the higher the molecular weight of the solvent. Thus one part by weight of ether dissolved in 100 parts of water, glacial acetic acid, or in benzene gives the following depressions:—

In water . . . . . . 0°·23
In glacial acetic acid . . . . 0°·53
In benzene . . . . . . 0°·67

The last two numbers are very nearly proportional to the molecular weights of the compounds represented, viz.—

Glacial acetic acid . . . $C_2H_4O_2 = 59\cdot 86$
Benzene . . . . . $C_6H_6 = 77\cdot 82$

For we have
$$0.53 : 0.67 = 1 : 1.26$$
$$59.86 : 77.82 = 1 : 1.30$$

Similar relations are found to obtain for other solvents, with the single exception of water.

Making use of this observation, Raoult has been able to extend this law and express it in the following terms:—

If the molecular weight of any compound be dissolved in one hundred times the molecular weight of any liquid, then the freezing point of this liquid will be depressed by about $0°·62$ C.

The majority of inorganic acids and salts when dissolved in water form exceptions to this law.

The molecular weights of other bodies, then, can be determined by aid of Raoult's law in the following manner:—

A weight P of the substance is dissolved in a large excess (a quantity L) of a solvent having the molecular weight M, and the reduction in the freezing point E is then determined. If m is the molecular weight to be found, then we have, approximately,

$$\frac{P}{L} : \frac{m}{100\,M} = E : 0°·62 ;$$

from which
$$m = \frac{P \cdot 62° \, M}{L \cdot E}.$$

The value of m so obtained is then to be corrected by the stœchiometric composition of the substance in question. It is, as a rule, more convenient to take, instead of m, the smallest quantity q, which represents a whole number of atoms and to calculate the reduction e brought about by this quantity in its solution in 100 M, thus:—

$$\frac{P}{L} : \frac{q}{100\,M} = E : e.$$

Then to try with what whole number x, the value of e, must be multiplied so that the product approximates as nearly as possible to $0°\,62$; the required molecular weight m is then equal to $x\,q$.

§ 79. **Exceptions to Raoult's Law.**—The exceptions to this law already mentioned are of two kinds. In the first place there are those substances, one molecular weight of which dissolved in 100 molecular weights of water (in round numbers 1800, or more exactly 1796 parts of water) does not give the normal depression of 0°·62, but one which is about 1° C. In order to bring the freezing point to 0°·62 it is necessary to add more water, some 2700 to 3000 parts, or 150 to 160 molecular weights to one molecular weight of the body dissolved. So water behaves as though its molecular weight were greater than the weight represented by the formula H_2O. One may imagine in fact that in water near its freezing point molecular aggregates exist, some of the formula H_4O_2 or the formula H_6O_3, and so on. The existence of such aggregates would explain the abnormal expansion below 4° C.

Cold water, therefore, may be looked upon as a solution of ice in water, and indeed in the light of a mixture consisting of one molecular weight, H_4O_2, with one of the molecular weight H_2O, or one molecular weight, H_6O_3, to three molecules of the formula H_2O.

The second class of exceptions is formed of many acids and salts, the smallest amount of which represented by the stœchiometric formula depresses the freezing point of water much more than the molecular weight of any indifferent organic substance, in some cases the depression being twice as great. According to the above table, for instance, a solution of 58·37 grammes of common salt in a litre of water freezes at $-3°·5$, whereas a solution containing 341·2 grammes of cane sugar ($C_{12}H_{22}O_{11}$) would freeze at $-1°·85$. Common salt, therefore, behaves as though it were composed, not of an amount represented by the formula NaCl, but by an amount almost equivalent to two molecules. To explain these facts S. Arrhenius has suggested that the greater portion of the salt exists in solution dissociated into sodium and chlorine. A somewhat similar proposal was formerly made by Clausius to explain the decomposition of its solution in electrolysis (compare §§ 12 and 99). Improbable as this hypothesis may at first sight appear, very weighty arguments have been advanced in support of it.

§ 80. **Diffusion.**—If the composition of a solution is different in different parts, then even when the temperature throughout is the same there arises without any external cause a gradual adjustment, inasmuch as all the constituents of the solution are gradually and uniformly distributed throughout the mass.

The movement by which this uniform distribution is effected was styled 'diffusion' by Graham This diffusion takes place slowly and consequently the substances mixing with one another may often take weeks and perhaps months in passing through a distance of a few decimetres only. Inasmuch as this admixture takes place spontaneously, it must result from the motion of the particles in the liquid state, and must also take place in perfectly homogeneous and uniformly mixed liquids.

The difference between this case and that in which the mixture is not uniform is to be found in the fact that as each of the particles in any given position moves in one direction, an equal number of particles will move in the opposite direction ; whereas in the case of mixtures lacking this uniformity, then from that portion of the liquid containing a larger number of particles in a given space, more particles will come in consequence of this excess, assuming that the temperature, and consequently the velocity of the particles on both sides, is equal. The uniform distribution of the concentration will therefore occur the more readily the greater the difference in the contents of the two layers of liquids in contact with each other.

From the considerable amount of heat which is rendered latent in the passage from the solid into the liquid state, one may conclude that the liquid particles have considerable motion imparted to them. That these particles, despite this motion, only move slowly from one position to another may arise from the fact that they interfere with one another's free movement, and consequently only with great difficulty and very slowly are they able to force their way through the crowd of surrounding particles

The velocity with which a substance diffuses depends, not only upon its nature, but also upon the nature of the solvent, and further upon the temperature. · These phenomena have been chiefly investigated for aqueous solutions. One might at first be inclined to believe that the smaller and lighter particles would diffuse more rapidly than the larger and heavier particles. Whilst this frequently is the case, it does not obtain universally, and especially is this found not to be so with bodies which are very nearly allied to one another. In illustration of this, a comparison may be made by taking an equal number of molecular weights of different substances dissolved in an equal volume of the same solvent. For instance, if the weight in grammes of potassium chloride, 74·4, represented by the formula KCl, of common salt the amount 58·37, of lithium chloride the amount 42·38, represented by their respective formulæ, be dissolved in a litre of water, and the several solutions brought in contact with pure water, then by determining the quantities of each which pass in equal times under otherwise similar conditions into the water we obtain values for the diffusion of these different substances which may be compared with one another. Experiments of this character conducted by J. H. Long have shown that the number of molecular weights of each of these bodies which diffuse in equal times are represented by the values given under d in the following table :—

—	d	—	d
KCl = 74 4	803	KNO_3 = 100 9	607
NaCl = 58 4	600	$NaNO_3$ = 84 9	524
LiCl = 42 4	541	$LiNO_3$ = 68 9	512
KBr = 118 8	823	KI = 165 6	823
NaBr = 102 8	509	NaI = 149 5	672

These examples show that potassium salts, despite their greater molecular weights, diffuse more readily than the corresponding sodium compounds, and these latter more readily than the corresponding compounds of lithium. Such examples, which might be considerably increased, show that frequently the large molecules diffuse more readily than the small ones; still, on the other hand, there are substances having very large molecular weights, more especially complicated organic compounds, which diffuse with extraordinary slowness. The substances mentioned in the foregoing section diffuse at a comparatively rapid rate, and these bodies, according to the hypothesis advanced by Arrhenius, must be supposed to exist in their solutions in a state of dissociation

§ 81. **Osmosis and Dialysis.**—If two liquids capable of diffusing into one another are brought, not into immediate contact, but are separated by a septum which is permeable to one or other of the constituents and not the other, or only permeable to a lesser degree, then we have produced that remarkable phenomenon to which Dutrochet has applied the term *osmosis*, from ὠσμός, an impulse As this term implies, the liquid to which the septum is permeable is driven through in such a way that a considerable inequality of pressure on each side of the separating wall is produced. Substances which swell up when moistened (compare § 72) are the best adapted for such septa. Animal or vegetable membranes, parchment paper, gelatinous precipitates, such as copper ferrocyanide or tanned gelatine, and also caoutchouc and other bodies, are examples of the materials which may be used for such septa; still there are also many substances which act in a similar manner, although they do not swell up when moistened. But what may and what may not pass through such septa is determined by the nature of the septum itself and also of the liquid. The cuticle of plants and animals and also many membranes which are produced from aqueous solutions are permeable by water, but are impermeable to many substances easily or only slightly soluble in water. Caoutchouc does not allow water to pass through it, although many organic substances diffuse readily through this material. The most remarkable fact observed in connection with the phenomenon of osmosis is that the portion of the liquid by which the wall is permeated will force its way through the membrane, despite the greater pressure existing on the opposite side. For instance, supposing an aqueous solution of salt be separated from pure water by a membrane permeable only to water; still, as has been shown by Nollet in 1748, and later by Fisher, Magnus, Dutrochet, and others, the water passes through the membrane to the salt, so that on the salt side an increased pressure is produced. The water therefore moves in opposition to the pressure which has been produced by its own movements. As soon, however, as the pressure reaches a certain amount, then this increase in volume ceases. This maximum pressure, the so-called 'osmotic pressure,' has been studied and measured for different substances by W. Pfeffer, and in many cases has been found to be very considerable and to be proportional to the concentration of the solution. At one time it was believed that this pressure was due to the attraction of the salt or other dissolved solid for the water. This explanation is no longer permissible, for De Vries has found that in a very large group of substances this pressure for the solution of two different substances is approximately the same when both solutions contain in equal volumes an equal number of molecules of the dissolved bodies. De Vries did not measure the 'osmotic pressure' directly, but determined the concentration of those solutions of different substances which give up as much water to certain plant cells as they receive from the membranes of these cells. These solutions are spoken of as *isotonic* (from ἴσος, equal, and τόνος, pressure). De Vries found that in order that the solutions of those organic substances investigated by him should be isotonic, they must contain in equal volumes an equal number of molecular weights, whilst solutions of inorganic salts were found to be isotonic with the former when less concentrated. Consequently very different substances exert equal osmotic pressures; the phenomenon, therefore, cannot be dependent upon the material composition of the bodies nor upon an attraction exerted by them upon water, which certainly could not be the same for substances so very different from each other.

We cannot, therefore, accept such an attraction to explain this phenomenon. If on one side of the wall there were water particles only, and on the other, particles of another substance, for instance, sugar, for which the wall is not permeable, then upon this side the number of water particles coming in contact with the wall would be smaller the smaller their number, and consequently the larger the number of particles of sugar contained in a unit volume. The smaller the number striking the wall so much the smaller will be the number passing into and through the wall, consequently a smaller number of particles of water pass from this sugar solution towards the pure water than from the water to the sugar solution. The amount of water on the side of the sugar solution must therefore increase. If the water so passing through the wall can flow away in any other manner, then the passage will continue so long as the concentration on both sides of the wall remains unequal. If, however, the solutions are contained in closed vessels, then in consequence of the advent of the water the pressure will be increased. In proportion as this increase proceeds the amount of water passing through the wall in a given time diminishes, and will finally cease when the pressure has reached a certain maximum; then the interchange ceases entirely. This arises from the fact that the pressure produced by the water particles is more strongly exerted upon the wall, and consequently they press through it. In this way the equilibrium of the materials passing from both sides is established.

If the pressure be increased artificially above this maximum then more water passes out than is returned, till the equilibrium is again established.

This osmotic pressure is dependent upon the condition of the wall, and not alone upon its composition, but also upon its thickness; for naturally it is easier to force the water through one kind of wall than it is for it to pass through another of a different material If, however, one brings consecutively in contact with the same wall, solutions of different materials, then the osmotic pressure will gradually become equal, the equality being established when the solution on each side of the wall contains an equal number of molecules of the substances to which the wall is impermeable If these two solutions are divided by a partition only permeable to the solvent, then no alteration in pressure is produced; if, however, one solution contains in a given space more molecules than the other, then the pressure rises in this solution. The osmotic pressure as well as the depression of the freezing point may be used for the purpose of comparing and determining molecular weights. This method is, however, less convenient than the former and suffers from the fact that these septa are, as a rule, not absolutely impermeable to dissolved substances In this method also it is found that acids and salts exhibit an exceptional behaviour similar to that described in § 79.

§ 82. **Evaporation and Ebullition.**—If a liquid be brought into a vessel which it does not completely fill, then a portion of the liquid passes as vapour into the space above. When this formation of vapour takes place only at the surface of the liquid it is styled 'evaporation,' but when it also proceeds in the interior of the liquid itself it is described as ebullition, or boiling. Which of these two forms of vaporisation obtains, is determined by external conditions, especially by the pressure on the liquid and by the temperature. Evaporation may also take place from the surfaces of solid bodies.

When the space above the liquid is completely void, then, as a rule, evaporation takes place very quickly; but if it be filled with air or other gas the vaporisation proceeds more slowly. The mass of the vapour increases, but only until a maximum density is reached, that is, until every unit of space contains a certain definite weight of vapour : this maximun density is dependent upon the nature of the substance and also upon the temperature. This is true whether the space be filled with air or not. The vapour tends to expand and consequently exerts a pressure on the walls of the vessel, which pressure with constant temperature is approximately, but not absolutely, proportional to the density. To this maximum density there is a corresponding maximum of pressure styled the pressure or tension of the saturated vapour. The maximum density is always reached when a sufficient amount of liquid is present. If another gas exist in the space with the vapour, then both exert a pressure, giving a total pressure equal to the sum of the two. The component pressures are spoken of as the 'partial' or 'individual' pressures

When the space filled with a saturated vapour is reduced, and therefore the vapour compressed, neither the pressure nor the density is altered, but a portion of the vapour is converted into liquid and separates out as such If the reverse happen, then an amount of vapour is formed until the conditions of the maximum of density and of pressure are again restored It must not, however, be concluded that by reason of the impossibility of exceeding this maximum, the production of vapour ceases when this condition has been reached; for the vaporisation continues, but as much vapour condenses and liquefies as there is fresh vapour formed. The condition of a saturated vapour therefore is no condition of rest, is not a statical but a dynamical equilibrium, a state of motion which has become stationary.

The maximum pressure of the vapour of a substance is determined by the material composition of the body and also by the temperature. At low temperatures it is frequently immeasurably small, whilst at higher temperatures it is considerable; still there are many bodies which cannot withstand the necessary rise of temperature without suffering decomposition, and therefore in the case of many liquids it is not known whether they can in any way be converted into vapour.

When the pressure of the vapour is as great or a little greater than the pressure surrounding the liquid, then the production of vapour proceeds, not at the surface alone, but also in the interior of the liquid itself, and the liquid boils. The formation of bubbles of vapour in the mass of the liquid itself does not necessarily take place as soon as the required temperature and pressure have been reached, just as the crystallisation of a solid from its solution does not begin immediately the condition of saturation has been reached. A liquid heated to a temperature above its boiling point is described as 'superheated.' This condition is analogous to that of supersaturation in the case of solutions. When the formation of vapour takes place in a 'superheated' liquid, it proceeds rapidly and suddenly, just as crystallisation in a supersaturated solution, and may consequently occasion violent explosions. Various agencies are found to be active in giving an impetus to the production of vapour—for example, shaking—but perhaps the most effectual is the contact of solid bodies, the surfaces of which are covered with a very thin layer of air or gas, or a solid which forms a gas when brought into the liquid will also promote the production of vapour. In this thin layer of air the first vapour production takes place, which rapidly extending forms a larger bubble, into the interior of which evaporation takes place from all sides. Bodies which condense air easily upon their surface, like platinum, or porous substances containing air in the pores, like burnt clay, charcoal, &c. are specially active in promoting this production of vapour. The walls of the containing vessels, more especially those constructed of glass or porcelain, act in the same way, by reason of the thin layer of air which is retained adhering to their surfaces. If this layer of air has been removed either by strongly heating the vessel or by long continued boiling of the liquid in it, then sudden and violent ebullition may set in, which can be avoided by bringing into the liquid, platinum wire, sand, or pieces of clay pipe-stems, &c.

The nature of the relationship between vapour pressure and

temperature is so far alike for all volatile substances that with a rise in temperature the pressure increases at first slowly, then rapidly and more rapidly until at last the increase takes place with extraordinary rapidity. If these phenomena are represented graphically with the abscissæ for the temperature and the pressure as ordinates, then the curve is found to be convex to the axis of the abcissæ, and is at first almost parallel to this axis, and finally almost perpendicular to it; as yet such representations have been made in only a few isolated cases. The law underlying this relationship has not yet been completely elucidated As a rule, it has been deemed sufficient to fix and determine the boiling points of different substances, *i e.* the temperatures at which the liquids boil under the ordinary atmospheric pressure. But since this pressure varies from time to time, and is different in different places, such determinations are of little value unless the height of the barometer be also measured. For instance, in consequence of the higher position of Tübingen or Munich, the majority of substances boil 1° or 2° lower at these places than they do at Berlin or Königsberg.

§ 83 **Boiling Points** —The comparison of the boiling points of substances of analogous composition has shown the existence of a very intimate relationship between the boiling point and the composition. These relationships were first brought to light by the investigations of H Kopp and of H. Schroeder, and have since been amplified and extended by numerous investigators. It is chiefly amongst the organic compounds that such investigations have been made, and among these it has been shown that regular changes in composition correspond to similarly regular alterations in the boiling points.

Among the numerous series of organic compounds of like atom-linkage, the members of which differ from one another by CH_2, or a difference of 13 97, or approximately 14 units, in their molecular weights, the boiling points and the molecular weights form arithmetical series with approximately equal differences; still the differences in the boiling points are not exactly equal, as is the case with those of the molecular weights.

The following examples are taken from the chlorides, bromides, iodides, alcohols, and acids derived from the series of so-called paraffins (hydrocarbons of the general formula C_nH_{2n+2}) The boiling points in each of the five series increase with the number of carbon atoms; still, this alteration is somewhat different in each series.

n	CHLORIDE $C_nH_{2n+1}Cl$	BROMIDE $C_nH_{2n+1}Br$	IODIDE $C_nH_{2n+1}I$	ALCOHOL $C_nH_{2n+1}OH$	ACID $C_nH_{2n}O_2$
1	$-22°$	$+4°·6$	$40°$	$66°$	$100°$
	35	34	32	12	19
2	$+12°·5$	$38°·4$	$72°$	$78°·5$	$119°$
	34	33	30	19	21
3	$46°·4$	$71°$	$102°$	$97°·4$	$140°$
	32	29	28	20	22
4	$77°·9$	$100°$	$129°·6$	$117°$	$162°$
	28	29	26	20	23
5	$106°·6$	$129°$	$155°·4$	$137°$	$185°$
	26	27	24	20	20
6	$133°$	$156°$	$179°·5$	$157°$	$205°$
	26	23	22	19	19
7	$159°$	$179°$	$201°$	$176°$	$224°$
	21	20	21	19	13
8	$180°$	$199°$	$222°$	$195°$	$237°$ (?)

Greater differences are found among the more easily volatile substances than between the less volatile members. Still in the case of bodies of approximately equal volatility the increase is greater in one family than in another. In consequence the remarkable relation obtains that the iodides and bromides of the radicals C_nH_{2n+1}, containing a smaller number of carbon atoms, boil at a lower temperature than the hydroxyl compounds, whereas with higher values of n the iodides and bromides are less volatile than the alcohols. With increasing values of n the chlorides approximate more nearly to the alcohols; whereas when $n=1$ the alcohol boils 88° C. higher than the chloride, and when $n=8$ the difference is only 15° C.

Relationships between the boiling point and molecular weight similar to the above are exhibited in many other series. A. Winkelmann has shown that similar differences are observed whatever be the pressure at which the boiling point is determined; the smaller the pressure the smaller the differences.

These approximately regular differences in the boiling points are only found when the substances compared have similar atomic linkage. Even minute differences in this respect may give rise to considerable deviations in the boiling point. For instance, the 'normal' hydro-carbons, containing carbon atoms united in a single chain, must not be compared with their isomerides containing side-chains of carbon atoms; the former boil at considerably higher temperatures than the latter. Inasmuch as by the replacement of hydrogen by an elementary atom or radical the volatility is affected, and the extent and manner of this alteration is determined by the position of the hydrogen so replaced, those compounds can alone be regarded as homologous in which there is complete analogy in the position of the substituting elements or groups. It is, in fact, this far-reaching influence exerted by the mode of the atom linkage in the boiling point which has made the volatility of compounds of great service in the investigation of the linking of the atoms in different compounds; organic chemistry provides numerous illustrations of the application and value of this method of determining the constitution of compounds.

§ 84. **Vapour Pressure of Mixed Liquids.**—If several liquids are contained in the same vessel, each of these will give off vapour into the part not occupied by the liquid. Regnault has shown that in such cases the phenomena may be divided into three distinct classes.

When liquids do not mix with one another, then each constituent gives off as much vapour as if it existed alone, and the total pressure is equal to the sum of the partial pressures of the vapours of both. Therefore, a mixture of two such liquids will boil at a lower temperature than either of the constituents. For instance, if water be poured on to bromoform ($CHBr_3$), which boils at 151° C., then ebullition commences at the surface separating the two at a temperature of 93° C., because at this temperature the sum of the vapour pressures of water and of bromoform is sufficient to overcome the pressure of the atmosphere. The boiling point remains constant so long as there is a sufficient quantity of each liquid present. Carbon bisulphide and water, ethyl iodide and water, and many other combinations behave in a similar manner. This property may lead to very considerable error in the determination of boiling points. Thus ethyl iodide in presence of a little water will boil 10° C. lower than the boiling point of the pure substance.

When liquids mix only to a limited extent with each other,

as for instance ether and water (*vide* § 75), then the vapour pressure of the mixture is less than the sum of the pressures of the single constituents, and in fact is only as great as that of the more volatile constituent; in the instance cited it would only be as great as that of ether. In such cases the boiling point of the more volatile liquid could be correctly determined in presence of the other. The more volatile component having distilled over with a portion of the less volatile liquid, the boiling then ceases, to commence again when the temperature at which the latter boils has been reached.

When liquids mix in all proportions, the vapour pressure of each reduces that of the other, so that the pressure of the mixture is considerably less than that of the more volatile constituent, and lies between their separate pressures. The pressure in such cases varies very considerably with the proportion of the constituents. If such a mixture is distilled, then the boiling point gradually rises in proportion as the more volatile constituent distils over. Separation by distillation in such cases is much more difficult than in either of the above instances. Separation is then only possible when the distillation is frequently interrupted, as in fractional distillation, when the distillate, as well as the residue, are each separately redistilled.

§ 85. **Relation of Density and Pressure of Vapours to Molecular Weights.**—If a vapour be examined under a pressure much smaller than the maximum of its vapour pressure at the temperature of experiment, then it is found that Avogadro's law (§ 17) holds true for the vapour, *i.e.* equal volumes of different vapours contain the same number of molecules, and as many as are contained in the same volume of a gas, provided that gases and vapours alike are measured under the same conditions of temperature and pressure. Under these conditions the densities are proportional to the molecular weights, and may serve, therefore, for the determination of the latter, in the manner already described in §§ 19–21.

When gases and vapours or several vapours are contained within the same space, and provided these gases and vapours exert no chemical action upon one another, and do not when in the liquid state mix with one another or dissolve in one another, then the sum of all the molecules is the same as would be the case were the space filled by a single gas or vapour under like conditions of temperature and pressure. In fact, the proportion of the pressure of each constituent to the total pressure is determined by the number of its molecules existing in the space. Methods for the determination of molecular weights have been based upon this property.

Thus, substances which cannot be heated without decomposing at the temperatures at which Avogadro's law can be applied may be mixed with indifferent gases, and the weight, pressure, and temperature of the mixture determined. Deducting from this the known or subsequently determined proportion of the admixed gas, the pressure and weight of the vapour are obtained, from which the density and molecular weight are calculated.

According to Alex. Naumann, the molecular weight of a volatile liquid can be determined by distilling it with another liquid with which it does not mix. For, in such cases, the pressure which each constituent of the mixture of vapour exerts is proportional to the number of its molecules in the vapour. The amount converted into vapour, and consequently that distilling over, is greater the larger the number and the greater the weight of the particles or the molecules. If P be the total pressure, and p and p_1 the partial pressures, $i.e.$ the vapour pressures of each of the separate vapours, then

$$P = p + p_1.$$

Further, let m and m_1 be the molecular weights and g and g_1 the weights of each substance distilling over, then

$$g : g_1 = pm : p_1 m_1.$$

If m_1 is already known and the pressure p_1 be measured for the temperature at which the mixture distils, then we have

$$p = P - p_1, \quad m = \frac{p_1}{P - p_1} \cdot \frac{g}{g_1} \cdot m_1.$$

For instance, from a mixture of toluene and water, 86.6 grammes of toluene and 21.1 grammes of water distil over at 84° 3 C. and 754.4 mm. At this temperature the pressure of aqueous vapour alone is 422.0 mm.; consequently we have—

$P = 754·4$ mm, $p_1 = 422$ mm, $p = P - p_1 = 332·4$ mm.
$$m = \frac{422}{332·4} \times \frac{86·6}{21·1} \times 17·96 = 94·5.$$

The molecular weight of toluene, according to the formula, C_7H_8, is 91·8. The agreement between these numbers is sufficiently satisfactory to leave no doubt as to the value of the molecular weight. This method can be used in many cases where others cannot be applied.

The vapour pressure may, according to Raoult, also be utilised to determine the molecular weights of substances in the liquid state. When a comparatively small amount of a solid or liquid is dissolved in a volatile liquid, such as ether, the vapour pressure of the solvent is thereby reduced and the reduction is almost proportional to the number of the molecular weights of the substance dissolved. For instance, the vapour pressure of ether is reduced almost by $\frac{1}{100}$ when 1 molecular weight of a substance is dissolved in 99 molecular weights of ether; with 2 molecular weights in 100, i.e. dissolved in 98 molecular weights of ether, the pressure is reduced by about $\frac{2}{100}$, and so on; still, the proportion of the substance dissolved must not be too great, otherwise this rule ceases to be reliable.

If f be the vapour pressure of pure ether, f' that of a solution containing g parts by weight of the dissolved substance in 100 parts of the solution, and consequently $(100-g)$ per cent. of ether, m the molecular weight to be determined, m_1 the molecular weight of ether ($C_4H_{10}O = 73·84$), and n the unknown number of molecules of the dissolved substance in 100 molecular weights of the solution, then the following proportion holds approximately:—
$$f' : f :: 100 - n : 100,$$
and therefore
$$n = 100 \frac{f - f'}{f}$$

Further we have also the following relations:—
$$g : 100 - g = n \times m : (100 - n) . m_1,$$
and consequently
$$m = \frac{(100-n) . g}{n . (100-g)} . m_1.$$

The molecular weights determined in this manner are only approximations and need correcting by the stœchiometric formula, just as do the molecular weights deduced from the vapour density.

§ 86. **Critical Temperature.**—As the pressure of a vapour increases with the temperature, and, in fact, the increase is the more rapid the higher the temperature, consequently the higher the temperature the greater the pressure required for the condensation of a vapour. For every vapour there exists a temperature above which no pressure, however great, can effect the liquefaction of that vapour. Andrews, the discoverer of this property, has styled this temperature the 'critical temperature,' and the pressure required to effect the liquefaction at temperatures a little below this is spoken of as the 'critical pressure.' There is a critical temperature for every vapour, provided it is not decomposed by the heat necessary to raise it to this temperature.

This discovery of Andrews indicated the method to be employed in the liquefaction of the so-called permanent gases, such as hydrogen, oxygen, nitrogen, carbon monoxide, marsh gas, &c., which Natterer had attempted but without success, although he had employed a pressure of several thousand atmospheres. These gases were first successfully liquefied by Raoult Pictet, who not only compressed the gases, but also at the same time cooled them to temperatures much below their critical temperatures.

According to the recently published investigations of Cailletet and Collardeau, the conclusions of Andrews require certain limitations, insomuch that the possibility of a liquid existing as such does not suddenly cease at the critical temperature, but only the sharp definition of the liquid from the vapour disappears, to be replaced by a misty, ill-defined intermediate layer. At a little above the critical temperature the liquid still remains more dense, and is therefore heavier than the vapour, and also possesses other properties than those belonging to the vapour. This difference between the liquid and gas disappears more and more as the temperature rises.

Despite this limitation the critical temperature, which is also known as the absolute boiling point, still remains an important and characteristic constant.

The critical temperatures of different substances are very different, varying with their nature and composition, as shown by the examples in the table below, in which the critical temperatures are given under the heading C T, and the critical pressure in atmospheres under C P.

In the case of many other substances the critical temperatures are much higher, and probably the critical temperatures of many of the metallic elements are higher than any available artificial temperatures.

The fact that no pressure, however great, should liquefy a gas at temperatures above the critical temperature finds its explanation in the fact that above this temperature the particles are in such rapid motion that they seldom if ever remain attached to one another, and the attraction of the particles exhibited as forces of cohesion or of capillarity is completely overcome.

		C T	C P
Hydrogen	H_2	below $-220°$ C.	?
Nitrogen	N_2	$-146°$	35
Carbon Monoxide	CO	$-140°$	—
Oxygen	O_2	$-119°$	50
Carbon Dioxide	CO_2	$+32°$	77
Nitrous Oxide	N_2O	$+35°$	75
Hydrogen Chloride	HCl	$+52°$	93
Hydrogen Sulphide	H_2S	$+100°$	92
Cyanogen	C_2N_2	$+124°$	62
Ammonia	NH_3	$+130°$	113
Chlorine	Cl_2	$+141°$	84
Marsh Gas	CH_4	$-74°$	57
Ethylene	C_2H_4	$+10°$	51
Ethane	C_2H_6	$+35°$	45
Acetylene	C_2H_2	$+37°$	68
Amylene	C_5H_{10}	$192°$	34
Benzene	C_6H_6	$292°$	60
Methyl Chloride	CH_3Cl	$142°$	76
Ethyl ,,	C_2H_5Cl	$183°$	54
Propyl ,,	C_3H_7Cl	$221°$	49
Chloroform	$CHCl_3$	$268°$	55
Carbon Tetrachloride	CCl_4	$282°$	58

This conception finds strong support in many other observations; for instance, the flow of liquids, capillarity, and other phenomena all show that the cohesion of fluids is gradually weakened by rise in temperature. That this should be the case is shown also by the fact that in the conversion of a liquid into vapour or gas, the higher the temperature so much the less heat is absorbed or rendered latent. At the critical temperature or absolute boiling point the latent heat of vaporisation is probably zero, or is at any rate extremely small

§ 87. **Nature of the Gaseous State.**—It has already been shown (§ 20) that, according to the generally accepted views, the particles which in a liquid are more or less coherent, are in vapours or gases completely separated, and have free and independent motion. The fact that vapours and gases, unless under great pressure, fill a space many times greater than that filled by the liquid from which they are produced proves that in the vaporisation or the conversion into gas the particles are separated widely from one another. It is known as the result of numerous observations that, apart from gravity and universal gravitation, the particles of matter can only act upon one another at extremely minute distances, the particles of a gas or vapour must therefore be beyond the sphere of mutual attraction. A body left entirely to itself will, however, continue to move on in a straight line with the velocity imparted to it unless deflected from this path by some external influence This is assumed to be the case with the particles of a gas or vapour, and, as shown in § 20, the pressure of a gas can in every detail be satisfactorily shown to be a consequence of this rectilinear motion of the particles.

According to the kinetic theory of gases, the pressure is proportional to the density, since the larger the number of particles, so many more particles must strike the walls of the containing vessel Further, the pressure is proportional to the square of the velocity of these particles, for the frequency and the force of the impacts must increase with the velocity. The pressure is found to be proportional to the absolute temperature of a gas: that is, to the temperature reckoned from $-273°$ C., or more exactly from $-272°·6$ C.; it follows, therefore, that the velocity of the rectilinear motion of the particles must increase in proportion to the square root of the absolute temperature. This velocity must be very great, because the momentum of every impact is proportional to the product of the velocity into the mass; but the latter is very small Clausius has succeeded, by very ingeniously combining theoretical considerations with the results of observation, in determining these velocities in absolute measures, the calculations being based upon the following considerations

The pressure of a gas is equal to the change of momentum of every single impact (*i.e.* to the product of the mass of the moving particle into the change of its velocity) multiplied into the number of impacts on any unit of area exposed to the pressure; again, the pressure may be measured by a column of mercury: that is, in terms of the action of the force of gravity on a column of this metal of a certain height and of a sectional area equal to the unit of area. Placing these two different measures of the pressure on opposite sides of an equation, we then obtain an expression of the relationship between the velocity of the particles and a value expressed in metres per second or any other convenient unit of measurement. The equation in any case contains still an unknown factor, the number of the particles, and also the unknown mass of an individual particle But of these unknowns the product alone occurs, representing a measurable quantity, viz. the mass of the unit of volume of the gas.

In the above it is assumed that the velocity of all particles is alike; in reality this can never be the case, since by the collision of the particles the velocities will undoubtedly vary, as is the case with a large number of billiard balls colliding freely. There will, however, always be found a value for the velocity, which, supposing all the particles to be uniform, would produce the same pressure as the variable values of the real velocities. Clausius has calculated that this velocity (v), which is known as 'the velocity of mean square,' is expressed in metres per second as follows:—

$$v = 485 \cdot \sqrt{\frac{T}{d \cdot 273°}}.$$

In this expression T is the absolute temperature and d the density of the gas, air being the unit.

As the density of a gas has been shown in § 21 to be proportional to the molecular weight, we may replace d by the expression

$$d = \frac{m}{28 \cdot 87},$$

and then obtain the following as the relation between the velocity and the molecular weight:—

$$v = 485 \cdot \sqrt{\frac{T}{273} \cdot \frac{28 \cdot 87}{m}} = 2605 \cdot \sqrt{\frac{T}{273 \cdot m}}.$$

In accordance with this formula the following numbers represent the velocities in metres per second of the particles of oxygen, nitrogen, and hydrogen at 0° C., *i.e.* T = 273, and at the critical temperatures −119°, −146°, and −220°.

Oxygen $v_0 = 461$ $v_K = 346$;
Nitrogen $v_0 = 492$ $v_K = 288$;
Hydrogen $v_0 = 1844$ $v_K = 953$.

The velocities, therefore, are considerable even at temperatures near those at which the gas may be liquefied, and at the freezing point the velocities are much greater than the velocity of sound, for instance

§ 88. **Constitution of Gases.**—Many of the different properties of gases, such as the constant expansive tendency, their rapid filling of empty spaces, and many other qualities, find an easy and simple explanation in the great velocities of gaseous particles. On the other hand, at first sight many of the properties do not appear to be consistent with so great a velocity. In opposition to the acceptance of these views it has been pointed out that the mixing or diffusion of gases, which certainly takes place more rapidly than in the case of liquids, is still comparatively slow, so that even with small quantities of different gases their complete admixture may require hours and in some cases even days. This apparent contradiction is, however, entirely due to the conception that, in consequence of the great velocity of the particles of gases, the admixture of gases should be effected instantly.

Clausius has, however, shown that the tardiness of gaseous diffusion and the low conductivity for heat and other properties of gases may be satisfactorily explained, despite the velocity of the particles. A single particle which, if alone, would move through several hundred metres in a second, is retarded by others which it meets in its path, and colliding with these is reflected back just like an elastic ball, in the same way that a man running rapidly would be retarded so soon as he came into a throng. The crowding together of the gaseous particles cannot, however, be so great, for a comparison of the density of gases and liquids shows that the particles of a gas fill only a thousandth of the space taken up by the mass; consequently in the spaces between them there must exist for their movements to and fro a thousand times as much space as that filled by the mass. But at the same time the average distance between the particles can only be very small when their number is great and the mass of each correspondingly small. Starting with these assumptions from the known rate of diffusion, the conductivity for heat, the internal friction of gases, &c , the average distance which a particle must travel before it collides with a second has been calculated—this distance Clausius has styled the mean free path.

The length of path is shown to be extremely small—less, in fact, than any length microscopically visible in the case of gases at normal pressure. With the majority of gases at the average temperature and a pressure of an atmosphere the distance is less than the ten-thousandth part of a millimetre. With a velocity of several hundred metres per second the number of times which a given particle must collide with others is quite inconceivable, and, according to calculation, it must be from four to ten thousand million times per second.

These calculations show the subdivision of matter in the gaseous state to be excessively great, since at the average temperature and under the pressure of one atmosphere a cubic centimetre of any given gas, and therefore in accordance with Avogadro's law, of all gases, will contain approximately some twenty trillion particles. As the weight of this mass can be determined, and, in fact, is known, the weight of a single molecule may be approximately ascertained. The weight of a molecule of hydrogen has thus been found to be

$$0\ 000,000,000,000,000,000,004 \text{ milligramme};$$

or a quadrillion of particles of hydrogen would weigh about four grammes Although these numbers cannot lay claim to any special accuracy, still they serve to give some idea of the magnitude (or, rather, the minuteness) of molecules and of atoms also.

Not only may the weight but also the dimensions of the particles be similarly estimated. The hindrances to its free movement experienced by a particle produced by collision with others is determined, not only by its velocity, but also by its dimensions; for the larger the particles the more they will interfere with one another. The path, therefore, will be shorter the larger the particles. The knowledge of the frequency of their collisions may further serve to enable us to form an estimate of and to measure approximately their dimensions. According to the calculations of O E Meyer, a cubic centimetre of hydrogen measured at 20° C. and under pressure of 760mm. contains so many molecules that if they were laid side by side they would cover 9500 square centimetres, or very nearly a square metre. Accordingly for each twenty trillion particles but a very small surface would be required, for in the length of a millimetre some four to five million particles could be arranged in a series.

The relative size of the molecules of two different gases or vapours may be calculated with greater exactness than can their absolute dimensions. By similar calculation it has been shown by the author that in the case of most substances the actual spaces filled by the gaseous particles stand to one another approximately in the same proportion as that which obtains in the liquid state.

§ 89. **Boyle's Law.**—The behaviour of gases under all conditions is determined by the dimensions, the mass, and the velocity of the particles. The deviations from the fundamental laws of gases exhibited in individual cases can be explained in a satisfactory manner as arising from these several influences. According to Boyle's law, the volume of a given mass of gas is inversely proportional to the pressure upon it, and therefore the product of the pressure into the volume or the quotient of the pressure and density remains constant. This law is not, however, absolutely true of any gas; for every gas, with the single exception of hydrogen, exhibits a greater diminution in volume with increase in pressure than should be the case if the law were absolutely true, *i.e.* the value of the product P V diminishes. So soon, however, as the pressure increases to a considerable number of atmospheres then the value of the product P V becomes greater, arising from the fact that the volume decreases less rapidly than the pressure increases. Hydrogen as far as it has been investigated always shows this increase in the value of the product P V, and not the diminution. The first of these deviations from the theoretical laws is explained by the assumption that the particles of the gas at temperatures much above that at which liquefaction takes place exert an action upon each other, showing itself as an attraction, becoming stronger the more frequently the particles strike one another. The deviation in the opposite direction finds its explanation in the reduction by increased pressure of the space between the particles, and not of that occupied by the particles themselves. The proportion which the latter bears to the total space occupied by the gas, increases with the pressure.

Van der Waals has shown that both these deviations from Boyle's law afford an explanation of the lack of exact proportion to the absolute temperature and the changes in pressure and volume with alterations in temperature.

The kinetic theory of gases, although it still requires further extension and further experimental investigation, is capable of giving a very satisfactory explanation of the behaviour and properties of gases; consequently this theory, in opposition to which at first many facts were cited, has now received general acceptance and recognition.

§ 90. **Mixture of Gases. Diffusion Effusion. Transpiration.** When two or more gases come in contact with one another, each will flow into the space filled by the others, even when they are both under the same pressure. The origin of this mixing or diffusion is the exceedingly great velocity of the particles, which, as already mentioned in § 88, despite its magnitude, can only effect a slow and gradual admixture on account of the frequent collisions of the particles with one another. The diffusion takes place most quickly with gases of small molecular weight, the particles of which have consequently greater velocities. In this respect hydrogen far exceeds all other gases; the rate of diffusion depends also upon the dimensions of the particles of the several gases themselves, since they form the barrier opposed to the free movement of the gaseous particles. It follows, therefore, that for any particular gas the nature of the gas into which it diffuses is important, and its rate of diffusion, therefore, is determined by the nature of the other gas.

When the surface separating the two gases is relatively large then the pressure, being the same on both sides, remains unchanged during and after the mixing of the gases. If the gases are separated by a porous partition or by a partition with a small opening, then the pressure will rise on the side towards which the gas with smaller molecular weight diffuses, because the other gas cannot pass through at a rate sufficiently great to compensate for the inequality of pressure. In course of time, however, this difference in pressure disappears.

In the flow of gases through narrow tubes or channels, which Graham styled 'transpiration,' the internal friction comes into play, and this being dependent upon the free path of the particles may be utilised for the purpose of determining the same.

The flow through a narrow opening in a very thin wall, described as 'effusion' by Graham, takes place with velocities which are inversely as the square root of the densities, and are consequently proportional to the velocities of the rectilinear motion of the particles. This property may therefore, as was proposed by Bunsen, be utilised to measure these velocities and also to determine the molecular weights.

§ 91. **Mixing of Gases and Liquids. Absorption of Gases.**—When a gas comes in contact with a liquid, then, as a rule, the gas passes into the liquid as it would into a vacuum or a space already filled by another gas, whilst at the same time the liquid evaporates to some extent into the gas. The taking up of the gas by the liquid is, when there is no chemical action between the two, spoken of as *absorption*. It is, however, frequently difficult, if not impossible, to draw a sharp line of distinction between absorption and chemical combination. The solution of a gas in a liquid is spoken of as absorption when it takes place in accordance with Henry's law, *i.e.* when it is proportional to the pressure of the gas, and is described as chemical combination when it is independent of the pressure. There are many instances which stand midway between these two extremes, in which whilst the amount of gas absorbed varies with the pressure it is not proportional to it. Such cases will be considered later in the discussion of chemical change (§ 92 *et seq*)

True absorption, which is proportional to the pressure, takes place very slowly when the gas is in simple contact with the surface of the liquid. When the two are brought into more intimate contact by shaking, then the absorption takes place rapidly. The absorption of the gas by the liquid proceeds until a certain relation between the density of the gas absorbed and that of the unabsorbed gas is reached, at which point equilibrium between the particles of gas absorbed and passing out of the liquid is maintained. This relation is called the *coefficient of absorption*: it is dependent upon the nature of the gas and of the liquid, and also upon the temperature. Many liquids, as for example mercury, and possibly other molten metals (perhaps with the exception of silver, which absorbs oxygen), are practically impervious to gases; others absorb but little; whilst others, again, are capable of absorbing considerable proportions of gases. The following table contains the coefficients of absorption by water of several gases at 0° C., 10° C., and 20° C., as found by Bunsen :—

	0° C.	10° C.	20° C.
Hydrogen	0·0193	0·0200	0·0207
Nitrogen	0·0203	0·0167	0·0150
Carbon Monoxide	0·0329	0·0273	0·0248
Oxygen	0·0411	0·0337	0·0305
Marsh Gas	0·0545	0·0453	0·0376
Olefiant Gas	0·2563	0·1904	0·1597
Nitrous Oxide	1·3052	0·9532	0·7191
Carbon Dioxide	1·7967	1·2281	0·9674

These numbers show that the quantity of gas taken up by a unit volume of water is in some cases greater, in others considerably less, than is contained in an equal volume of the free gas itself. In the case of hydrogen the amount of gas absorbed by the unit volume of water is about 2 per cent. of the quantity of hydrogen contained in the unit volume; in fact, this proportion is maintained for parts by weight or for volume, assuming that in the latter case the volumes are measured under the same conditions of pressure and of temperature as those at which the absorption takes place.[1]

A litre of water at 10° absorbs only 20 c.c. of hydrogen

[1] For practical reasons Bunsen measures all the gas absorbed at 0°; consequently his coefficients at 10° and 20° would differ somewhat from those given in the above table.

16·7 c.c. of nitrogen, 33·7 c.c. of oxygen, but takes up as much as 1228·1 c.c. of carbon dioxide.

A comparison of the coefficients of absorption with the critical temperatures given in § 86 shows that the order is very nearly the same, and therefore those gases which require for their liquefaction the greatest cooling and pressure are the least easily absorbed by water. Absorption of gases by liquids would therefore appear to be a phenomenon analogous to that of their liquefaction. It is further to be remarked that the unit gas, which does not under any conditions show a decrease in P.V. with increase of pressure (§ 89), viz. hydrogen, exhibits no diminution in the coefficient of absorption with a rise of temperature from 0–20° C.

Absorption would appear, therefore, to proceed as follows : a certain fraction of the gaseous particles coming in contact with the liquid is taken up by the liquid, the proportion being the greater with the more easily liquefied gases. On the other hand, a portion of the gas is always given off again, and equilibrium is established when as much passes out as is taken up by the liquid. If the pressure on the gas is increased, then so many more particles impinge on the liquid in a given time, and consequently more is absorbed; when the pressure is reduced, then more particles pass out than in, until a new condition of equilibrium is established.

From a mixture of gases each gas is absorbed as though it alone were present, and therefore in proportion to its coefficient of absorption and its share of the total pressure, which Bunsen has described as the 'Partial Pressure.'

§ 92. **Chemical Change.**—The phenomena discussed in the foregoing section are concerned with changes affecting the aggregation of molecules, but not of the molecules themselves, in which the nature of the atoms entering into their composition undergoes a change. The changes in composition of the molecules themselves form the true chemical phenomena, or, as they are usually styled, 'chemical decompositions.' Every element and every compound is capable of such change, but in varying degrees. Whilst many substances resist in a remarkable manner all tendencies to produce changes in their composition, others are so unstable that they retain their individuality only under very special conditions, and are destroyed by the slightest alteration in external conditions. Between these extremes every possible and conceivable state of stability and instability is known.

Chemical changes may assume different forms, which are characterised by the alterations in the molecules produced by the changes.

(1.) A molecule may be formed by the immediate union of the atoms (pure synthesis).

(2.) Or it may be resolved into atoms.

(3.) Two or more molecules may combine to form a single molecule. When the molecules are alike, the phenomenon is spoken of as polymerisation; *e.g.*

$$3C_2H_4O = C_6H_{12}O_3$$
3 mols. of aldehyde 1 mol. of paraldehyde.

When the molecules are different, the combination is described as 'addition,' *e.g.*

$$Hg + Cl_2 = HgCl_2$$
Mercury Chlorine Corrosive sublimate.

$$C_2H_4 + Br_2 = C_2H_4Br_2$$
Ethylene Bromine Ethylene bromide.

(4.) On the other hand, a molecule may split up into several others, either like or unlike. The change when permanent is described as 'decomposition,' and as 'dissociation' when the products of decomposition reunite on withdrawal of the cause producing the change.

(5.) A substance may withdraw a constituent from another substance, or expel a constituent and take its place. The following changes,

$$HgBr_2 + Cl_2 = HgCl_2 + Br_2; \quad Cd + HgCl_2 = CdCl_2 + Hg,$$

may either be interpreted as the expulsion of bromine by chlorine, of mercury by cadmium, or as the chlorine withdrawing bromine from mercury, and the cadmium withdrawing the chlorine. The replacement of a substance (*e.g.* bromine) by another (chlorine) is described as 'substitution' of the second in place of the first.

164   OUTLINES OF THEORETICAL CHEMISTRY

(6.) The most frequent form of chemical change is that of 'double decomposition,' in which two substances mutually interchange some of their constituents, *e.g.*

$$HH + ClCl = HCl + HCl$$

$$HI + AgCl = HCl + AgI$$

$$C_2H_5OH + HONO_2 = C_2H_5ONO_2 + HOH.$$
Alcohol   Nitric acid   Ethyl nitrate   Water

Formerly, many of the changes belonging to this category were regarded as syntheses or additions, but such views are now regarded as erroneous, *e.g.*

$$\cancel{H + Cl = HCl}, \text{ or } H + Cl = HCl.$$

(7.) Triple and even more complex interactions are not infrequent; *e.g.*, the oxidation of carbon monoxide (according to Dixon), or of metals (according to Traube), by moist oxygen, the bromination of benzene by the agency of ferric chloride (according to Scheufelen), and even the solution of zinc in dilute sulphuric acid:

$$CO + O \;\; H_2 + O \,|\, O + H_2 \,|\, O + CO = CO_2 + H_2O + OH_2 + CO_2$$

$$Zn + 2\,(OH \,|\, H) + O \;\; O = Zn\,(OH)_2 + H_2OO$$

$$C_6H_6 + BrBr + FeCl_3 = C_6H_5Br + HCl + FeCl_2\,Br$$

$$HO \,|\, H + Zn + H\,.\,OSO_2\,OH = H\,.\,H + HO\,ZnOSO_2OH.$$

Considering the final result of the first change, one might conclude therefrom that oxygen and carbon monoxide alone take part in the action, since there is as much water present at the end as there was at the commencement of the action. This view is nevertheless incorrect, as it has been shown that this oxidation does not take place in the absence of water, or, if at all, only at high temperatures.

(8.) A rearrangement of atoms may take place in the molecules themselves, resulting in a change of the atomic linkage; such cases are described as metameric changes, *e g.*

$$\text{O}{=}\text{C}{=}\text{N}-\text{NH}_4 = \text{O}{=}\text{C}{<}^{\text{NH}_2}_{\text{NH}_2}$$
Ammonium isocyanate   Urea

$$\text{N}{\equiv}\text{C}-\text{S}-\text{NH}_4 = \text{S}{=}\text{C}{<}^{\text{NH}_2}_{\text{NH}_2}$$
Ammonium thiocyanate   Thio-urea

As a matter of fact, many of these main forms of chemical change frequently occur simultaneously; consequently the complete change may be a very complex one.

§ 93 **Causes of Chemical Change.**—Every chemical compound, if left to itself, would in all probability remain unaltered, retaining its composition and properties for all time. Alterations in composition may be produced by external causes of different kinds. The ability to withstand the action of such agencies is described as the 'stability' of a chemical compound. The stability varies within the widest limits. Compounds are known in which, the atoms being in a condition of unstable equilibrium, the slightest change, such as shaking or a touch, suffices to disturb their arrangement and induce a decomposition; whilst in others the mode of arrangement is so stable that they withstand the action of the strongest and most powerful agencies.

The following are the main forces active in effecting chemical changes: (1) mechanical disturbance, (2) heat, (3) light, (4) electricity, (5) the action of other substances, which action is usually ascribed to their powers of attraction or affinity. It is seldom that one or other of these causes is alone active; consequently it is difficult to distinguish and separate their individual effect. Heat is always concerned in such changes, for we are unacquainted with any means whereby all the heat may be withdrawn from a body; and, moreover, it is highly improbable that, supposing its particles perfectly motionless, a substance would still be capable of undergoing a chemical change.

§ 94. **Heat as Cause and Effect of Chemical Change.**—The relation between heat and chemical change is a very intimate one, so that not only is heat productive of chemical changes, but as a rule is a consequence of such actions, and is either positive or negative, according to whether in the change heat is produced or used up

The mode of action of heat in producing and favouring

chemical changes is easily understood; since heat consists of a rapid movement of particles not only of the molecules but also of the atoms composing them, it follows, therefore, that with the acceleration of this motion the atoms move farther and farther apart, and thus the coherence of the molecules is gradually loosened, and finally destroyed. It is not essential that the molecule should be thus broken down into single atoms; but these may, in consequence of the loosening of the already existing bonds, and their altered positions, find opportunities to enter into new states of combination, producing in this manner compounds more stable at the higher temperature than the original. In the case of more complex changes in which several substances take part, heat may, by loosening the bonds of union holding the atoms together, facilitate the action, and thus bring about the change, which might perhaps not have taken place without the aid of heat.

The mechanical theory of heat was at one time supposed to give a satisfactory explanation of the production of heat in chemical changes, this heat-production being regarded as due to the affinity, the force by which the atoms were supposed to be mutually attracted to one another. Assuming that the atoms are provided with these forces of attraction, which are only effective at short distances, then the atoms will obey these forces so soon as they are brought within the sphere of their mutual action, and will acquire velocities which will become greater the stronger the attraction and the smaller the mass to be moved. When the atoms clash with one another, then their kinetic energy must either become converted into heat or some other form of motion, or do work, $i.e.$ move some mass under the influence of opposing forces. If heat is produced, then this will be greater in proportion to the strength of the active affinities, and this heat must therefore offer a very suitable means of measuring the strength of these affinities. When work is done, then, as a rule, this work consists in overcoming the forces of attraction of some other atoms, and consequently the atoms so held together are expelled. This very plausible theory was for a long time received as the true explanation, but was only tenable so long as no reliable method existed for measuring the strength of the affinities. So soon as it was possible to make such measurements it became evident that the greatest heat-production is not necessarily associated with the most powerful affinities, and therefore the calorific effect is not a suitable measure of the combining power. Further, it has been most clearly shown that the amount of heat produced depends upon the changes of state in each of the reacting substances, and not upon the reciprocal action of two bodies, and therefore not on their mutual affinity.

Since the early conception of the origin of the heat of combination must be abandoned, there only remains the hypothesis that this heat has its origin entirely or in part in the motion of the atoms, which they lose when combination takes place, and which must be imparted to them when this union is destroyed. It certainly may be assumed that this heat, at any rate in part, is the product of the forces of affinity; but such an assumption is at the present time quite useless, and only complicates the problem unnecessarily.

Inasmuch as the hope that the heat produced or used up in chemical changes might be utilised as a measure of affinity has not been realised, the investigations of these calorific actions declined in interest, but are now again becoming important, as the numerous results of observations in this field are studied and investigated free from and unprejudiced by preconceived notions, with the object of learning something of the changes in state which accompany chemical action.

§ 95 **Propagation of Chemical Change. Temperature of Ignition. Explosion** —Whether a chemical change produced at any given point in a body or a mixture will spread throughout its mass depends as a rule not only upon the cause of the change, but also upon the heat produced by the action. For instance, supposing a mixture of a combustible gas and oxygen be heated at any given point by an electric spark, or any other means, to such a degree that the combustion begins, it does not necessarily follow that the burning will spread throughout the whole of the mixture. Whether it does so depends upon the amount of heat produced by the combustion. If this suffices to raise the immediate layers of combustible material to the temperature required for its inflammation, i.e. to the 'temperature of ignition,' then these layers are burnt up, and in turn yield heat sufficient to ignite the next stratum, and so on until the whole is consumed. Since, however, in cases of this kind a portion of the heat produced is always given out either by radiation or conduction to the surrounding bodies not concerned with the reaction, it may happen that the progress of the combustion is interrupted before the entire mass has been attacked. This will be the less liable to occur the more the heating consequent upon the reaction exceeds the temperature of ignition. In case the mixture contains non-combustible bodies, *e.g.* nitrogen, then, as such bodies have their temperatures raised at the expense of the heat produced by the combustion, the temperature is thereby reduced, and with a considerable admixture of such bodies the temperature may sink so low that the advance of the combustion ceases. Every combustible mixture may therefore be rendered non-inflammable by the admixture of a sufficient quantity of non-combustible material. If no such disturbing influences are to hand, and the heat of combustion be great, then the heating may rise far above the temperature of ignition. Further, if the products of the combustion are gaseous or vaporous, then a considerable sudden expansion results, which may increase until it becomes an explosion.

Something of the same kind takes place in the case of substances which can be exploded by mechanical disturbance or by percussion. This property is alone exhibited by substances in which the atoms are in a state of more or less unstable equilibrium, from which condition they can pass with production of heat, or corresponding amount of work, into a more stable state of equilibrium. Examples of this class of bodies we have in the chlorine, bromine, and iodine compounds of nitrogen, in the organic nitrates and nitro-organic compounds. When such bodies yield gaseous or vaporous products of decomposition, and produce much heat, they may also act as explosives.

The liquid chloride of nitrogen, for instance, is decomposed by very slight causes; this decomposition is expressed by the following equation:—

$$NCl_3 + NCl_3 = N_2 + Cl_2 + Cl_2 + Cl_2.$$

This action is attended by a considerable heat-production, and consequent marked expansion of its gaseous products.

Glyceryl nitrate (commonly but erroneously described as nitroglycerine) $C_3H_5(ONO_2)_3$, in which $\frac{2}{3}$, or in reality $\frac{5}{9}$, of the oxygen is combined with the nitrogen, yields gaseous and vaporous oxidation products of carbon and hydrogen, whilst the nitrogen is also set free in the gaseous state. This decomposition can be brought about by percussion or detonation as well as by heat. If the nitrate be ignited in an open space, it burns slowly and quietly, for the gaseous products pass freely away If the nitrate be enclosed so that this free passage is prevented, or if it be ignited by a powerful blow, then the violent shock and pressure produced will immediately decompose the particles near those first struck, and thus the decomposition will spread in the form of an explosion. If the decomposition does not produce heat or do work sufficient for its extension, then the reaction ceases.

These explosives are quite analogous to gunpowder, with the single exception that in the case of gunpowder the combustible constituents, charcoal and sulphur, are only mechanically mixed with the nitre, which contains the oxygen, whilst in the former the oxygen is combined chemically with the other constituents.

§ 96. **Dissociation of Gases.**—One of the simplest forms of chemical change, which is in the main produced by heat, is that which H Sainte-Claire Deville styled dissociation. Dissociation is characterised by the decomposition lasting only so long as the cause is active, the substances returning to the original state on withdrawal of the cause. Many substances are found to undergo dissociation; still it is often difficult to observe and demonstrate the dissociation. More especially is this the case when very high temperatures are needed to bring about the decomposition. In many instances the action is associated with a change in colour, and can be recognised by this, thus, for example, the colourless vapours of nitrogen peroxide, N_2O_4, dissociate into dark brown vapours of NO_2. Dissociation is recognisable in the increase in the number of molecules resulting from it; for, as Avogadro's Law still holds, the density of the gas or vapour is also altered. In the case just mentioned, viz.

$$N_2O_4 = NO_2 + NO_2,$$

the number of molecules, and consequently the volume, is doubled, and therefore the density is reduced to one-half. Observations have, however, shown that this change does not occur suddenly, but takes place gradually as the temperature rises, so that the progress and extent of the dissociation may be calculated from the changes in volume and density.

The density of the compound NO_2 in relation to air is 1·59; therefore that of the non-dissociated compound, N_2O_4, is twice as great, viz. 3·18. Mixtures of these two, such as are produced by the dissociation, would have densities lying between these values; the more nearly the observed density approaches the lower value, the more advanced the dissociation. If in 100 particles, x have been dissociated, and therefore $100-x$ are still unaltered, then we have

$$100\,(N_2O_4) = (100-x)\,N_2O_4 + 2x\,NO_2.$$

Consequently there are now $100+x$ particles instead of 100, the volume is increased in the proportion of $100 : 100+x$, and the density, D, decreased in the inverse proportion, viz. of $100+x : 100$. To determine x, the percentage of dissociation, we have the following proportion:—

$$100+x : 100 = 3·18 : D$$
$$x = 100 \times \frac{3\,18-D}{D}.$$

By this formula the percentage of dissociation can be calculated for every observed density; in this way the following values have been obtained:

Temperature	Density d	Dissociation x	Increase for 1° C.
		per cent.	per cent
26 7°	2·65	19·96	0 65
35 4°	2·53	25 65	0 81
39 8°	2 46	29 23	1 10
49 6°	2 27	40 04	1 21
60 2°	2 08	52 84	1 30
70 0°	1 92	65 57	1 04
80 6°	1 80	76 61	0 88
90 0°	1 72	84 83	0 44
100 1°	1 68	89 23	0 31
111 3°	1 65	92 67	0 35
121 5°	1 62	96 23	0 18
135 0°	1 60	98 69	
154 0°	1 58	100 00	

The average increase in the dissociation for each degree centigrade rises until a maximum is reached, when the dissociation is about half completed, and then it gradually diminishes, until at 140° C. the dissociation is complete.

One might imagine that the dissociation having once begun, it must be suddenly translated through the mass so soon as the temperature required for its commencement has been reached. That this is not the case finds an explanation in the fact that in consequence of the frequent and irregular collision of the particles they do not all retain an equal velocity, and as the temperature is determined by this motion, the particles have not all the same energy. The particles having the greatest energy, *i.e.* those in the most rapid motion, are first dissociated, and those having the least heat-motion will be the last to dissociate. What we measure as the temperature of a gas is only the mean or average temperature of all the particles; some of the particles may have temperatures differing considerably from this. As great differences are seldom found, but smaller differences more frequently occur, dissociation will proceed most rapidly when the mean temperature is the same as the temperature of dissociation. At this temperature 50 per cent. of the entire mass is dissociated, and in the case of nitrogen peroxide this point is reached at 60° C.

When the temperature of dissociation is too high to permit of exact measurements of density, then, in order to make it evident, other means must be employed. Deville has employed many ingenious devices for this purpose. For instance, by diffusion through porous septa he separated the hydrogen from the oxygen formed by the dissociation of steam at a white heat, which gases, if not separated at this temperature, would recombine at a somewhat lower temperature. By rapid cooling carbon monoxide and carbon were separated from the dissociated carbon dioxide, and chlorine in a similar manner was obtained from hydrochloric acid gas.

Bunsen has shown from the pressure produced by the explosion of a mixture of two volumes of hydrogen and one volume of oxygen that combination ceases as soon as the temperature has reached about 3000° C., and therefore above this temperature steam cannot exist, but is resolved into its elements. Whether in this decomposition the molecules are resolved into atoms, thus,

$$H_2O = H + O + H$$

or whether elementary molecules are formed,

$$2H_2O = 2H_2 + O_2$$

has not as yet been satisfactorily determined.

On the other hand, it is known that the partial decomposition of hydrogen iodide into hydrogen and iodine takes place at 440° C., whilst the decomposition of the iodine molecules into atoms begins at 600°, and that of the hydrogen molecule, if at all, at much higher temperatures So it is probable that the dissociation of hydrogen iodide at 400—500° C. takes place as follows :—

$$2HI = HH + II.$$

The compound is, therefore, not resolved into atoms, and the decomposition is not a case of simple dissociation, but an instance of a chemical exchange.

§ 97 **Dissociation of Liquids and of Solids.**—Liquids, both homogeneous and mixed, undergo dissociation just as gases do ; but in the case of liquids it is less frequent, and also much more difficult of demonstration. Still, the colourless liquid nitrogen peroxide, N_2O_4, is observed to assume a reddish colour when warmed; showing that even in the liquid state, as is the case with the gas, it is dissociated into the red compound, having half the molecular weight and the formula NO_2. Liquids, and many solids also, are frequently dissociated when boiled. Concentrated sulphuric acid is not volatile as such, but at 325° is resolved into the anhydride and water, thus :

$$H_2SO_4 = SO_3 + H_2O$$

and these compounds on cooling reunite with each other.

This volatilisation is not true boiling, and therefore even under reduced pressure it takes place only at the same temperature as under the atmospheric pressure (Mendeléeff). Carbonic acid, H_2CO_3, and sulphurous acid, H_2SO_3, exhibit a similar decomposition, but at much lower temperatures.

Chloral hydrate when vaporised decomposes into chloral and water, thus:
$$CCl_3CO_2H_3 = CCl_3COH + H_2O$$

and these recombine on cooling. The iodides, bromides, and chlorides of many tertiary alcohols behave in a similar manner, thus, amyl iodide yields amylene and hydriodic acid:
$$C_5H_{11}I = C_5H_{10} + HI.$$

Inorganic chlorides, bromides, and iodides exhibit dissociation, e.g. phosphorus pentachloride:
$$PCl_5 = PCl_3 + Cl_2.$$

Phosphorus pentafluoride is, however, volatile without decomposition.

The salts of ammonia and of substituted ammonias form a group of compounds which can only be volatilised by first undergoing dissociation. Thus ammonium chloride is decomposed into ammonia and hydrochloric acid:
$$NH_4Cl = NH_3 + HCl$$

and tetra-ethyl ammonium iodide is resolved into tri-ethylamine and ethyl iodide:
$$N(C_2H_5)_4I = N(C_2H_5)_3 + C_2H_5I.$$

In the case of many liquids it has been observed that the density of their vapour is much greater at temperatures near their boiling points than at higher temperatures. Thus, according to Cahours, the density of acetic acid vapour at 250° C. is 2·08, air being the unit, which gives a molecular weight corresponding to the formula $C_2H_4O_2$. At 125° C the density is found to be 3·2 in comparison with air. This is generally explained by assuming that at the lower temperature the vapour consists in part of particles of greater molecular weight, e.g. $C_4H_8O_4$, which are dissociated by further heating, as also by reduction of the pressure on the vapour.

Sulphur, aluminium chloride, and many other substances behave in a similar manner.

§ 98. **Dissociation in Solution.**—Dissociation may be more frequently observed in mixed liquids, in solutions, than with homogeneous fluids. The occurrence may be evidenced by a change in colour, as, for instance, when a coloured hydrated salt loses or changes its colour in consequence of a loss of water (*cf.* § 78). Thus the red compound $CoCl_2 + 6H_2O$ dissolves in water, and also in dilute spirit, forming a red solution; but on warming the solution becomes blue, either because an anhydrous compound or one containing less water is produced. On cooling the solution the red compound is again formed.

Crystallisation may in many cases be used to prove dissociation. At low temperatures from a solution of sodium sulphate, Glauber's salt, $Na_2SO_4 + 10H_2O$ separates out; whilst at 33° C. the anhydrous salt Na_2SO_4 is deposited. Many other salts behave in a similar manner.

In the case of double salts and analogous compounds dissociation may be demonstrated, as has been done with gaseous compounds, by diffusion. For example, if an open vessel filled with a solution of alum, $K_2SO_4, Al_2(SO_4)_3 + 24H_2O$, be placed in a larger vessel filled with water and allowed to remain, then, according to Graham's observations, in course of time the upper layers of water are found to contain more potassium sulphate and less aluminium sulphate than correspond to the composition of the alum. The two simple salts have, therefore, separated from each other in the solution; the double salt has been dissociated. This separation takes place because the potassium salt diffuses more rapidly than the aluminium sulphate, and therefore passes out before the other; the separation is consequently only recognised at first, as later on the inequality is compensated for. Almost all double salts behave in a similar manner, but their dissociation can only be demonstrated when the products have different rates of diffusion.

§ 99. **Electrolysis.**—Electricity offers a very powerful means of separating the dissociated products from one another. It has been known since the end of the last century that when an electric current is conducted through certain liquids the constituents are separated from one another at the points where the electricity enters and leaves the liquid. Faraday, to whom we are indebted for the investigation of the fundamental laws of this phenomenon, styled this kind of decomposition 'electrolysis,' i e. analysis by electricity. Those substances capable of undergoing this species of decomposition are styled ' electrolytes,' and described as 'conductors of the second class,' conducting electricity only when simultaneously decomposed, and are distinguished in this way from (1) the ' conductors of the first class,' or ' metallic conductors,' which allow the passage of electricity without decomposition, (2) from the ' non-conductors,' or ' insulators,' which do not conduct electricity at all. The conductor of the first class, which serves to bring into and carry away the electricity from the electrolyte, is styled the ' electrode' (from $\dot{\eta}$ $\delta\delta\delta s$, the way). The electrode situated upstream as regards the positive current is called the ' anode,' whilst that situated down-stream is styled the ' cathode.' Finally, the constituent passing up-stream and deposited at the anode is called the ' anion' ($\tau\grave{o}$ $\dot{a}\nu\iota\grave{o}\nu$), whilst that going down to the cathode is the 'cation' ($\tau\grave{o}$ $\kappa a\tau\iota\grave{o}\nu$). Both are spoken of as the ' ions.'

For a long time electrolysis was regarded as the result of the decomposition of the electrolyte by electrical attraction, until in 1857 Clausius adduced the proof that electricity is not the cause of the decomposition, but that it can only effect the separation of the constituents of compounds already decomposed by the action of other forces. For if electricity is needed to effect the decomposition of a compound in which the constituents are held together by the force of affinity, then electrical energy in the conductor cannot produce the decomposition so long as it remains weaker than the affinity, and must, therefore, give rise to a very violent decomposition so soon as its strength somewhat exceeds this. Experience, however, shows this not to be the case, for the smallest force produces a current the intensity of which increasing in proportion to the force is sufficient to cause the ' ions' to collect together at the electrodes, or, as it is technically described, to produce the 'polarisation at the electrodes.' Since, therefore, the smallest electromotive force is sufficient to produce this effect, no expenditure of force can be needed for the decomposition of the electrolyte; this must have already taken place, the electrolyte must have been dissociated. This dissociation must have an origin similar to that spoken of in the preceding sections, and have been wrought by the rapid motion of the particles communicated as heat to the substances.

The recent investigations of Arrhenius have drawn attention to the fact that electrolytes are exactly those substances which, as already shown in § 78, produce a greater depression in the freezing point of water than is consistent with the proportion in the solution of their molecules as represented by the generally accepted formulæ. Thus, whilst in the case of non-electrolytes, when their molecular weights in grams are dissolved in a litre of water, giving a so-called 'normal solution,' the freezing point of water is depressed by $-1.8°$ C., the haloid salts of the alkalis, for instance, give twice as great depression, for

$$NaCl - 3.5°, KCl - 3.3, \text{ etc. (v. § 78).}$$

If it be assumed that these salts are entirely or in part dissociated, in the following manner.

$$NaCl = Na + Cl, KCl = K + Cl$$

then the depression of the freezing point would appear to be normal; for, as there are twice as many particles present, the depression of the freezing point must be twice as great as in the case of substances which are not dissociated.

At first sight it does appear not a little remarkable that the substances which are supposed to decompose so easily should be exactly those which are formed by bodies uniting with one another with considerable energy, and to which consequently strong mutual affinities are ascribed. A further consideration shows, however, that these very same substances take part easily in the most diverse kinds of chemical change, and therefore their constituents cannot be so firmly and indissolubly attached to one another. Clausius did not suppose that when, for instance, common salt is dissociated into sodium and chlorine, the individual atoms are permanently set at liberty, but rather was of opinion that reunion and decomposition recur continually, each atom combining not only with the one with which it was previously united, but with any others which it may meet in the throng of atoms. This conception would appear still to be permissible; making clear, as it does, why in a solution of common salt we find neither free chlorine nor free sodium, so long as they are not brought together at the electrodes by the passage of an electric current.

§ 100. **Faraday's Law.**—According to the law discovered by Faraday, the passage of electricity from one electrode to the other, through the electrolytes, takes place in such a way that for a certain amount of electricity passing through the electrolyte a given fixed quantity of each 'ion' separates out at the electrodes; so that the ions are not only equivalent to one another, but also the amount of each liberated is proportional to the quantity of electricity passing through the system. From this we must conclude that every equivalent weight of the ions can be charged by a fixed and definite amount of electricity, which it carries through the electrolyte from one electrode to the other; just as a ship takes up a given load and carries it across the ocean. The anode charged with positive electricity gives up positive, the negatively charged cathode an equivalent quantity of negative electricity. The electrolyte takes up these charges, but in return discharges an amount of each ion equivalent to the electricity at each electrode, at the anode the electro-negative anion, e.g. chlorine, and at the cathode the electro-positive cation, e.g. sodium, is discharged.

The origin of the distinction of the ions as positive and negative is to be found in the observation mentioned in § 37, that different substances when brought in contact with one another become electrically excited, one becoming charged with positive, the other with negative electricity; and the greater the difference in the chemical characters of the substance, so much the stronger is the charge; and, further, those substances which by such contact become electro-negative in electrolysis appear as 'anions'; conversely, the electro-positive appear as 'cations.' The hypothesis has been advanced that ions united with one another in compounds are charged in like manner, and retain their charge even when dissociated. Such a supposition explains how it comes about that the positively charged anode should attract the negatively charged anion, and that the cation should be drawn to the cathode, the electrodes repelling the ions charged similarly to themselves; consequently one receives an impulse in one direction, the other in the opposite direction. When the attracted ion comes in contact with the electrode the opposing electricities neutralise one another, and the ion remains in an unelectrified state. Now two ions, e.g. two chlorine atoms, which were previously charged with the same kind of electricity, and in consequence would repel one another, may combine to form a molecule of free chlorine, Cl_2, and as such appear at the anode.

By this discharge of electricity at the electrodes the liquid receives at these points an excess of the opposite electricity, that is, of the same kind as that with which the electrode is charged, and this moves with the ions through the electrolyte to the other electrode. For the transport of the electricity it is not necessary that the particles repelled by one electrode should reach the other. This movement takes place simultaneously throughout the whole of the electrolyte situated between the electrodes, the cations going always with the current, the anions against the stream; and this takes place in such a way that in every sectional area of the current there is as much electricity passing in a given time as through any other similar section, namely, as much as each electrode gives off or takes up respectively.

§ 101. **Relationship between Conductivity and Dissociation.**—As the electricity is transferred by the ions, and can only pass through the electrolyte by their aid, the undecomposed molecules taking no part in the transport, it follows that only substances capable of dissociation can act as electrolytes; and, further, they must conduct the more readily the more advanced the dissociation. In fact, Arrhenius has shown by numerous examples that all electrolytes described in § 79, whose aqueous solutions give an abnormal depression of the freezing point, are therefore partially or entirely dissociated, and that their conductivity is proportional to the extent of the dissociation as measured by the reduction of the freezing point. Those bodies, such as the chlorides of the alkali-metals, which give a reduction almost twice as great as that produced by an equal number of molecules of non-dissociable substances, are almost completely decomposed in their dilute solutions, and therefore are good conductors of electricity. In more concentrated solutions the conductivity does not increase in proportion to the amount present, but more slowly, because in such cases the dissociation is not so great. If the share in the conduction of electricity taken by each molecule be calculated by dividing the conductivity, by the number of equivalent weights (expressed in grams) contained in the unit volume (1 litre), then we obtain a series of quotients which Kohlrausch has styled the specific molecular conductivity;[1] and which increases with increased dilution, and therefore with increasing dissociation. The conclusions arrived at in § 79 find a most satisfactory confirmation in this behaviour of electrolytes.

The knowledge of the interdependence of dissociation and electrolytic conductivity enables one to explain the statement made by F. Kohlrausch that at the ordinary temperature only mixtures conduct electricity, the several constituents of which are, however, non-conductors. Thus, whilst a mixture of water and hydrochloric acid gas is a good conductor of electricity, because the hydrochloric acid gas is almost completely dissociated, still neither pure water nor liquefied hydrochloric acid gas is a conductor. At a red heat, when the tendency to decomposition is greater, many homogeneous substances are electrolytes.

§ 102 **Migration of the Ions.**—As the positive electricity is alone transported by the cations, and the negative by the anions, and as exactly equal amounts of each are simultaneously deposited at both electrodes, one might be inclined to think that what holds true for the different kinds of electricity will also apply to the ions, and that equal quantities of each ion must pass simultaneously through any section of the current. This is, as Hittorf has shown, not the case; nor is it necessary that it should be, for, as far as the transport of electricity is concerned, it is immaterial whether a number of positive ions move to one side or an equal number of negative ions pass to the other side. A deficiency of one kind may therefore be compensated by an excess of another. The transference of electricity, however, is proportional to the sum of the quantities of both the ions deposited; the electrolytic conductivity is also proportional to this amount, which consequently may be used as a measure of the conductivity.

The ratio of the velocities of the anions and cations may also be determined. It is only necessary, after the electrolysis has

[1] Strictly speaking, the addition 'molecular' is not correct, as the specific conductivity is given in terms, not of molecular, but of equivalent weights.

N 2

gone on for a little time, to determine, by an analysis of those portions of the liquid surrounding the electrodes, what quantities of each ion have passed through the central and still unaltered portion of the liquid. Hittorf has made a large series of such determinations, and found that the migration of the ions, as he styles it, takes place with very unequal velocities. If the anion and cation were to move at equal rates, then for every single equivalent weight of each deposited at the electrodes one half of this amount of each must during this time pass through the intermediate layers of the electrolyte; for by the complete symmetry of the operation one half of the positive electricity released at the cathode is provided by the positive ions, coming from the side of the anode; the other half is thus free, so that the negative ions may pass from the cathodes towards the anode. This, according to Hittorf's investigations, happens in some cases, for example, in a moderately dilute solution of potassium chloride, in which for every equivalent of potassium, $K = 39.03$, deposited at the cathode, and every equivalent of chlorine, $Cl = 35.37$, deposited at the anode, and giving up their charge of electricity, the half of each of these quantities passes from one half of the solution to the other. If now we take the case in which, for instance, the cation of an electrolyte is entirely or almost completely immovable, electrolytic conduction and decomposition may still take place; in such a case, however, the transport of electricity is effected by the anion entirely, of which, therefore, an entire equivalent must pass from the side of the cathode to the anode, so that a loss of anion takes place in the portion of the liquid surrounding the cathode, and the loss in that portion surrounding the anode produced by the deposition of the anion is completely compensated for by this migration. Moreover, as one equivalent of the cation is deposited at the cathode, it is evident that the entire expenditure is borne by that portion of the electrolyte surrounding the cathode. At this point the liquid must become very much diluted, whilst in other parts the concentration will remain unaltered. Such an extreme case has certainly never been observed; but all those hitherto investigated lie between this and the first case considered.

The number expressing the fraction of an equivalent of an ion transferred from one electrode to the other in the time during which an equivalent of each is liberated at the electrodes Hittorf has styled the 'transport number, and represents it by 'n.' For example, from a solution of 1 part of crystallised copper sulphate, $CuSO_4 + 5H_2O$, whilst 0·2955 gram of copper is deposited on the cathode, 0·0843 gram only passes through the intermediate and unaltered layers of the liquid from the side of the anode to the cathode. In this instance, then, we have n for copper equal to 0·285.

$$\frac{0·0843}{0·2955} = 0·285.$$

Instead of half an equivalent of the metal passing through the unaltered section of the current, little more than a quarter passes. This portion of the electrolyte does not contain the free ions but simply the neutral salt, proving that the ions exist in equivalent proportions; it therefore follows that the quantity of the anion passing against the current has proportionately increased—in fact, 0·715 equivalent of SO_4, thus:—

$$1 - n = 1 - 0·285 = 0·715 \text{ equivalent } SO_4$$

The sum of the transport numbers of the two ions is always equal to unity. They are not quite invariable, but vary somewhat with the concentration, and in some cases considerably.

For instance, in the case of potassium bromide, the 'transport number' for bromine changes. For a solution of 1 part of the salt in 2·36 parts of water it is 0·493, in 116·5 parts of water it is 0·546. The transport number of the potassium falls in a corresponding manner from 0·507 to 0·454. In the more dilute solutions the velocity of the bromine compared to that of the potassium is somewhat increased.

§ 103. **Velocities of the Ions.**—By the aid of these numbers and the determinations of the conductivity of solutions, F. Kohlrausch has calculated the velocities of the single ions. The electrical conductivity of a body depends not only on its material composition, but also on its dimensions and the temperature. According to Ohm's Law it is proportional to the sectional area, and inversely proportional to the length of the conductor; in electrolytic conduction it rises with increased temperature, but decreases with rise in temperature in case of metallic conduction. By maintaining the temperature and dimensions constant, in other words, by comparing conductors of exactly the same form at the same temperature. and in the case of liquids using vessels of exactly the same width and length, results are obtained which enable us to fix the relation between the conductivity of the electrolyte and the quality and quantity of its constituents.

As pure water does not conduct, the conducting power of an aqueous solution depends chiefly upon the nature and amount of the substance dissolved in it, and in fact is determined, not by the total amount dissolved, but only by the portion dissociated (*cf.* § 101). If the specific molecular conductivity of such a solution be calculated, a number is obtained which is dependent not only on the number of molecules dissolved but also upon the extent of their dissociation. Since this dissociation is complete only when the dilution is infinitely great, only such diluted solutions should be used for comparison, which is by no means easily done. These difficulties may be avoided by comparing only solutions which contain in a given volume not only an equal number of molecules, but contain these in a similar state of dissociation If this be at least approximately the case, and both contain an equal number of ions in a given volume, the differences in the specific conductivity can only be due to the difference in the mobility of the ions, and may, therefore, serve to determine this.

The specific conductivity λ can be represented as the sum of two values, one u proportional to the velocity of the cation, the other v proportional to that of the anion; thus

$$\lambda = u + v.$$

But as the proportion of both these parts is given by the transport numbers, we have

$$u : v :: 1-n : n$$

n representing the transport number of the anion. Two equations are thus obtained for the determination of the unknown u and v, viz.

$$u = (1-n)\lambda, \; v = n \cdot \lambda.$$

Calculating by the aid of this expression the velocity of one and the same ion from the conductivity of its different compounds, satisfactory results are obtained, as has been shown by Kohlrausch, so long as salts of monobasic acids only are compared with one another. The following table contains the velocities of ions calculated by Kohlrausch and expressed in terms of an arbitrary standard, in which λ is measured in terms of the ten-millionth part of the conductivity of mercury, or the latter is set down as 10^7.

Cations	$u.\,10^7$	Anions	$v.\,10^7$
H = 1	272	OH = 16·96	143
Li = 7	24	F = 19·06	30
Na = 23·0	32	Cl = 35·37	54
K = 39·0	52	Br = 79·76	53
NH_4 = 18·01	50	I = 126·54	55
Ag = 107·66	40	CN = 25·98	50
½Mg = 12·15	26	NO_3 = 61·89	48
½Ca = 19·95	26	ClO_3 = 83·25	42
½Sr = 43·65	28	$C_2H_3O_2$ = 58·86	26
½Ba = 68·45	30		
½Cu = 31·59	29		
½Zn = 32·55	24		

If these velocities are expressed in absolute terms, it is then seen that they are very small even under the influence of a strong electromotive force, and the particles move in a second through a few hundredths or a tenth of a millimetre, and consequently at a snail-like speed. It is evident that they meet with considerable opposition to their movement.

§ 104. **Relation between Electrolytic Conduction and Diffusion.**—The intimate relationship between electrolytic conduction and the motion of the particles is shown also in the fact that those movements which take place independently of electricity exhibit corresponding variation. J. H. Long has proved experimentally that the velocities with which different salts of analogous composition diffuse into water stand to one another in approximately the same relation as their electrolytic conductivities, so that the compounds which diffuse the most easily are the best conductors. This statement is not absolutely true, but holds only for certain groups of compounds of similar composition, because in different groups the extent of the dissociation is different, and undecomposed molecules diffuse with velocities other than those of the ions.

That many salts are in reality resolved into their ions and do not, or only in part, diffuse undecomposed, is also shown by Long's observations; for the comparison of compounds containing the same anion—for example, the chlorides—has shown that the rate of diffusion is inversely proportional to the transport number of the anion; but the comparison of salts with the same cation— for example, the potassium salts—has demonstrated the rate of diffusion to be directly proportional to the transport number of the anion. This practically amounts to saying that, if two salts have the same ion in common, then the salt with the more mobile second ion is the more easily diffusible The rate of diffusion would therefore appear to be the sum of the velocities of the ions.

§ 105. **The Function of the Ions in the Production of Electric Currents.**—The near relationship between the electrolytic ions and the movement of electricity is seen also in the fact that electric currents are produced by the contact of unequally concentrated solutions of electrolytes simultaneously with the diffusion tending to compensate for the inequality in concentration. The intensity of the currents can be shown, both experimentally and theoretically, to be related to the velocities of the ions.

The electric currents produced ordinarily by contact of two or more metals with one another or with one or more electrolytes appear to owe their origin to the free and mobile ions set at liberty by dissociation. The chemical affinity of the metals for the anions exercises an attraction on these. By the deposition of the anions on the metal and the giving up of their negative electricity the metal becomes so charged with electricity that the further approximation of the anions is prevented The strength of this charge of negative electricity is greater the greater the affinity of the metal for the anion. For instance, if two metals, like copper and zinc, are immersed in a liquid, then the metal, in this case zinc, possessing the stronger affinity will be charged more strongly with negative electricity than the other, viz. the copper. If the two metals are united by a metallic conductor, then the more strongly charged zinc will give up its negative electricity to the copper, and in return receive a charge of positive from the copper. Thus the equilibrium at the points of contact of the two metals and the electrolyte is disturbed; in consequence of the reduced negative charge of the zinc, more anion is attracted, and the increased negative charge of the copper induces a repulsion of the anion; and cations are attracted by reason of their positive charge. In addition, at the point of contact of both metals there is a separation of electricity opposite to the charge produced by the ions. Equilibrium cannot be established so long as both the metals are in contact with each other and the electrolyte. But as the ions collect more and more on the metals and cover them, the negative anion on one, and the positive cation on the other, the ions take the place of the metal and thus reverse the action completely, for the positive cation attracts the anion, and the reverse. This separation of the ions which produces a current opposed to the original is styled 'electric polarisation.'

In order, therefore, to produce a constant current the separation of the ions at the electrodes must be prevented, or in other ways made innocuous, which end can be attained by suitable choice of the electrolyte. In this way constant electric batteries can be produced. Daniell's battery is one of the oldest of this kind, and consists of a plate of copper surrounded by a solution of copper sulphate, $CuSO_4$, and a plate of zinc immersed in dilute sulphuric acid, and separated from the copper by a porous cell. The zinc attracts to itself the anion, SO_4, and repels the cation, H_2, and is charged with negative electricity, which passes over to the copper on which the positive cation, Cu, collects; whilst if the copper and zinc were not in contact the copper would also be surrounded with the anion, SO_4. The precipitate of copper on the copper plate leaves the latter unchanged; the zinc remains unaltered, because by combining with the anion, SO_4, zinc sulphate, $ZnSO_4$, is formed which dissolves in the water.

The combination remains, therefore, almost entirely unchanged so long as zinc, acid, and copper sulphate are present.

According to this conception, put forth recently by L. Sohncke, and developed uniformly by the use of the older representations, the source of the electric current, respecting which there has been so much discussion, is to be sought neither in the contact of the metals nor in the chemical action of the metals, but in the dissociated state of one or other of the electrolytes in contact with the metals. The observation made by F. Kohlrausch, that simple unmixed liquids are not as a rule electrolytes, and are therefore incapable of developing a current unless in the fused state and at high temperatures, fully confirms this view. Dissociation produced either by mixing with other liquids or by the application of heat is therefore essential to the action of electrolytes.

That in aqueous solutions hydrogen chloride exists to a large extent in a state of dissociation (*cf.* § 109) can be demonstrated by the depression of the freezing point (*cf.* § 78). Still, the mode of dissociation cannot in this case be determined; for by the electrolysis of concentrated solutions hydrogen and chlorine are the ions, whilst from dilute solutions hydrogen and oxygen are formed. It would hence appear probable that in the first case the hydrogen chloride is decomposed into hydrogen and chlorine, and in the second case the solution contains the compound $HCl + H_2O$, or H_3ClO, the existence of which Thomsen assumes, and this is resolved into H_2 and $HClO$, the latter yielding oxygen, O, and hydrochloric acid, HCl, at the anode.

§ 106. **Dissociation a Condition Preparatory to Chemical Change.**—In the majority of cases it would appear that dissociation must precede chemical change; for those electrolytes which are most easily dissociated belong to the class of substances distinguished by their ability to take part in chemical actions. This ability ceases so soon as the possibility of this dissociation taking place is removed. Anhydrous hydrogen chloride, liquefied by pressure and cold, does not attack the metals, which are easily dissolved by the aqueous solutions.

This extremely interesting and remarkable phenomenon becomes perfectly clear in the light of the hypothesis that pure hydrogen chloride cannot be dissociated and remain so, because each of the separated ions must come in contact with others and be fixed by these, whilst in the aqueous solutions they would both be separated by the water, and remain apart for a short time.

The behaviour of many elements is very remarkable according as they exist in compounds which are electrolytes or non-conductors, *i e.* in compounds which do not undergo dissociation. Thus, for instance, chlorine, bromine, and iodine are separated from their compounds by solutions of silver salts only when the compounds are such as easily dissociate, and these elements form the ions. The majority of organic compounds containing these halogens are either incapable of being dissociated or dissociate at high temperatures only, and then only in some cases is the dissociation such that the halogens chlorine, bromine, and iodine appear as ions. In complete agreement with these facts, the chlorine, bromine, and iodine of such compounds either do not react at all with silver nitrate or only slightly; many other compounds of these and other elements behave in a similar manner. The chlorine of chlorates and perchlorates in which the metals are the cations and the radicals ClO_3 and ClO_4 the anions, does not in solution give any silver chloride, but forms first silver chlorate and perchlorate, from which the chloride can be produced by their decomposition. The sulphates with the anion SO_4 in the ordinary course of things give rise to sulphates with the same 'anion,' and many other salts and similar compounds behave in the same way. The compounds may decompose in other ways if the manner of the dissociation, and consequently the nature of the ions, be changed by heat or by the action of other bodies.

If by the study of a series of compounds capable of undergoing dissociation the ions contained in them are known with any degree of certainty, the majority of the reactions of these compounds may be predicted, for the combinations and changes always result from the union of the ions with those of the other active bodies. These facts afford an explanation of the principle known as the 'conservation of the type'—a rule which has been recognised for a considerable length of time, and which states that the bodies produced in any given reaction belong to the same types as those from which they are formed; in other words, they represent compounds analogous to those from which they are produced. An acid and a salt yield usually by their mutual reaction a salt and an acid, thus:

$$H \cdot Cl + Ag \colon NO_3 = Ag \; Cl + H \; NO_3.$$

A sulphate and a nitrate act upon one another to form by exchange of metals another sulphate and nitrate:

$$K_2 \colon SO_4 + Ba \; 2NO_3 = Ba \cdot SO_4 + 2K \colon NO_3$$

188   OUTLINES OF THEORETICAL CHEMISTRY

Again, a hydroxide and a salt form another salt and hydroxide:

$$Ba(OH)_2 + Mg(NO_3)_2 = Mg(OH)_2 + Ba\,2NO_3,$$

and so on. Changes of this kind take place in all probability even when the final result is different from what this rule would lead one to expect; the instability of one or other of the compounds formed may lead to the formation of new substances. Thus copper iodide should be formed by the action of potassium iodide on copper sulphate:

$$2KI + CuSO_4 = K_2SO_4 + CuI_2$$

But cuprous iodide and iodine are formed by reason of the instability of cupric iodide·

$$2CuI_2 = Cu_2I_2 + I_2.$$

The action of potassium hydroxide on silver nitrate affords another example of a similar kind; the product should be silver hydroxide and potassium nitrate:

$$K:OH + AgNO_3 = KNO_3 + Ag.OH$$

but the silver hydroxide dissociates into silver oxide and water, thus:

$$2AgOH = Ag_2O + HOH$$

Numerous other examples might be given in which the 'type' is not maintained.

For the commencement of the reaction it would appear to be sufficient if one of the reacting substances is capable of dissociation, although the other is entirely incapable of being dissociated. Thus benzene and many other hydrocarbons do not undergo dissociation at the ordinary temperature, yet when brought in contact with nitric acid, which is easily dissociated, the ions of the acid act energetically and the hydrocarbon is nitrated, thus:

$$\underset{\text{Benzene}}{C_6H_6} + \underset{\text{Nitric acid}}{HO\,NO_2} = \underset{\text{Nitrobenzene}}{C_6H_5NO_2} + \underset{\text{Water}}{HOH}$$

When neither of the substances dissociate, then as a rule no reaction takes place, or a rise in temperature is needed to start the reaction, which aids or simply induces dissociation.

Free oxygen, O_2, does not appear to be easily dissociated, for the oxidation of most bodies by its aid can only be effected at high temperatures. It is, however, dissociated by electricity, and ozone produced, which probably has the formula O_3, and which itself is extremely easily dissociated, and, as is well known, acts as a powerful oxidising agent.

It is very remarkable that many substances, such as phosphorus, are less easily oxidised by pure oxygen than by air, in which it is mixed with a considerable proportion of nitrogen, or even by oxygen diluted by reduction of pressure. As phosphorus when slowly oxidised is luminous in the dark, these facts may be easily observed.

In pure oxygen at 20° C. and under a pressure of 760 mm. no light is given out, the phosphorus becomes gradually luminous as the pressure is reduced, and is very distinctly so when the pressure has fallen to 150 mm., or to about $\frac{1}{5}$ of an atmosphere. This remarkable phenomenon is probably in part due to the fact that the dissociation of the oxygen particles is favoured by the dilution.

§ 107. **Rates of Chemical Change.**—Every chemical action requires a certain length of time for its completion. The time required is, however, very different, varying with the nature of the reacting substances, with their amounts, and the conditions under which they are brought in contact. This subject has hitherto been thoroughly investigated only in comparatively few cases. In most cases the conditions are so complex that it is difficult to separate and estimate their various influences. Numerous observations show, however, that the rapidity of a chemical action is influenced by the quality, the quantity, the mass of the reacting bodies; also by their state of aggregation, as well as that of the products, further, by temperature and pressure, and by the presence of bodies taking no active part in the action, such as solvents and diluents, &c. The influence of mass, solubility, and volatility was submitted to a thorough investigation by Claude Louis Berthollet more than a hundred years ago; but only in recent years have his endeavours obtained their just recognition, and the work been resumed and extended by the aid of more modern methods

§ 108. **Simple Decomposition.**—The simplest case is that in which, with several active substances present, one only of these undergoes a change. Such a case we have in the inversion of cane sugar under the influence of a dilute acid,[1] whereby it is converted into a mixture of dextrose (grape sugar) and levulose (fruit sugar), which rotates the plane of polarised light in the opposite direction to that in which it is rotated by cane-sugar solutions. This decomposition, represented by the equation

$$\underset{\text{Cané sugar}}{C_{12}H_{22}O_{11}} + H_2O = \underset{\text{Grape sugar}}{C_6H_{12}O_6} + \underset{\text{Fruit sugar}}{C_6H_{12}O_6}$$

has been carefully investigated by Wilhelmy, and more recently by Ostwald. If a given quantity of sugar dissolved in water be mixed with a definite amount of an acid, capable of producing the inversion, then in every interval of time an amount of the sugar is inverted which is proportional to the amount of sugar still remaining unchanged. If A be the quantity of sugar originally present, and x the quantity of sugar inverted during the time, t, of mixing, then the amount dx inverted in the infinitely short interval of time dt is proportional, the amount $(A - x)$ remaining unaltered. In this manner we obtain the differential equation:

$$\frac{dx}{dt} = K \cdot (A - x), \quad \frac{dx}{A - x} = K \cdot dt$$

in which K represents a constant, or in this case at least an invariable quantity. By integration the following expression is obtained for the amount x inverted in the time t

$$-\log_e (A - x) = K \cdot t + \text{constant}.$$

Reckoning t from the moment of mixing, when $t = o$, so also x becomes o; consequently the integration constant is

$$-\log_e A = \text{const}.$$

$$\log_e \frac{A}{(A - x)} = K \cdot t$$

---

[1] We may neglect the part played by the water in this reaction, as also that of the acid, the proportion of which remains unchanged

and from these we have
$$\frac{A}{A-x} = e^{K \cdot t}$$
$$x = A\left(1 - \frac{1}{e^{Kt}}\right) = A(1 - e^{-Kt})$$

in which e represents the base of natural system of logarithms, viz. $e = 2 \cdot 71828$.

The general correctness of these equations has been proved to such an extent, that the quantity $\log_e \frac{A}{A-x}$ may be calculated from the value of x, determined experimentally, and divided by the corresponding values of t. The values of
$$K = \frac{1}{t} \cdot \log_e \frac{A}{A-x}$$

have thus been found to be constant, as is required by theory. The quantity of sugar, therefore, inverted every moment is proportional to the amount of unaltered sugar present; and of this equal portions are always inverted in the same time.

The invariable quantity K is not absolutely constant, but varies with the nature as well as the amount of the acid used for inversion, and also with the proportion of sugar contained in a given volume of the solution, consequently with the concentration of the solution. An alteration in the mass of the acid is of much greater influence than a change in the quantity of the sugar. According to Ostwald's experiments, by increasing the sugar to ten times the amount whilst the hydrochloric acid remains constant, the value of K is only increased by half its original value. The increase in the proportion of acid, with the sugar remaining constant, produces a different effect, according to whether the acid is strong and easily dissociated, or weak and one which does not easily dissociate.

With the strong acids, such as nitric, hydrochloric, and hydrobromic acids, the inversion is approximately proportional to the acid, but decreases with the dilution to a somewhat greater extent than would correspond to the amount of the dilution. In the case of the weaker organic acids—formic, acetic, propionic, butyric, and succinic acids—the inversion takes place more slowly than the increase in the dilution warrants; so that without doubt the more dilute acids have a stronger action, because they are more completely dissociated.

Many other reactions take place in accordance with Wilhelmy's formula, the amount decomposed at each interval of time being proportional to that which still remains unaltered. This, according to Harcourt and Esson, is the case in the reduction of permanganic acid by a large excess of oxalic acid, and also in the reduction of hydrogen peroxide by hydriodic acid. According to Ostwald, the so-called saponification of ethereal salts soluble in water, such as methyl acetate by dilute acids, follows this law also; this reaction is no doubt analogous to the inversion of sugar, for the ethereal salt by the assimilation of water is resolved into alcohol and acid. According to Van't Hoff the replacement of chlorine or bromine in organic compounds by hydroxyl (OH) with or without subsequent splitting off of water affords another instance to which this logarithmic formula may be applied; many other reactions also might be cited

§ 109. **Double Decomposition.**—The case is somewhat less simple when two substances are simultaneously changed. Strictly speaking, this is the case in some of the reactions discussed in the foregoing section, inasmuch as water takes part in the change. Its influence is not perceived, because, for example, in the inversion of sugar the amount of water assimilated scarcely alters the large excess of water present. Similarly, in the reduction of permanganic acid and of hydrogen peroxide by so large an excess of the reducing agent, the changes in the amounts of these do not come into consideration.

If in any reaction the two active substances are in solution, their masses are then most conveniently calculated in equivalent weights, *i.e.* according to the number of these proportions which react with one another. If A be the number of equivalents of one substance, and B that of the other, and x the number of equivalents of each decomposed in the time t, then, assuming the change is always proportional to the reacting mass, the reaction would be represented by the following differential equation :—

$$\frac{dx}{dt} = K (A-x)(B-x); \quad \frac{dx}{(A-x)(B-x)} = K \cdot dt$$

For equivalent amounts of both substances, that is, when A = B, the equation assumes the form

$$\frac{dx}{(A-x)^2} = K \cdot dt;$$

and when integrated, with $t=o$ and $x=o$, the following expression is obtained:—

$$\frac{x}{A-x} = A \cdot K \cdot t.$$

According to this expression the relation of the amount of the decomposed to the amount of the unaltered substances is variable with, and proportional to the time. For a long time no single case had been observed which corresponded to this rule, until it was shown by Hood to apply in the oxidation of ferrous sulphate by chloric acid. The amounts of these substances equivalent to one another in this case are $1HClO_3$ and $6FeSO_4$. Instead of using these substances, $1KClO_4$ and $6FeSO_4$ were mixed together with dilute sulphuric acid, and the proportion of unoxidised iron was determined by the titration from time to time of a sample taken from the mixture. The results are in accord with the above equation. It has been also shown by R. Warder that the saponification of ethyl acetate by an aqueous solution of caustic soda proceeds in a manner confirmatory of this law, and Van't Hoff and Schwab have shown the same to be the case with the conversion by caustic soda of monochloracetic acid into glycollic acid, and according to Ostwald the decomposition of acetamide by dilute acids into ammonium salts and acetic acid proceeds in a similar manner.

If A and B are different the integration of the above equation yields the following expression:—

$$\log_e \frac{B(A-x)}{A(B-x)} = (A-B) \cdot K \cdot t;$$

or by introducing the proportion of A to B

$$A : B = 1 : n$$

we obtain

$$\log_e \frac{A - \frac{x}{n}}{A - x} = A(n-1) \cdot K \cdot t.$$

o

This equation has also been confirmed by a certain number of observations.

It must, however, be confessed that the number of quantitive observations hitherto made to test the theory is altogether out of proportion to the innumerable chemical investigations undertaken in this century, despite the desirability and necessity for such observations.

§ 110. **Reversible Reactions.**—Remarkable relationships are observed when the products of a reaction so react upon one another as to form again the original substances, and thus reproduce the condition from which they started. This is the case when two or more electrolytes in solution react, and their ions combine in such a way as to produce all the several possible combinations. The simplest of all such cases is that when the substances produced by the combination of the ions are neither insoluble in the solvent used, nor volatile, and consequently neither separate out in the solid nor in the gaseous state. When this possibility is excluded, and all remain in solution, the reaction then proceeds according to the law discovered by Guldberg and Waage, which is but the corrected form of the law proposed about a century ago by C. L. Berthollet. This is usually described as the 'Law of the Action of Mass.'

This law comes into play when, for instance, an acid is brought into a solution of another salt; when alcohol is added to an acid or an ethereal salt treated with water. In the first case the free acid decomposes a portion of the salt, so that the solution contains both the free acids and salts of each of them; for instance, if hydrochloric acid be added to a not too concentrated solution of nitre the solution will then contain, not only unaltered potassium nitrate, but also potassium chloride, free nitric and free hydrochloric acids. In fact, for the ultimate division of the constituents it does not matter whether the nitrate has been treated with hydrochloric acid or the chloride decomposed with nitric acid, provided only that in both cases the proportions of all substances concerned are the same.

In the second instance the acid and alcohol produce an ethereal salt and water, which in turn give rise to the alcohol and acid; and here, also, if sufficient time elapses, the final condition in which all four substances are present is the same, whether we start with one or the other set of combinations. If, for example, acetic acid and alcohol are mixed in the proportion of their molecular weights, then, according to Berthelot and Pean de St. Gilles, they react upon one another in accordance with the following equation:—

$$(C_2H_3O)OH + (C_2H_5)OH = (C_2H_3O)O(C_2H_5) + HOH$$
Acetic Acid   Alcohol   Ethyl Acetate   Water

forming ethyl acetate and water until two-thirds of the whole mass is decomposed in this manner. On the other hand, when the ether and water are mixed in molecular proportions, the reverse reaction proceeds until one-third is converted into alcohol and acid. Consequently, in the final condition, whether this be reached from one side or the other, the mixture contains one molecular proportion of alcohol and of acid for every two molecular proportions of ether and of water, so that the condition of equilibrium in the mixture is represented as follows:—

$$(C_2H_3O)OH + (C_2H_5)OH + 2(C_2H_3O)O(C_2H_5) + 2HOH.$$

This condition of equilibrium is not to be looked upon as a state of rest, in which, when once reached, no further reaction takes place, but is to be regarded rather as a state in which just as many particles react in one way as there are particles reacting in the opposite, the two opposing reactions maintaining the equilibrium.

A simple consideration shows that each of these reactions will take place the more frequently the larger the number of particles of the active bodies present. Since the particles must come in contact with each other in order that they may combine or react, it is apparent that the space in which they are confined must be of influence; for, indeed, generally speaking, the reaction will be the more complete the larger the number of particles contained in a given space in the unit of volume. Yet, again, it is to be remembered that every particle present is not to be looked upon as taking part in the action. The number of such active particles present is dependent upon the degree of dissociation, which, as has been already shown, usually changes with the dilution of a solution, and, as a rule, the extent of the dissociation increases with the increase of the dilution. If, however, the dissociation, and consequently the chemical activity, be so far advanced that any further alteration in the concentration no longer exercises any great influence, the change is then almost proportional to the masses of the active bodies present in the unit volume; for example, in a litre.

Guldberg and Waage's theory of the action of mass is based upon this supposition, the truth of which has been confirmed by numerous observations.

§ 111. **Guldberg and Waage's Theory of the Action of Mass.** —Let A and B' represent two bodies which interact according to the equation

$$A + B' = A' + B;$$

and let the reaction be reversible,

$$A' + B = A + B';$$

then, if the two bodies A and B' are brought together, both reactions will go on concurrently until a state of equilibrium ensues, in which the two opposite reactions take place to the same extent.

Let p, q, p', and q' denote the number of particles which are present in this state; then

$$p \cdot A + p' \cdot A' + q \cdot B + q' \cdot B'$$

will represent the composition of the mixture in the state of equilibrium. Assuming that the action is proportional to the mass, the change represented by the first equation is proportional to the number of particles A and B', and is consequently proportional to the product $p \cdot q'$, and the reverse reaction represented by the second equation is proportional to $p' \cdot q$. The action in the unit of time is expressed by the formulæ $K \cdot p \cdot q'$ and $K' \cdot p' \cdot q$; K and K' being factors which depend on the nature of the bodies and on external conditions such as temperature, but they remain constant so long as these conditions are unchanged. The state of equilibrium in which the reaction takes place to the same extent in one direction as it does in the reverse is represented by the equation

$$K \cdot p \cdot q' = K' \cdot p' \cdot q;$$

or
$$\frac{p'}{p} = \frac{K}{K'} \cdot \frac{q'}{q} = \chi^2 \frac{q'}{q},$$

in which $\frac{K}{K'}$ is replaced by the symbol χ^2. If the values $\frac{p'}{p}$ and $\frac{q'}{q}$ are termed *quotients of decomposition*, then the law may be expressed in the following words: In the state of equilibrium the quotients of decomposition bear a fixed relation to each other.

For example, let A and B be acids and A' and B' salts of these acids; then the quotients of decomposition indicate for each acid the ratio the non-neutralised bears to the amount of neutralised acid. When the constant χ^2 is once determined this ratio can be calculated for any given case.

§ 112. **Experimental Proof of Guldberg and Waage's Law by Etherification.**—Different methods have been proposed for determining the constant of affinity, χ^2. It can be easily determined in the process of the formation of an ethereal salt from an acid and alcohol. If R is an alcoholic radical and S an acid radical, the formation of an ethereal salt is represented by the equation

$$ROH + SOH = ROS + HOH,$$

and the state of equilibrium by

$$p \, ROH + q' \, SOH + p' \, ROS + q \, HOH;$$
$$\frac{p'}{p} = \chi^2 \frac{q'}{q}.$$

If P molecular weights of alcohol and Q molecular weights of acid are used, and the amount of free acid q' in the state of equilibrium is determined by titration, then χ^2 and the coefficients p, p', and q can be determined by means of the following equation:—

$$P = p + p'; \qquad Q = q + q'; \qquad \chi^2 = \frac{p' \cdot q}{p \cdot q'}.$$

If only acid and alcohol are mixed together without the addition of ethereal salt or water, $p' = q$.

For the sake of simplicity let $P = Q = 1$; then

$$p = 1 - p' = 1 - q = q'; \qquad \chi^2 = \left(\frac{1-q'}{q'}\right)^2.$$

In this case if $R = C_2H_5O$ and $S = C_2H_3O$ the result of experiment for acetic acid and ethyl alcohol is that $q' = \frac{1}{3}$.

It therefore follows that $\chi^2 = 4$ and the state of equilibrium is represented by $1ROH + 1SOH + 2ROS + 2HOH$. That is to say, if we take equivalent quantities of alcohol and acetic acid, two-thirds will interact to form ethyl acetate and water and one-third will remain unaltered.

After determining the value of χ^2 in this way, the validity of the theory can be tested by taking any other values for P and Q and determining the quantity q' of free acid and comparing the experimental result with the value calculated by means of the factor $\chi^2 = 4$. The agreement between the experimental and calculated results has been found to be most satisfactory, even when certain quantities of water and ethereal salt were added, provided that the water was not added in sufficient quantity to cause the liquid to separate out into two layers.

In this case the value of χ^2 is not greatly influenced by temperature, and it varies within rather narrow limits for different organic acids and alcohols, possessing analogous atomic linking. According to Menschutkin, in the case of the action of the fatty acids, $C_nH_mO_2$, on isobutyl alcohol, χ^2 increases with the molecular weight of the acid; $\chi^2 = 3.2$ when $n = 1$ (formic acid) and $\chi^2 = 5.9$ when $n = 8$ (caprylic acid). In spite of this rather large difference in the constants, the difference in the quantity of undecomposed acids is not very large.

For instance, when $P = Q = 1$ the following results are obtained:—

		$q' = p$	$q = p'$	χ^2	χ
Formic Acid [1]	$C_1H_2O_2$	0·358	0·642	3 22	1·79
Acetic Acid	$C_2H_4O_2$	0·326	0 674	4·28	2 07
Propionic Acid	$C_3H_6O_2$	0·313	0·687	4 82	2·20

[1] At 100° C, the other acids at 154°.

		$q^1 = p$	$q = p^1$	χ^2	χ
Butyric Acid .	$C_4H_8O_2$	0·305	0·695	5·19	2·28
Caproic Acid .	$C_6H_{12}O_2$	0·302	0 698	5 34	2·31
Caprylic Acid	$C_8H_{16}O_2$	0·291	0·709	5·94	2 44

The state of equilibrium is slightly different for different acids: this is seen under χ in the preceding table, which contains the number of equivalents of acid etherified for each equivalent of unaltered acid (assuming that the acid and alcohol were present in equivalent quantities).

§ 113. **Avidity of Acids.**—Julius Thomsen and W. Ostwald have investigated the changes which take place when two acids act upon one base, which is not present in sufficient quantity to neutralise them both, or when two bases act on one acid under similar conditions The constant χ which determines the ratio between the amounts of the two acids neutralised is termed by Thomsen the *avidity* of the acid, its striving for neutralisation, but Ostwald calls it *affinity*.

In order to investigate the reaction Thomsen made use of the liberation or absorption of heat accompanying the reaction, and Ostwald made use of the changes in volume and density which accompany the change Both chemists agree that the reaction is very rarely complete.

If one equivalent of soda (NaOH = 39·96, or in round numbers 40 parts by weight) in dilute solution is exactly neutralised by the equivalent quantity of sulphuric or nitric acid ($\frac{1}{2}H_2SO_4$ = 48 91, or in whole numbers 49 parts by weight and HNO_3 = 62 89, or 63 in round numbers) more heat will be produced in the first than in the second case.

With sulphuric acid	.	.	.	15689 cals.
,, nitric acid	.	.	.	13617 cals.
			Difference	2072

A caloric, or thermal unit, is the amount of heat required to raise the temperature of the unit weight of liquid water 1° C.

It is a general law in the mechanical theory of heat that the amount of heat evolved or absorbed depends only on the initial and final state of a system, and not on the order in which the change takes place.

The heat evolved is consequently the same when sulphuric acid and soda unite together, directly forming sodium sulphate, thus:—

(1) $2\text{NaOH} + \text{H}_2\text{SO}_4 = \text{Na}_2\text{SO}_4 + 2\text{H}_2\text{O}$

and when sodium nitrate is first formed, and afterwards converted into sulphate:—

(2a) $2\text{NaOH} + 2\text{HNO}_3 = 2\text{NaNO}_3 + 2\text{H}_2\text{O}$
(2b) $2\text{NaNO}_3 + \text{H}_2\text{SO}_4 = \text{Na}_2\text{SO}_4 + 2\text{HNO}_3$

It is assumed that the nitric acid in (2b) assumes the state in which it first occurred.

Reaction (1) yields 15689^c for each 1NaOH, but (2a) only yields 13617^c; therefore (2b) must yield the difference 2072^c for each equivalent of NaOH taking part in the reaction.

On the other hand, if the sulphate could be completely decomposed by the nitric acid, the reaction

$$\text{Na}_2\text{SO}_4 + 2\text{HNO}_3 = 2\text{NaNO}_3 + \text{H}_2\text{SO}_4$$

would yield -2072^c, i.e. as much heat would be absorbed as is evolved in the opposite reaction.

Thomsen found that when an equivalent of sodium nitrate (NaNO_3) in dilute solution is mixed with one equivalent of sulphuric acid ($\frac{1}{2}\text{H}_2\text{SO}_4$) only 288^c instead of 2072^c are evolved, and, on the other hand, one equivalent of sodium sulphate ($\frac{1}{2}\text{Na}_2\text{SO}_4$) and one equivalent of nitric acid produce -1752^c instead of -2072^c. It follows from these observations that in neither of these cases does a complete decomposition take place in accordance with the equations, but that an intermediate stage of partial decomposition ensues, which is the same in both cases.

By adding these two results together we obtain $288^c + 1752^c = 2040^c$, which agrees approximately with the difference in the heat of neutralisation of the two acids. Apparently the reactions could be represented respectively by

$$\frac{288}{2040} = 0\cdot 14 \text{ and } \frac{1752}{2040} = 0\cdot 86,$$

i.e. 14 per cent. of the nitrate is decomposed by the equivalent of sulphuric acid and 86 per cent. of the sulphate is decomposed by the nitric acid. But this interpretation is erroneous, for in both cases each free acid not only acts on the salt of the other acid but on its own salt with absorption of heat. By special experiments Thomsen found for

$$\tfrac{1}{2}(Na_2SO_4 + nH_2SO_4) : -\frac{n}{n+0.8} \cdot 1650^c,$$

and for $\qquad NaNO_3 + HNO_3 : -36^c.$

On mixing equal equivalents the solution contains in a state of equilibrium

$$p\tfrac{1}{2}H_2SO_4 + (1-p)\tfrac{1}{2}Na_2SO_4 + (1-p)HNO_3 + pNaNO_3;$$

$$\frac{p}{1-p}H_2SO_4 \text{ acts on } 1Na_2SO_4; \text{ therefore } n = \frac{p}{1-p},$$

and the amount of sulphate present gives with the free acid a calorific effect

$$\frac{1-p}{2}\left\{\frac{\dfrac{P}{1-P}}{\dfrac{P}{1-P}+0.8}\right\} \cdot 1650^c = -\frac{p(1-p)}{0.2p+0.8} \times 1650^c.$$

In both cases the total effect is represented by

1. $(1-p) \cdot 2072^c - \dfrac{p(1-p)}{0.2p+0.8} \cdot 1650^c - (1-p)36^c = 288^c.$

2. $-p \cdot 2072^c - \dfrac{p(1-p)}{0.2p+0.8} \cdot 1650^c - (1-p)36^c = -1752^c.$

In these equations p is very nearly equal to $\tfrac{2}{3}$.

Replacing p by $\tfrac{2}{3}$ in equation 1, we obtain 286^c instead of 288^c and in 2, -1786^c instead of -1752^c.

The state of equilibrium is represented by the formula

$$2 \cdot \tfrac{1}{2}(H_2SO_4) + \tfrac{1}{2}(Na_2SO_4) + 1HNO_3 + 2NaNO_3;$$

$$\frac{p'}{p} = \chi^2\frac{q'}{q} = \frac{1}{2} = \chi^2\frac{2}{1} : \chi^2 = 0.25;$$

and the avidity $Av = \chi = 0.5$, i.e. when equal equivalents are taken the relative quantities of sulphuric and nitric acids neutralised are as 1 to 2.

§ 114. **Avidity calculated for Molecular Weights.**—These interactions are more accurately represented by molecular formulæ, and the state of equilibrium in this case can be expressed by the formula

$$2H_2SO_4 + Na_2SO_4 + 2HNO_3 + 4NaNO_3,$$

or as sulphuric acid acts on its salts and converts the greater part of them into acid sulphates—

$$H_2SO_4 + 2NaHSO_4 + 2HNO_3 + 4NaNO_3.$$

Now let us consider what will be the result when equal molecular weights (not equivalent weights) of the two acids take part in the reaction. The general formula for the state of equilibrium is

$$p\tfrac{1}{2}H_2SO_4 + p'\tfrac{1}{2}Na_2SO_4 + qHNO_3 + q'NaNO_3$$

and the values for the total equivalents of

$$\text{Sulphates} = p + p' = 2 \text{ equivalents}$$
$$\text{Nitrates} = q + q' = 1 \text{ equivalent}$$
$$\text{Salts} = p' + q' = 1 \quad ,,$$

The condition of equilibrium is

$$\frac{p'}{p} = \chi^2 \cdot \frac{q'}{q} = 0.25 \frac{q'}{q}.$$

From these four equations it follows that

$$p' = -\frac{1}{2} + \sqrt{\frac{11}{12}} = 0.46;$$

$$q = p' = 0.46, \ q' = 0.54, \ p = 1.54.$$

By introducing these values and changing the equivalent formulæ to molecular formulæ we obtain for the state of equilibrium—

$$0.54 H_2SO_4 + 0.46 NaHSO_4 + 0.46 HNO_3 + 0.54 NaNO_3$$

The ratio between the quotients of decomposition—

$$\frac{0.46}{0.54}=\chi^2 \cdot \frac{0.54}{0.46}; \quad \chi^2=\left(\frac{0.46}{0.52}\right)^2=0.73,$$

and the molecular avidity $(Av)_M = \chi = 0.85$

When equal molecules of nitric and sulphuric acid act on a quantity of sodium hydroxide solution equivalent to the nitric acid, 85 molecules of sodium hydrogen sulphate ($NaHSO_4$) are formed for every 100 molecules of sodium nitrate produced.

	Molecular Formula	$(Av)_E$	n	$(Av)_M$
Nitric Acid	HNO_3	100	1	100
Hydrochloric Acid	HCl	98	1	98
Hydrobromic Acid	HBr	89	1	89
Hydriodic Acid	HI	79	1	79
Trichloracetic Acid	$HC_2Cl_3O_2$	80	1	80
Sulphuric Acid	H_2SO_4	49	2	83
Selenic Acid	H_2SeO_4	45	2	75
Dichloracetic Acid	$H_2C_2HCl_2O_2$	33	1	33
Oxalic Acid	$H_2C_2O_4$	26	2	40
Orthophosphoric Acid	H_3PO_4	13	3	24
Monochloracetic Acid	$HC_2H_2ClO_2$	7	1	7
Tartaric Acid	$H_2C_4H_4O_6$	5.2	2	7
Citric Acid	$H_3C_6H_5O_7$	5.0	3	9
Glycollic Acid	$HC_2H_3O_3$	5.0	1	5
Hydrofluoric Acid	HF	5.0	1	5
Formic Acid	$HCHO_2$	3.9	1	3.9
Lactic Acid	$HC_3H_5O_3$	3.3	1	3.3
Malic Acid	$H_2C_4H_4O_5$	2.8	2	4
Succinic Acid	$H_2C_4H_4O_4$	1.45	2	2.07
Acetic Acid	$HC_2H_3O_2$	1.23	1	1.23
Propionic Acid	$HC_3H_5O_2$	1.04	1	1.04
Butyric Acid	$HC_4H_7O_2$	0.98	1	0.98
Isobutyric Acid	$HC_4H_7O_2$	0.92	1	0.92

Thomsen's investigations were confirmed and further developed by Ostwald. Both investigators determined the avidity of a large number of acids. In the preceding table $(Av)_E$ denotes the avidity for equivalents and $(Av)_M$ the molecular avidity with the formation of acid salts. The avidity of nitric acid = 100 serves as the standard of comparison; n indicates the number of equivalents contained in the molecule.

§ 115. **Relation between the Avidity and Composition of Acids.**—The numbers in the preceding table clearly show the connection between the avidity of an acid and the nature and arrangement of its atoms. The fatty acids

$$C_nH_{2n}O_2 = C_{n-1}H_{2n-1}, CO\!-\!OH$$

grow weaker as the value of n increases, that is, as the mass of the hydrocarbon radical united to the carboxyl increases:—

		Av
Formic Acid	H—CO—OH	3·9
Acetic ,,	CH_3—CO—OH	1·23
Propionic ,,	C_2H_5 . CO . OH	1·04
Butyric ,,	C_3H_7 . CO . OH	0·98

The avidity is increased by replacing hydrogen by hydroxyl (OH).

		Av
Acetic Acid	CH_3 . CO . OH	1·23
Glycollic ,,	HO . CH_2 . CO . OH	5
Propionic ,,	C_2H_5 . CO . OH	1·04
Lactic ,,	HO . C_2H_4 . CO . OH	3·3

		$(Av)_E$	$(Av)_M$
Succinic Acid	HO . CO . C_2H_4 . CO . OH	1·45	2·07
Malic ,,	HO . CO . C_2H_3(OH) . CO . OH	2·8	4·0
Tartaric ,,	HO . CO . C_2H_2(OH)$_2$CO . OH	5·2	7·3

It is greatly increased when H_2 is replaced by O.

		$(Av)_E$	$(Av)_M$
Glycollic Acid	HO . CH_2 . CO . OH	5	5
Oxalic ,,	HO . CO . CO . OH	26	40

The same effect is produced by replacing hydrogen by chlorine:—

		Av
Acetic Acid	CH_3 . CO . OH	1·23
Monochloracetic Acid	CH_2Cl . CO . OH	7
Dichloracetic ,,	$CHCl_2$. CO . OH	33
Trichloracetic ,,	CCl_3 . CO . OH	80

All these examples show that the facility with which a chemical change takes place is determined, not only by the nature and arrangement of the atoms directly taking part in the reaction, but is also influenced by other more distant atoms in the chain, and frequently their influence is so powerful as to preponderate over that of all the others.

§ 116 **Connection between Avidity and other Properties of the Acids.**—The property termed *avidity* or relative affinity determines the behaviour of the acid in almost all its actions. The inversion of sugar by acids in dilute aqueous solution mentioned in § 108, where the acid remains unchanged, the analogous decomposition of ethereal salts soluble in water by dilute acids, and many analogous reactions, take place with a velocity which is directly proportional to the avidity. A relation also exists between the avidity and the rate of diffusion and the closely allied electric conductivity of acids. The strength of an acid is almost directly proportional to its rate of diffusion and to its conductivity.

This surprising connection between chemical and physical properties is explained by the fact that the apparently stronger acids dissociate more easily, and in proportion to the facility with which the acid dissociates into ions its power of entering into double decomposition and its conductivity and other properties increase.

What we term affinity or avidity is no other than the facility of entering into reactions, mobility. We can therefore do without the notion of strong or weak chemical affinity in these speculations, although at the present time we cannot safely substitute another cause for the combination of the atoms in its place. Our present views are essentially different from the earlier views What was formerly ascribed to a stronger attractive force is now accounted for as a result of greater mobility.

§ 117. **Influence of Insolubility and Volatility on Chemical Change.**—C. L. Berthollet has pointed out that an act of double decomposition is materially influenced by the state of aggregation of the bodies taking part in the reaction. Berthollet maintained that when a compound separates out in an insoluble or volatile form it then loses all influence on the reaction. He explained, for example, the nearly perfect precipitation of sulphuric acid by barium salts and similar changes by assuming that the two acids, for instance, sulphuric and hydrochloric acids, distribute themselves between the base, according to the relative quantities in which they are present and in the ratio of their affinities. But the state of equilibrium produced is disturbed by the precipitation of insoluble barium sulphate, and consequently a new distribution of the acids takes place, and this process continues until there is either no barium salt or no sulphuric acid in the solution.

In this particular instance, owing to the resistance which barium sulphate offers to chemical change, this hypothesis corresponds fairly well with what actually takes place; but, as a general rule, this is not the case, as the insoluble precipitates do not cease to interact with the compounds still remaining in solution.

The simplest problem which offers itself to our consideration is when two of the four bodies interacting on each other are soluble and two insoluble. In this case Guldberg and Waage's theory is applicable with a slight modification. Of the four bodies A . B . A' . B' (see § 111) taking part in the reactions let A' and B' be insoluble. The state of equilibrium is represented by $pA + p'A' + qB + q'B'$; the equation for the quotients of decomposition, $\frac{p'}{p} = \chi^2 \frac{q'}{q}$, is simplified by the fact that an increase in the quantities p' and q' of the insoluble compounds does not exert any perceptible influence. These quantities may therefore be regarded as invariable, provided that not too small a quantity of each of these bodies is present. Let $\chi^2 \frac{q'}{q} = \gamma$ = constant; then $q = \gamma \cdot p$; that is to say, in the state of equilibrium a definite relation exists between the quantities of the two soluble substances in the solution. This condition is established when the quantity of A acting on the insoluble B' is equal to the amount of B interacting with A' in the same interval of time. In order that this state of equilibrium may be rapidly attained the liquid must be brought into intimate contact with the precipitate by boiling or by shaking. The coefficient γ depends not only on the nature of the interacting compounds but also on the concentration and temperature, and is often greatly affected by these conditions. The more or less crystalline character of the precipitate frequently exerts a great influence.

Guldberg and Waage allowed mixtures of barium sulphate and potassium carbonate, and barium carbonate and potassium sulphate, to interact for a year at 3° C. The substances were present in the proportions—

(a) $1BaSO_4 + 1K_2CO_3 + 100H_2O$
(b) $1BaCO_3 + 1K_2SO_4 + 100H_2O$

The solution contained—

(a) $0·959K_2CO_3 + 0·041K_2SO_4$; $\gamma = 23·4$
(b) $0·929K_2CO_3 + 0·071K_2SO_4$; $\gamma = 13·1$

and consisted, therefore, almost entirely of carbonate: in (a) $23·4K_2CO_3$ and in (b) $13·1K_2CO_3$ to each molecule of K_2SO_4. The state of equilibrium had not been reached in this long period, as is evident from the marked difference in the values of γ.

At 100° the interaction goes on more rapidly, but γ is much smaller, i.e. there is much more sulphate in solution.

In three days $1BaSO_4 + 1K_2CO_3 + 100H_2O$
yielded $0·76K_2CO_3 + 0·24K_2SO_4$; $\gamma = 3·2$;
and $1BaCO_3 + 1K_2SO_4 + 100H_2O$
in the same time produced $0·72K_2CO_3 + 0·28K_2SO_4$; $\gamma = 2·6$. Here the state of equilibrium is nearly attained.

A strong solution contains more sulphate, a dilute solution more carbonate. This agrees with the directions H. Rose gave many years ago for decomposing barium sulphate by boiling with a strong solution of potassium carbonate, renewing the potassium carbonate solution when it contained a certain quantity of sulphate.

The chromates behave like the sulphates. According to James Morris, potassium carbonate and barium chromate interact until the solution contains $10K_2CO_3$ if cold, or $3·75K_2CO_3$ if boiling, for each K_2CrO_4. Here, again, γ decreases, and with it the amount of carbonate in solution, as the temperature rises.

According to Watson Smith, the insoluble calcium oxalate is very slightly attacked by sodium carbonate, but calcium carbonate is almost completely decomposed by sodium oxalate. The behaviour of the corresponding compounds of strontium, barium, and lead is exactly the reverse of that exhibited by calcium carbonate and oxalate.

§ 118. **One Insoluble Substance.**—The problem is not quite so simple when only one of the interacting compounds is insoluble. When aqueous solutions of oxalic acid and calcium chloride are mixed together, calcium oxalate is precipitated, and free hydrochloric acid, oxalic acid, and some calcium chloride remain in solution. The state of equilibrium is represented by the formula—

$$p\text{H}_2\text{Cl}_2 + p'\text{CaCl}_2 + q\text{H}_2\text{C}_2\text{O}_4 + [q'\text{CaC}_2\text{O}_4].$$

For the sake of uniformity the formula for hydrochloric acid is doubled. The formula of the insoluble compound is placed in brackets. Two reactions maintain equilibrium, viz :—

$$\text{CaCl}_2 + \text{H}_2\text{C}_2\text{O}_4 = \text{H}_2\text{Cl}_2 + [\text{CaC}_2\text{O}_4]$$

and

$$\text{H}_2\text{Cl}_2 + [\text{CaC}_2\text{O}_4] = \text{CaCl}_2 + \text{H}_2\text{C}_2\text{O}_4.$$

The frequency with which the first reaction takes place increases with the number of particles of the interacting bodies in solution; it is therefore proportional to the product $p' \times q$. The value of q', which is always relatively large, has no perceptible influence on the frequency of the reaction, and the relation between the reaction and the number p of acid equivalents is far from simple. It is certain that calcium chloride and oxalic acid can only exist together in solution in very small quantities; the first reaction preponderates over the second. When an excess of oxalic acid or of calcium chloride is used the first reaction takes place to the almost entire exclusion of the second.

§ 119. **Action of Mass in Gases.**—If one of the products of decomposition in a solution is a gas, and entirely escapes, it ceases to exert any further influence. But if the whole or a part of it remains absorbed, then the absorbed gas behaves like any other substance in solution—that is to say, it can reverse the reaction which led to its formation.

Gases are frequently formed by the dissociation of compounds in solution, e.g. carbonic anhydride is evolved from bicarbonates. If all the gas escapes the decomposition is complete and all the bicarbonate changes into carbonate. Such a change is more likely to occur in a hot than in a cold solution. If carbonic anhydride remains in solution, then some bicarbonate will remain undecomposed or will be re-formed According to Hufner's observations, the red colouring matter of the blood, so necessary for the life of men and the higher animals, loses the oxygen with which it is combined in a similar way unless there is at least a small quantity of free oxygen dissolved in the blood. If the free oxygen is removed, fresh oxygen will be formed by dissociation of the colouring matter This process may be repeated until the red colouring matter is completely decomposed, so that by means of the air-pump all the oxygen can be removed, although the greater part of it is in a state of chemical combination, and only a small fraction of it is physically absorbed.

Guldberg and Waage's law or a similar law is probably valid when all the bodies taking part in the reaction are gaseous. But experimental proof of this problem has only been adduced in a few special cases. The first experiments in this direction (or, indeed, on the action of mass since the time of Berthollet) were made by Bunsen, who proved that when two combustible gases are mixed with an insufficient quantity of oxygen for their complete combustion the amount of oxygen combining with either gas is proportional to the amount of that gas present. In the case of a mixture of carbon monoxide and hydrogen the oxygen will be equally divided between the two gases if the mixture consists of six volumes of carbon monoxide to one of hydrogen. In a mixture of equal volumes of the two gases the hydrogen takes up three or four times as much oxygen as the carbon monoxide. The quantities change in the manner indicated by Guldberg and Waage's law, but they do not obey this law as closely as might be supposed. Recent investigations of Harold Dixon have shown that the process is much less simple than was formerly held to be the case. Perfectly dry carbon monoxide burns in oxygen with great difficulty, although it burns readily when it is mixed with aqueous vapour; the aqueous vapour is reduced and the resulting hydrogen is again oxidised—

$$CO + H_2O = CO_2 + H_2;$$
$$2H_2 + O_2 = 2H_2O.$$

Probably the law of Guldberg and Waage is valid for the

first process, providing that the temperature is sufficiently high to prevent the water depositing.

The state of equilibrium is $pCO + p'CO_2 + qH_2 + q'H_2O$ and

$$\frac{p'}{p} = \chi^2 \cdot \frac{q'}{q}.$$

As the second reaction can only be reversed at a very high temperature the law does not, as a rule, apply to this case. Mass exerts considerable influence in the interaction of gases and solids, *e.g* the oxidation of red-hot charcoal by steam, when the chief products are carbonic anhydride, hydrogen, and a small quantity of carbon monoxide, but a portion of the steam remains undecomposed.

§ 120 **Exceptions to Guldberg and Waage's Law.**—Unexpected deviations from Guldberg and Waage's law are occasionally met with. For example, A. Bonz found that the formation of an amide by the action of ammonia on an ethereal salt is a reversible reaction.

$$\underset{\text{Ammonia}}{NH_3} + \underset{\text{Ethyl Acetate}}{C_2H_5\text{—O.COCH}_3} = \underset{\text{Acetamide}}{NH_2\text{—COCH}_3} + \underset{\text{Alcohol}}{HOC_2H_5}$$

At temperatures above 100° alcohol and acetamide interact, yielding ethyl acetate and ammonia. The proportion of ethereal salt produced increases with the temperature and with the molecular weights of the alcohol and amide

The influence of mass is in accordance with the law of Guldberg and Waage. The value of χ^2, however, is only constant when equal molecules of ethereal salt and ammonia are present, *i.e.* in the proportion in which they are formed by the action of alcohol on the amide. The addition of an excess of ammonia increases the decomposition of the amide by alcohol; the addition of the ethereal salt lessens the action; and in either case the effect produced is greater than it should be, according to Guldberg and Waage's law. In this case the effects of the two interacting compounds on the decomposition are opposed to each other. This is not usually the case.

§ 121. **Non-reversible Reactions.**—The law of Guldberg and Waage does not apply to non-reversible reactions. In these cases the rule appears to be that the quantity of any given substance exerts an influence, but the influence produced by the mass varies with different substances Menschutkin has shown that the formation of acetanilide from aniline and acetic acid—

$$NH_2.C_6H_5 + HOCOCH_3 = NHC_6H_5.CO.CH_3 + HOH$$
$$\text{Aniline} \quad \text{Acetic Acid} \quad \text{Acetanilide} \quad \text{Water}$$

is greatly facilitated by an excess of acetic acid, whereas an excess of aniline delays the operation, but increases the amount of the product. If Guldberg and Waage's law were valid both bodies would act in the same way. That it does not apply in this instance is probably due to the fact that the acetic acid dissociates, and that the aniline either does not dissociate or dissociates only to a slight extent.

A still more striking example of the difference in the influence of two interacting bodies on a reaction is afforded in the nitration of aromatic organic compounds, e g.—

$$C_6H_6 + HONO_2 = C_6H_5.NO_2 + H_2O$$
$$\text{Benzene} \quad \text{Nitric Acid} \quad \text{Nitro-benzene} \quad \text{Water}$$

The reaction is facilitated by increasing the amount of nitric acid, but it is delayed by the addition of benzene and also by the products of the decomposition, namely, water and nitro-benzene. An increased quantity of acid not only increases the absolute, but also the relative quantity, *i.e*, the percentage of acid taking part in the interaction. According to A. Kessler, by taking double the theoretical quantity of nitric acid, the yield of nitro-benzene in the first quarter of an hour is increased fourfold; and if the amount of nitric acid is trebled, the yield will be ninefold. The quantity of nitro-benzene increases in proportion to the square of the quantity of acid used. In order to make this observation it is necessary to mix the benzene with its equivalent of nitro-benzene and to keep the mixture cold in order to moderate the reaction, which would otherwise take place with explosive violence.

Without doubt the complete difference in the influence of these two interacting compounds is due to the fact that the power of dissociation is possessed by nitric acid in a very high degree, and not at all by benzene Nitric acid dissociates according to the equation

$$2HO.NO_2 = N_2O_5 + H_2O$$

and does not form the electrolytic ions HO and NO_2.

The anhydride then attacks the benzene thus:—

$$NO_2.O.NO_2 + 2C_6H_6 = 2C_6H_5 NO_2 + H_2O.$$

Diluting the acid with water, nitro-benzene, or even with benzene, tends to prevent the decomposition of the acid into anhydride and water, and the weak acid steadily grows weaker, and finally ceases to nitrate. The ease with which the nitration is effected also depends on the nature and composition of the organic body. When a portion of the hydrogen in benzene is replaced by other elements or radicals, the operation of nitration may be facilitated, or it may be rendered more difficult, and even impossible. This depends on the nature and the position of the elements replacing the hydrogen.

§ 122. **Contact Action.**—It occasionally happens that two or more bodies can only interact in the presence of a third, and this third substance either remains unchanged or experiences a change itself. Phenomena of the first class are termed *catalysis* by Berzelius and *contact action* by Mitscherlich The characteristic feature of this class of phenomena is that a small quantity of the substance which remains unchanged can bring about the decomposition of a very large quantity, frequently of an unlimited quantity, of another compound.

The ignition of hydrogen and oxygen by finely-divided platinum is a simple example of this contact action. The action of the metal depends on the property which platinum possesses of condensing gases on its surface and of bringing them into such intimate contact that combination ensues. Contact action is a term which is well adapted to describe this class of phenomena It is, of course, open to question whether the metal does act only by contact, or whether it forms an unstable compound either with oxygen or, like palladium, with hydrogen.

In other cases the participation of the 'contact substance' in the interaction has been definitely proved. Take, for example, the 'carriers of oxygen.' As the oxidation of sulphurous acid by the oxygen of the air takes place very slowly, nitric oxide is used as a carrier of oxygen in the leaden chamber of the vitriol works. The nitric oxide, NO, is oxidised at the expense of the oxygen of the atmosphere to the peroxide, NO_2, which oxidises the sulphurous acid and is reconverted into nitric oxide. The reaction is not quite as simple as it is here depicted. In the first place nitro-sulphonic acid (the crystals of the leaden chamber) $HO—SO_2—NO_2$ is first formed from nitric oxide, oxygen, steam, and sulphur dioxide. This compound decomposes, yielding sulphuric acid and oxides of nitrogen—

$$2HO—SO_2—NO_2 + H_2O = 2HO—SO_2—OH + NO_2 + NO.$$

The sulphates and other salts of manganese, copper, iron, and other metals act as carriers of oxygen to aqueous solutions of sulphurous acid, as they are reduced by the sulphurous acid and reoxidised by the atmospheric air. A cold solution of oxalic acid is not oxidised by chromic acid, except in the presence of a manganese salt, which reduces the chromic acid and oxidises the oxalic acid. Manganese sulphate also acts as a carrier of oxygen when oxalic acid is oxidised by permanganic acid. Indigo effects the oxidation of an alkaline solution of grape sugar by acting as a carrier of atmospheric oxygen, for the indigo is reduced to indigo-white by the grape sugar, but at once unites with oxygen and forms indigo-blue again.

The formation of ethyl ether from alcohol and sulphuric acid was formerly considered to be an example of catalytic or contact action—

$$2C_2H_5.OH = (C_2H_5)_2O + H_2O.$$

But Williamson proved that the sulphuric acid takes part in the change, thus:—

$$\underset{\text{Alcohol}}{C_2H_5.OH} + \underset{\text{Sulphuric Acid}}{H_2SO_4} = \underset{\text{Ethyl Sulphuric Acid}}{C_2H_5—HSO_4} + \underset{\text{Water}}{H_2O}$$

$$C_2H_5.OH + C_2H_5.HSO_4 = \underset{\text{Ether}}{C_2H_5.O.C_2H_5} + H_2SO_4.$$

The sulphuric acid does not act merely by its presence, but takes part in the interaction and is formed again. It is probable that something similar takes place in the case of the apparently simple decomposition mentioned in § 108. The decomposition of cane sugar into dextrose and lævulose is probably preceded by the formation of corresponding ethereal salts with the inverting acid, which are in their turn decomposed by water.

Emmerling observed and explained a very remarkable case of apparent contact action. Oxalic acid scarcely attacks crystalline calcium carbonate, *e.g.* marble. A thin insoluble crust of calcium oxalate forms on the surface of the marble, which prevents any further action taking place, but on the addition of a very small quantity of nitric acid or a nitrate the marble is rapidly attacked and converted into calcium oxalate. Apparently it is the nitric acid or the nitrate which incites the oxalic acid to attack the calcium carbonate, but in reality it is the nitric acid which was added or was liberated from the nitrate by the oxalic acid that attacks the marble, forming calcium nitrate. The oxalic acid interacts, forming calcium oxalate and liberating nitric acid.

Interactions which apparently take place between two substances but require the presence of a third body, are of frequent occurrence. Many metals remain unaltered in dry air which rust or oxidise in a damp atmosphere. M. Traube has shown that water takes part in this process of oxidation; a metallic hydroxide and hydrogen peroxide are first formed according to the equation—

$$Zn + 2HO\ H + O_2 = ZnO_2H_2 + H_2O_2.$$

The metal decomposes the water, forming hydroxyl (HO—) and hydrogen, but the latter unites with a molecule of oxygen. The molecule of oxygen consists of two atoms, and at the low temperature the hydrogen is unable to effect their separation. The hydroxide loses water and passes into oxide, the hydrogen peroxide loses oxygen, forming water. In this way the water which took part in the interaction reappears as water when the reaction is completed.

Certain bodies act as carriers of chlorine in a similar way to the oxygen carriers. Pure nitro-benzene is practically unattacked by chlorine, but in the presence of anhydrous ferric chloride substitution of the hydrogen by chlorine takes place;

but the ferric chloride remains unchanged in quantity and has apparently taken no part in the reaction.

When bromine is substituted for chlorine the following reaction takes place, according to A Scheufelen :—

$$Br_2 + C_6H_5NO_2 + FeCl_3 = Br.C_6H_4.NO_2 + HCl + FeCl_2Br$$

and the analogous change in the case of chlorine is

$$Cl_2 + C_6H_5NO_2 + FeCl_3 = Cl.C_6H_4 NO_2 + HCl + FeCl_2.Cl.$$

The chlorine of the ferric chloride unites with an atom of hydrogen of the benzene to form hydrochloric acid, and both atoms are replaced by free chlorine or bromine. All three bodies consequently take part in the interaction

The numerous and varied forms of fermentation were formerly regarded as cases of catalytic action. It was believed that simple contact with the ferment, *e.g.* yeast, brought about the decomposition of the fermentable substance, sugar. Fermentation is now considered to be due to the action of minute living organisms, which devour the fermentable substance for their nourishment and excrete the decomposition products. The yeast ferment feeds on sugar and produces carbon dioxide and alcohol. The process is much more complicated than was formerly supposed to be the case.

This example, taken from a large class of similar phenomena, clearly shows that those changes which were formerly described as the result of contact action must be generally regarded as the interaction of three or more different bodies, or are even much more complex reactions. Berzelius explained this class of phenomena by the hypothesis of a special catalytic force contained in those substances which apparently take no part in the interaction. This hypothesis is now known to be unnecessary and superfluous.

§ 123. **Kinetic Nature of Affinity.**—An examination of the various forms of chemical change as described in the preceding paragraphs leads of necessity to the conclusion that the hypothesis of an attractive force known as affinity, such as was formerly accepted and even survives to the present time, is of little or no use in explaining chemical phenomena.

We might conclude from the fact that cupric sulphate is

reduced to a cuprous salt by sulphurous acid that sulphurous acid has a stronger affinity for oxygen than copper has in the form of cuprous oxide; we should consequently expect that cuprous oxide will take up oxygen from the air less readily than sulphurous acid does. As observation shows that the reverse is the case, we come to the conclusion that this view of the matter is incorrect; nor is the explanation satisfactory in many other cases. We have gradually receded from the idea of a static state of equilibrium of the atoms brought about by their powers of affinity, and we now consider the atoms, and the molecules which are built up of atoms, as particles in an active state of movement. Their relations to each other are essentially determined by the magnitude and form of their movements. Chemical theories grow more and more kinetic, and although, partly from habit and partly from want of a better expedient, the existence of an attractive force between the atoms is frequently used in explaining chemical phenomena, this only happens in the conviction that this hypothetical affinity is merely an expression for the real though imperfectly known cause of the internal cohesion of chemical compounds.

INDEX

ABS

ABSORPTION of gases, 160
Action of mass, 196, 197, 203, 208
Affinities, unsaturated, 69
Affinity, 71, 215
Aggregation, state of, 104
Alcohols, atomic linking of, 85
— isomeric, 89
Alexejeff, 131
Allotropy, 95
Andrews, 152
Anion, 175
Anode, 175
Arrhenius, 138, 176, 178
Asymmetrical atoms, 99
Atomic heat, 21-29
— hypothesis, 8
— linking, 76, 80
— — determination of, 83, 85
— — of alcohols, 85
— — theory of, 84
— volume, 57, 120
— weight of beryllium, 63
— — — caesium, 63
— weights, accuracy of, 50
— — Berzelius, 13
— — Dalton's, 13
— — determination of, 11, 39, 45, 48
— — unit of, 11
Avidity, 199-205
— of acids, 203, 204, 205
Avogadro, 30, 33

BAEYER, 116
Benzene theory, 92-95
Bernouilli, 32
Berthelot, 195
Berthollet, 6, 194, 205
Beryllium, atomic weight, 63
— specific heat, 25

CON

Berzelius, 7, 10, 13, 20, 30, 46, 50, 212, 215
Boiling points, 146
Bonz, 210
Boyle's law, 158
Bruhl, 127
Bunsen, 161, 162, 171, 209

CAESIUM, atomic weight, 63
Cahours, 173
Cailletet, 152
Cannizzaro, 30
Capillarity, 119, 128
Carbon, atomic heat, 25
— asymmetrical, 99
— monoxide, combustion of, 209
Catalysis, 212
Chemical change, 2, 162
— — rates of, 189
— combination, 7
— equivalents, 13
— symbols, 10
— theories, development of, 5
Chemistry, definition of, 1
— relation to other sciences, 2
Classification of the elements, 53
Clausius, 32, 175
Cohesion, 119
Collardeau, 152
Combining volumes, 28
— weights, 8
— — determination of, 44
Combustion, Lavoisier's theory, 5
Compounds, constitution of, 75
— unsaturated, 68
Constant batteries, 185
Constitution of chemical compounds, 75, 77, 80
Contact action, 212

Continuous etherification process, 213
Couper, 76
Critical pressure, 152
— temperature, 152
Crystallisation, 132
Crystallographic equivalents, 17

DALE, 124
Dalton, 7, 9, 10, 13
Decomposition, double, 192
    simple, 190
— quotients, 197
Density, 120
— of elements. 58
— — gases, 34
— — — abnormal, 41
— — solids, 108
Deville, 169, 171
De Vries, 142
Dialysis, 140
Diffusion, 138, 159
— and electrical conductivity, 183
Dimension of molecules, 158
Dimorphism, 96
Dissociation of gases, 169
— — liquids, 172
— — nitrogen peroxide, 169
Dixon, H , 209
Doebereiner's triads, 52
Double decomposition, 192
Dualistic formulæ, 81
Dulong and Petit, 21, 25
Dumas, 53
Dutrochet, 141

EBULLITION, 143, 145
Electric polarisation, 185
Electro-chemical properties of elements, 60
Electrolysis, 174, 177
Electrolyte, 175
Electrolytic conduction and diffusion, 183
— — — dissociation, 178
— equivalents, 16
Elements, 5
— classification of, 52, 54
— density of, 58
— electro-chemical properties of, 60
— fusibility of, 59
— malleability of, 59
— melting points of, 113
— physical properties of, 57
Equivalents, chemical, 13
— crystallographic, 17

Equivalents, electrolytic, 16
— thermic, 21
Esson, 192
Etherification, continuous process, 213
— rate of, 197
Evaporation, 143
Expansion by heat, 123
Explosion, 167

FARADAY, 16, 91, 174
Faraday's law, 177
Fischer, 141
Formulæ, dualistic, 81
Freezing point of solutions, 133
Friction of liquids, 119
Friedel, 87
Fusibility of elements, 59
Fusion, 112

GALLIUM, 56
Gaseous state, 154, 156
Gases, density of, 34
— dissociation of, 169
— kinetic theory of, 31
— molecular weights of, 33
Gauss, 50
Gay Lussac, 28, 31
Germanium, 56
Gladstone, 124
Graham, 139, 160, 174
Guldberg and Waage, 194, 196, 206, 209

HARCOURT, 192
Heat and chemical change, 165
Henry's law, 160
Hittorf, 180
Hoff, van t', 99, 193
Hüfner, 209
Humboldt, 28
Hydroxides, 68
Hypothesis, 4
— Avogadro's, 30
— Prout's, 51

IMBIBITION, 128
Investigation, method of, 3
Ions, 175
— migration of, 179
— velocity of, 181
Iso di-morphism, 96
Isomeric alcohols, 89
— benzene derivatives, 93

Isomeric tartaric acids, 101
Isomerism, 76, 97
— optical, 98
— physical, 95, 97
Isomorphism, 17

JUNGFLEISH, 117

KEKULÉ, 76, 92, 94
Kessler, 211
Kinetic nature of affinity, 215
— theory of gases, 31, 156
Kohlrausch, 179, 181, 183
Kopp, 120
Kundt, 106

LANDOLT, 124
Lavoisier, 82
Lavoisier's theory of combustion, 5
Law of action of mass, 194, 206, 209
— Dulong and Petit, 21
— Faraday, 177
— Guldberg and Waage's, 196
— of multiple proportions, 7
— Raoult's, 137
Le Bel, 99
Lellmann, 85
Light, refraction of, by liquids, 123
Liquids, dissociation of, 172
— friction of, 119
Long, 140
Lorentz, 123
Lorenz, 123

MAGNUS, 141
Marignac, 52
Mass, action of, 194, 196
Melting points of benzene derivatives, 117, 118
— — compounds, 115
— — elements, 114
— — mixtures, 118
— — organic acids, 116
Mendeléeff, 63
Menschutkin, 198, 211
Metamerism, 76
Metastasis, 76
Meyer, O. E., 158
Meyer, V., 71
Migration of ions, 179
Mitscherlich, 17, 212
Molecular refraction, 124
— volumes, 108, 121

Molecular weights, 36, 42
Molecules, dimensions of, 157
Morris, 207
Multiple proportion, law of, 7

NASCENT state, 44
Natterer, 152
Naumann, 150
Newlands, 53
Nilson, 25, 64
Nitrogen peroxide, dissociation of, 169
Nollet, 141
Non-reversible reactions, 210

OPTICAL isomerism, 98
Osmosis, 140
Osmotic pressure, 141
Ostwald, 199
Oxides, 67

PÉAN DE ST.-GILLES, 195
Periodic system, 55
Periodicity of atomic volumes, 57, 58
— — density, 58
— — fusibility, 59
— — physical properties, 56
— — valency, 64
Petit, 21, 25
Pettenkofer, 53
Pettersson, 25, 64
Pfeffer, 111
Phlogiston, theory of, 5
Physical isomerism, 95, 97
Pictet, 152
Pleomerism, 76
Polymerism, 76
Polymorphism, 96
Prediction of properties of elements, 63
Pressure, critical, 153
Prout's hypothesis, 51
Proust, 61

RADICALS, 82
Raoult's law, 137
— — exceptions to, 138
Reactions, non-reversible, 210
— reversible, 194
Refraction of light, 123
Regnault, 148
Richter, 6
Roscoe, 50

SCANDIUM, 56
Scheufelem, 164, 215
Schroeder, 146
Schuncke, 130
Schwab, 193
Seubert, 63
Simple decompositions, 190
Smith, W., 207
Sohncke, 106, 185
Solidification, 112
Solutions, 129
— freezing point of, 133
Specific heat, 21
— volume, 120
Stas, 48, 52
Stœchiometry, 6
Supersaturation, 132

TABLES of absorption of gases, 161
— atomic heats, 22, 23
— — volumes, 58
— — weights, 39, 40, 43, 55
— avidity of acids, 203
— boiling points of organic compounds, 147
— critical pressure, 153
— — temperature, 153
— density, 39, 40, 43, 58
— hydroxides, 68
— melting points of benzene derivatives, 117
— — — elements, 114
— — — organic acids, 116
— molecular weights, 39, 43
— oxides, 67
— periodic system, 55
— specific heats, 22
— velocity of ions, 183
Tartaric acids, 101
Temperature of ignition, 167

Theories, 4
— chemical, 5
Theory of atomic linking, 77
Thermic effect, 166
— equivalent of beryllium, 25
— — of carbon, 24
— equivalents, 21
Thomsen, J., 199
Transpiration, 159
Traube, 164, 214
Triads, Doebereiner's, 52

UNIT of atomic weights, 11
— — molecular weight, 35
Unsaturated affinities, 69
— compounds, 68

VALENCY, determination of, 64
— periodicity of, 64
Vanadium, 50
Vapour density, 28
— pressure, 144, 148
Velocity of gaseous particles, 155
— of ions, 181
Viscosity, 119
Volumes, combining, 28

WAAGE and Guldberg, 194, 196, 206, 209
Waals, J. D. van der, 123, 159
Warburg, 106
Warder, 193
Weber, 25
Wilhelmy, 192
Williamson, 213
Winklemann, 147
Wishcenus, 103
Wollaston, 11

ements.

	VII.	VIII.		
	Fluorine F 19·06			
	Chlorine Cl 35·37			
	Manganese Mn 54·8	Iron Fe 55·88	Cobalt Co 58·6	Nickel Ni 58·6
	Bromine Br 79·75			
		Ruthenium Ru 101·4	Rhodium Rh 102·7	Palladium Pd 106·35
	Iodine I 126·54			
		Osmium Os 191	Iridium Ir 192·3	Platinum Pt 194·3

To be pasted on a Wooden or Card-board Cylinder 75mm. Diameter and 175mm. high (v. p.).

Natural System

Hydr...

I.	II.	III.	IV.	
Lithium Li 7·01	Beryllium Be 9·08	Boron B 10·9	Carbon C 11·97	Nitr... N 14
Sodium Na 23·00	Magnesium Mg 24·3	Aluminium Al 27·04	Silicon Si 28·3	Phos... P 3(
Potassium K 39·03	Calcium Ca 39·91	Scandium Sc 43·97	Titanium Ti 48·0	Van... V 5
Copper Cu 63·18	Zinc Zn 65·10	Gallium Ga 69·9	Germanium Ge 72·3	A... A
Rubidium Rb 85·2	Strontium Sr 87·3	Yttrium Y 88·9	Zirconium Zr 90·4	Ni... Nl
Silver Ag 107·66	Cadmium Cd 111·7	Indium In 113·6	Tin Sn 118·8	... S
Caesium Cs 132·7	Barium Ba 136·9	Lanthanum La 138	Cerium Ce 139·9	
		Ytterbium Yb 172·6		T T
Gold Au 196·7	Mercury Hg 199·8	Thallium Tl 203·7	Lead Pb 206·4	
			Thorium Th 232·0	

f the Elements.

H = 1.

	VI.	VII.	VIII.		
	Oxygen O 15·96	Fluorine F 19·06			
	Sulphur S 31·98	Chlorine Cl 35·37			
	Chromium Cr 52·45	Manganese Mn 54·8	Iron Fe 55·88	Cobalt Co 58·6	Nickel Ni 58·6
	Selenium Se 78·87	Bromine Br 79·75			
	Molybdenum Mo 95·9		Ruthenium Ru 101·4	Rhodium Rh 102·7	Palladium Pd 106·35
	Tellurium Te 125·0	Iodine I 126·54			
	Tungsten W 183·6		Osmium Os 191	Iridium Ir 192·3	Platinum Pt 194·3
	Uranium U 239·0				

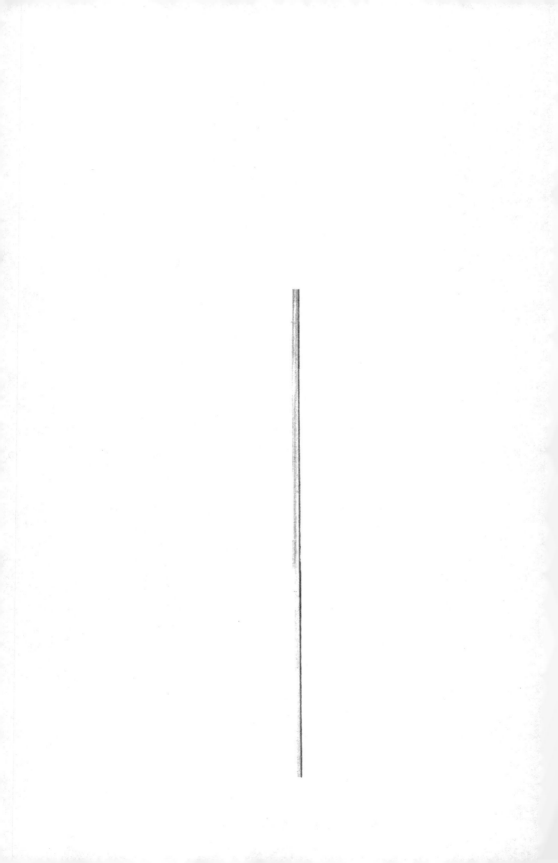

CPSIA information can be obtained
at www.ICGtesting.com
Printed in the USA
BVHW061021030920
587910BV00001B/159